ARIS AND PHILLIPS CLASSICAL TEXTS

CATULLUS

Poems 61–68

John Godwin

Aris & Phillips is an imprint of Oxbow Books

First published in the United Kingdom in 1995. Reprinted 2015 by
OXBOW BOOKS
10 Hythe Bridge Street, Oxford OX1 2EW

and in the United States by
OXBOW BOOKS
908 Darby Road, Havertown, PA 19083

Paperback Edition: ISBN 978-0-85668-671-9

A CIP record for this book is available from the British Library

For a complete list of Aris & Phillips titles, please contact:

UNITED KINGDOM
Oxbow Books
Telephone (01865) 241249
Fax (01865) 794449
Email: oxbow@oxbowbooks.com
www.oxbowbooks.com

UNITED STATES OF AMERICA
Oxbow Books
Telephone (800) 791-9354
Fax (610) 853-9146
Email: queries@casemateacademic.com
www.casemateacademic.com/oxbow

Oxbow Books is part of the Casemate Group

Printed and bound by CPI Group (UK) Ltd, Croydon, CR0 4YY

Contents

Preface

Catullus is the most appealing of Latin poets. Most students begin their reading of Latin poetry with the short poems of this most direct author, and most come away with the idea that the poet is brutally and appealingly honest about himself and his contemporaries. The long poems (61-68) are less instantly attractive: they are more oblique in style and in content than the shorter poems and need more thought and more explanation.

This is, to my knowledge, the first edition entirely given over to these long poems on their own. They may have been intended to be published as a single volume by the poet – we cannot be certain quite what the poet intended as his *libellus*. They certainly have a great deal of internal coherence and shared interest, such that the reader who studies all eight poems together cannot but be struck by the unifying features and the symmetry of the whole, whereby the themes of marriage, love, and adultery run through the collection – with variations – as a *Leitmotif*. Such themes are also found in the elegiacs and the polymetrics, of course: but to read these poems as a sequence gives a wonderful view of the power and the literary finesse of this most urbane of poets; and there is no better way of achieving that than by publishing them as a single volume in themselves.

This poet's work is often the first Latin poetry which the student reads, and many students are unfamiliar with technical terms of literary theory and criticism. To avoid either excessive repetition or needless obscurity I have appended a glossary of such terms at the end of the book; the terms marked with an asterisk in the body of the Introduction and Commentary are briefly explained there.

Commentaries on this poetry multiply every year, and much of the present work inevitably rests on the shoulders of those who have published such work before; my debt to the commentaries of Kroll, Fordyce, Quinn and Goold is as great as it is obvious. The space allowed me by a generous publisher has also allowed me to publish and discuss some of the massive secondary literature on the poet which appears every year in books and journals around the world, and again my debt to their work will be obvious to those familiar with the literature.

Producing this sort of edition is, then, something of a team effort between the editor and his fellow-scholars both past and present. He also relies heavily and thanklessly on his friends to shoot down the wilder kites he flies and to spot the mistakes which pepper the draft typescript. In all this I have been fortunate enough to secure the assistance of Professor Malcolm Willcock, who has been unstintingly generous with his time and his patience in wrestling an unruly manuscript into some sort of shape. Time after time he has saved me from myself and the final version owes a great deal to his scholarship and his generosity. All the mistakes which escaped his eagle eye are, alas, my own.

John Godwin   Shrewsbury, September 1995

Introduction

CATULLUS' LIFE AND TIMES

Catullus certainly lived in 'interesting times'. During his lifetime the military leaders who controlled Rome's army began to assume a more and more dominant role in society: the aristocrat Sulla took over the state and attempted to impose a constitution which would give the Senate total power and stability to the state, but his constitution crumbled within a few years of his death. There followed a period of thirty years in which military leaders, senators and urban demagogues vied with each other for power, culminating in the Civil War of 49 B.C. which left Julius Caesar in total power. Frequently towards the end of Catullus' lifetime elections were abandoned because of violence and corruption, and the history of the period is peopled with few heroes and many villains: Catiline, whose abortive attempt at revolution in 63 B.C. gave Cicero his hour of glory but almost brought down the state, Clodius, whose popularity was secured by a blend of demagogy and thuggery and who met his end in a street brawl in 52 B.C., Verres, the rapacious governor of Sicily, and so on. One of the interesting features of Catullus' work is the small amount of direct political comment we find there: there is plenty of abuse of politicians, but precious little of what we might call political ideals. Catullus had no answers to the evils of late-republican government: but he seems to have had neither faith nor interest in it either. Catullus' great contemporary Lucretius denounced the corrupt world of politics and advocated an apolitical Epicurean stance, even attempting to persuade Catullus' sometime praetor Memmius to follow his example: Catullus responded to the political chaos in a different manner.

On the one hand, then, there is no evidence that Catullus ever engaged in political life in Rome or anywhere else, and he only mentions politicians to abuse them either by insult (57), irony (49), studied indifference (93) or mockery (84). He also insults his 'friends' and so we should not take his abuse as itself a political gesture, but it does show him making no sign of any attempt to ingratiate himself with men who might have helped his political career. On the other hand, Catullus clearly believed that his poetry would have a future (1.10) and he seems to have channelled his energies into his art, carving out for himself and his friends a haven of poetry, friendship and love which eschewed the world of politics: and to mark this rejection of the world of politics he used the vocabulary of politics for the business of love. Ross ((1969) 83) perhaps overstates the case in saying that the poet used the '(almost technical) terminology of the workings of party politics and political alliances in Rome', but the Roman reader would have been in no doubt that words like *amicitia*, *fides, foedus* were found more often in the forum than the bedroom. Lyne contests Ross' case and points out that in Rome the state was largely in the hands of the amateur – which meant the aristocrat – and that such people naturally used the vocabulary of 'aristocratic commitment and obligation': so it is not Catullus taking over the language of 'politics' but rather politicians and Catullus alike taking over the language of the prevailing governing class (Lyne (1980) 26). This is no doubt true, but it does not affect the issue here: Catullus does not use the language of politics to talk about politics but rather to talk about love, and his use of such 'public' terms as *amicitia, foedus, fides* in a private context of sexual love is to some extent at least a reaction against the world of politicians who thundered high ideals in public but were guilty of all manner of corruption behind the scenes, just as his life of love is a reaction against the 'disapproving old men' of poem 5.

Of the external details of Catullus' life there is little independent evidence, and some of it is not especially reliable. St Jerome informs us simply that Catullus was born in Verona in 87 B.C. and died in 57 B.C.; the second date is disproved easily by the poet's reference to Caesar invading Britain in 55 B.C. (11.9-12). Catullus does not refer to events after 54 B.C., and so it is tempting to locate his death in that year: Ovid mentions that he died young (*Amores* 3.9.61). The problem is neatly sewn up if we assume that Jerome mistook the year of Catullus' birth by placing it in Cinna's first consulship when in fact it was his fourth consulship (84 B.C.) – this allows Catullus to live for thirty years and die in 54 B.C. and is thus accepted by Goold ((1983) 2).

Hard evidence is also obtained from the poems themselves, especially where they mention known individuals. Gaius Memmius, for instance, of whom a good deal is known, is named as the praetorian governor on whose staff the poet served in Bithynia; and his governorship can be securely dated from a letter of Cicero (*To his brother Quintus* 1.2.16) which tells us that Memmius was elected to be praetor in 58 B.C. If Memmius stayed in Rome for his year of office and then went to his province (as was usual), he will have been in Bithynia with Catullus from 57 B.C. until 56 B.C.

More famous even than Memmius are the names which crowd the pages of this poet: he wrote a poem addressed to Cicero, the finest orator of the period and a man of refined literary taste who knew a Neoteric hexameter line when he saw one (see below # 'The Metres'). More impressive still is the textual evidence linking Catullus with Julius Caesar, the future dictator of Rome: Suetonius records (*Julius Caesar* 73) that Caesar was a friend of Catullus' father – which suggests, as Wiseman points out (Wiseman (1985) 100) that Catullus *père* was an important man – presumably in business circles. What is interesting is that the poet felt relaxed enough with Caesar to compose grossly insulting poetry about his personal life (29 and especially 57) without fear of reprisal – Suetonius uses Caesar's pardoning of Catullus as an example of his famous clemency, and one can only wonder what would have become of Catullus if he had writen such verses fifty years later under a harsher regime.

The love poems – including 68 – appear so heartfelt and 'sincere' that few scholars have ever dared but take them at face value. The identity of the 'real' Lesbia was stated, according to Wiseman ((1985) 51-2), within a single generation of the poet's death by Julius Hyginus who was Librarian of the Palatine Library; it is stated as a matter of fact by Apuleius (*Apologia* 10) that Catullus gave Clodia the false name of Lesbia, a practice common in love-poets of the time. Scholars quickly inferred that this Clodia must have been the most famous woman of that name alive at the time – Clodia Metelli, sister of the popular activist (and enemy of Cicero) Publius Clodius and wife of Metellus Celer. This fits nicely with other facts: Catullus' mistress was married (68. 145-6 is unambiguous on that point), Metellus Celer was indeed governor of Cisalpine Gaul (where Verona is) in 62 B.C., and Cicero, in defending Marcus Caelius Rufus against Clodia's accusation of attempted murder, paints a scandalous portrait of this woman as having had an affair with Caelius and been subsequently spurned by him. All in all she appears rich, loose and thoroughly dangerous to know – exactly the sort, one feels, who would impress a sensitive poet and trample on his feelings in the heartless manner described in poems 11, 75, 76, etc. Add to that the name Caelius which appears in poems where the poet lays claim to 'our Lesbia' (58) and one might swiftly arrive at the certainty of the 1966 edition of the *Oxford Companion to Classical Literature* which states categorically (s.v. 'Caelius') that Caelius 'supplanted Catullus as lover of Clodia'. Such neat coincidence is all too appealing, but it is quite possibly wrong. For one thing, the Caelius referred to in poem 69 is a sick man with gout and smelly breath, while Cicero's client was nothing if not young and healthy.

We will never know for certain. Even if Apuleius is correct in giving Lesbia the name Clodia, there were other women of the same name at the same time and of the same family – Clodia Metelli's two sisters, for instance. The pseudonym theory is itself open to serious questioning: the references to 'Lesbia' might have denoted a Greek courtesan of that name (although Griffin ((1985) 28), who argues forcibly that Roman poets loved Greek girls, still regards Catullus' Lesbia as an 'amateur' – i.e. a Roman lady), or at least be intended to disguise her as one, and it is even possible that the poem which refers to the woman's husband (68. 145-6) without naming her may be describing another woman altogether. The dangers of the 'documentary fallacy' – whereby the creations of a poet are taken as a documentary account of real experiences enjoyed by the writer – are well known and argued against by Catullus himself with tremendous force in poem 16. We do not need biographical facts to appreciate the love-poetry he composed, and anyway the poet chose to hide the object of his feelings behind a pseudonym and so did not mean us to enquire too closely. We would do better to look at the poems on their own terms, as poetry.

NEOTERIC POETRY AND CATULLUS

Catullus was hardly a lone poetic voice in Rome at the time, nor was he the first. There was abundant literature before him in Latin – epic poetry, satire, comedy, tragedy, farce, historical writing, etc. – and before them there was the massive – and the massively influential – wealth of literature from Greece. It was not uncommon for poets to claim originality (cf. Lucretius 1. 926-30, Horace *Odes* 3.30.13-14) and the Catullan circle of poets which we now know as the 'New Poets' (*novi poetae*, the Neoterics) clearly felt that they were writing literature of a new and original kind. In fact they were attempting to recreate in Latin the literary style and the milieu of Greek Alexandria.

The Egyptian city of Alexandria (founded by Alexander the Great) was, in the time of Catullus, 'the greatest city in the world' (Wiseman (1985) 54). In the period from 280 to 240 B.C., as the cultural centre of the Greeks, Alexandria was the birthplace of some of the greatest literature produced in the ancient world. Poets such as Callimachus, Theocritus and Apollonius Rhodius reacted to the literature which preceded them and determined to be more than mere epigones: and it was their poetics and their example which inspired the Neoterics in Rome two centuries later.

The major 'Alexandrian' features which we find in the poetry of Catullus are as follows. In the first place, the poet rejects the school of long-winded epics and prefers the shorter narrative form, the miniature epic (subsequently named the *epyllion*: on the history of the term see Most (1982)) which would be minutely crafted in form and would be original in content – looking at a familiar story from an unfamiliar viewpoint, as in Callimachus' *Hecale*, or switching to another story by means of an *ecphrasis** as in Moschus' *Io* or Catullus poem 64. The short epic does not aim to tell the whole story. The short epic expects the reader to know the whole story and to be able to appreciate the artistry of the poet who has sculpted what appears to be a miniature fragment of it in such unfragmentary perfection. This leads us on to the second major Alexandrian feature: learning.

Reading Alexandrian literature is not always easy. These writers expected their readers to have a wide vocabulary and an even wider range of background knowledge with which to understand their works. The techniques of allusion to other literature and sometimes recondite periphrases to denote people and places suggests that this was literature meant for *literati*, not for the man in the street. Catullus' poetry imitates this style on many occasions, especially in poems 64 and 68: and we may assume that his readers found his style pleasing and even teasing but not frustrating. Finally, the Alexandrian writers appear to have cultivated an aesthetic of 'art for art's sake' which was in conscious reaction against the didacticism of earlier poetry, whose usefulness was traditionally accounted for in terms of the good advice or moral instruction it provided (Russell (1981) 84-98). Paradoxically, the Alexandrians produced the most thoroughly didactic poets of all – Nicander of Colophon's didactic epics on *Venomous Reptiles* and *Antidotes to Poisons* for instance – but the studied didacticism of these works fooled nobody. They were hardly material for the back-pocket of the hill-walker, but ingenious and artistic exercises designed to show off the skill of the poet in his ability to transform anything into refined verse. No longer did the poet concern himself with 'high' style and 'high' society, telling great tales of kings and heroes, either: the Alexandrians show a keen interest in the feelings and the everyday lives of working people, of women, even of working women. It is no great surprise to find Catullus giving us his close account of Cyclopean metallurgy, his intimate portrait of Ariadne, his delightful simile of the girl ashamed when her apple rolls out of her dress. These are the very stuff of neoteric – and Alexandrian – poetry: a new angle on old legends, the delightful detail rather than the thunder of grandeur, the artistic word-order and exquisite euphony which repays repeated readings, the arch periphrases and allusions, the refusal to employ a straight linear narrative and the complex symmetry of construction.

   All this and more can be seen most easily in poem 68, where the tale of Laudamia and Protesilaus is woven into the personal lament for the poet's brother and his love for his mistress – a novel twist to an old story. The symmetry is perfect, as the poet passes through the themes of his love, Laudamia and his brother and then retraces his steps through the same themes in reverse order – a closed example of 'ring-composition'. The poet weaves connections between the disparate elements in the poem with apparent ease – both his brother and Protesilaus went to Troy, both Laudamia and Lesbia came to a house for love-making – and even the similes are both arresting and also apt. The late-born grandson (119-124) typifies 'natural' family life and contrasts with the wife who is stolen by the poet from her husband (145-6) as also with the wife (Helen) who is stolen and starts the Trojan War (87), just as the concupiscent doves (125-8) mirror t ̣ ̣ ̣esire both of Laudamia and also of the poet. The style is mostly clear and limpid, with the occasional Alexandrian touch of elegant erudition as in the line: *audit falsiparens Amphitryoniades*, with the patronymic alluding to Hercules (son of Alcmene who was married to Amphityron: in fact, the son of Jupiter – hence 'of false parenthood'). There is Alexandrian use of anaphora*, of apostrophe*, above all of similes*.

   Other linguistic and metrical features of the Neoterics are picked out in the commentary: their penchant for the fifth-foot spondee in hexameter verse, for instance (e.g. 64.3), and Catullus' use of Grecisms of language (the accusatives of respect at 64. 64-5, the use of *ut* in 64. 116-23, the use of the nominative in indirect statements such as 4.2). More striking and important is the poet's use of contrasting themes (happy love and the sadness of death, for instance, in 68) and his interest in the bizarre (63), the obscure (66), the unexpected (the shifts of perspective in 64). These are the elements which make Alexandrian literature different from what went before, and these are the elements which characterise these poems of Catullus as essentially ironic.

Many of the poems end, for instance, with the poet himself, leaving us with a note of ironic self-reference as a closural* gesture which is almost his signature at the foot of the page as it leaves the reader in awe both of the 'enclosed' perfection of the art and therefore also of the skill of the artist. The illusion is broken with a return from 'sublimity' to 'reality', exploring the slippage between the finely crafted poem and the world which it both reflects and refracts. Sometimes this is also achieved by ironic distance between poems – the same Catullus who disapproves so strongly of adultery in 61. 97-99 is himself a happy adulterer in 68. 145-6 – sometimes within a single poem different attitudes are struck (the heroic *virtutes* in 64.51 turn out to be far from heroic in the depiction of Theseus). Irony pervades these poems: but irony of this kind does not imply that the poet took his material less seriously but rather the opposite – there emerges from the text a realisation that this is a *text* and therefore second-hand, stylised, derivative, open to question at every turn; 'Catullus, writing in an age of lost innocence, can only say: "I love you madly – as Sappho might say"' (Fowler (1994) 248). The artifice does not, again, render the emotional response invalid or 'insincere'. Reading the text as an ironic artefact preserves the awareness of the artistry involved without seeing the whole thing as merely intellectual play: sure, the poet has 'made it all up' – but then so do all lovers and all artists. The slippage between stances adopted, the self-awareness of having both said and heard it all before was a given of the writer's condition then as much as it is now, and the ironic attitude is thus the recognition of this and the exploration of the only 'reality' – i.e. contingent, fluid appearances – which is available to any of us. Part of the peculiar fascination and value of these poems lies precisely in the fluidity and inscrutability of the stances adopted, even where – especially where – they seem most 'moral' and didactic, as at the end of poem 64. The stance may be 'sincere' in the old-fashioned sense (in that it may accord with a genuine feeling of the poet's), but its expression in a work of high art can never be interpreted without consideration of the form in which the feelings are couched, its context and its intertext – which almost always set the sentiments expressed in a distanced frame of irony. The stories lack 'foundation' in that they are here not being presented simply as 'facts' but visions and fantasies spun in words and encountered in two-dimensional shape on the page: and the words themselves are loose and insubstantial, constantly open to questions of meaning and tone, frequently slipping into invisible quotation marks as attitudes are struck and images cast. The aesthetic vituosity of the poetry is of course itself a value-system which (it could be argued) is elevated by the poet as of supreme worth where values such as love, duty, religion are shown as hollow and contingent. But then that, too, is perhaps another contingent story being brought by this reader into the text.

LUCRETIUS AND CATULLUS 64

Lucretius is mentioned a good deal in the commentary on these poems: there are many points of similarity between the two poets, as is perhaps only to be expected since they were writing at much the same time. It is quite obvious that one of them read the other and imitated him, and it is usually believed that Catullus read and imitated Lucretius rather than vice versa: poem 64 in particular has a great many echoes of Lucretius, and it is more likely that Catullus was influenced by Lucretius at one stage in the composition of 64 than that Lucretius should have spread reminiscences of a single poem of Catullus throughout his entire *oeuvre* (so Jenkyns (1982) 130-1).

At first sight they are quite different poets. Lucretius composed an epic poem teaching his audience the details of Epicurean philosophy; his purpose was (ostensibly at least) sheer utility – people will only be convinced if they listen, and they will listen better if the words are arranged in a pleasing euphonious poem. The poetry is, in his famous phrase, the 'honey of the Muses' with which he smeared the lip of the cup of bitter medicine (1.936-50), the art is not for art's sake but simply designed to sell the ethical and scientific dogmas. Catullus on the other hand appears to have nothing like this utilitarian approach to literature. His verses are written for entertainment or at the highest level for the sake of artistic expression. If he has a philosophy to sell, it is simply that poetry is worth writing well and enjoying.

Similarities of theme and emphasis are, however, striking; and the similarities and differences between the two poets are instructive. The following pages will discuss the themes of pastoral idealism, love and human sacrifice.

PASTORAL IDEALISM

31 lines into his poem Catullus describes the folk of Thessaly leaving their homes and fields to flock to the wedding of Peleus and Thetis, gifts in their hands and joy on their faces (34). Catullus then (38-41) inserts a description of the abandoned countryside, a description hyperbolic in its emphasis on the enervating effects of the temporary idleness:

rura colit nemo, mollescunt colla iuvencis,
non humilis curvis purgatur vinea rastris,
non falx attenuat frondatorum arboris umbram
non glebam prono convellit vomere taurus,
squalida desertis robigo infertur aratris.

The interpretation of this passage is clearly problematic. In some ways it reminds us of the topos* of the golden age when men did not need to work, as in Vergil:

non rastros patietur humus, non vinea ²alcem

robustus quoque iam tauris iuga solvet arator (*Eclogues* 4.40-1) ('the earth will not endure the harrow, nor the vine the pruning-hook; the sturdy ploughman will also loose the yokes from off the oxen').

This in turn derives clearly from Hesiod's men of the Golden Race (*Works and Days* 112-8) as also does the image of Lucretius' gods for whom (3.23)

omnia suppeditat porro natura ('Nature supplies everything for them')

That is one set of images suggested. Bramble ((1970) 38-9) however sees it 'the decay of agriculture...wholesale dereliction', pointing out that the Golden Age imagery does not go on to offer the innocent earth producing crops of her own volition as we expect, but only decadent luxury of which (he says) the 'normal Roman' would have disapproved. We may discard the latter point as an overgeneral and premature judgement on the 'normal Roman' but still be uneasy about the agrarian dereliction which is quite unnecessary to support the argument that in lines 43-9 'Catullus is revelling in the sensuous luxury of what he describes.' (Jenkyns (1982) 91)

Parallels for the pejorative view of idleness are there, as for example in Vergil's *Georgics* 1.505-7:

tam multae scelerum facies, non ullus aratro

dignus honos, squalent abductis arva colonis,

et curvae rigidum falces conflantur in ensem

('there are so many faces of crime, no worthy honour is paid the plough, the fields lie untended as the farmers have been removed, and the curved sickles are bent into the stiff sword.').

Here the idle fields are the result of civil strife and a symptom of society in disarray.

This sort of pejorative language in a description which the narrative does not demand would suggest that a moral attitude is being struck by the poet, as Bramble suggests. Look now at Lucretius 5. 1287-96:

et prior aeris erat quam ferri cognitus usus,

quo facilis magis est natura et copia maior.

aere solum terrae tractabant, aereque belli

miscebant fluctus et vulnera vasta serebant

et pecua atque agros adimebant; nam facile ollis

omnia cedebant armatis nuda et inerma.

inde minutatim processit ferreus ensis,

versaque in opprobrium species est falcis ahenae,

et ferro coepere solum proscindere terrae,

exaequataque sunt creperi certamina belli.

('the use of bronze was discovered before that of iron, because it is more easily handled and in more plentiful supply. With bronze they tilled the soil. With bronze they whipped up the clashing waves of war, scattered a withering seed of wounds and made a spoil of flocks and fields. Before their armaments all else, naked and unarmed, fell an easy prey. Then by slow degrees the iron sword came to the fore, the bronze sickle fell into disrepute, the ploughman began to cleave the earth with iron and on the darkling field of battle the odds were made even.')

The link between metallurgy, agriculture and warfare is clearly shown in this passage – notice the striking metaphor of men 'sowing' wounds and stirring up 'streams of war', the language of peaceful agriculture being requisitioned just as the implements were. Catullus uses this as a poetic theme

> namque velut densas praecerpens cultor aristas
> sole sub ardenti flaventia demetit arva
> Troigenum infesto prosternens corpora ferro. (64. 353-5)

Yet Catullus is not pushing the line that agriculture is a symbol of the earth's corruption as he well could have done: the earth no longer produces everything we need of her own accord, which means that we have to work for our bread – which in turn means that we now have a reason to fight and kill each other. Catullus rather seems to be showing that the men of Thessaly could afford to leave their fields long enough to attend the wedding without dying of starvation: compare that with the picture of the disgruntled farmer in Lucretius:

> iamque caput quassans grandis suspirat arator
> crebrius, incassum magnum cecidisse laborem,
> et cum tempora temporibus praesentia confert
> praeteritis, laudat fortunas saepe parentis.
> tristis item vetulae vitis sator atque vietae
> temporis incusat momen saeclumque fatigat,
> et crepat antiquum genus ut pietate repletum
> perfacile angustis tolerarit finibus aevom,
> cum minor esset agri multo modus ante viritim;
> nec tenet omnia paulatim tabescere et ire
> ad scopulum, spatio aetatis defessa vetusto. (2. 1164-74)

('by now the ploughman of ripe years shakes his head with many a sigh that his heavy labours have gone for nothing; and, when he compares the present with the past, he often applauds his father's luck. In the same despondent vein, the cultivator of old and wilted vines decries the trend of the times and rails at heaven. He grumbles that past generations, when men were old-fashioned and god-fearing, supported life easily enough on small farms, though one man's holding was then far less than now. He does not realise that everything is gradually decaying and going aground onto the rocks, worn out by old age.')

The farmer arouses Lucretius' sympathy but not his agreement: and it is hard not to see an ironic mocking tone in the insertion of *pietate repletum* as an essential ingredient of successful farming in the old days. Lucretius insists throughout the poem that the gods do not interfere with the working of the world, and so there is no room for that sort of moral explanation of the decline of the earth's fertility due to a decline in piety – and yet something very similar finds itself in Catullus' epilogue to 64 where the evils of mankind now preclude the sort of familiarity which they used to enjoy, the urbane poet using a nostalgic tone such as we find in the mind of Lucretius' rustic.

The rural idleness is followed by the luxury of the palace: and opinions vary on whether the luxury is wallowed in sensuously or held up to stern disapproval. Again, a similar passage from Lucretius (2.24-33) may be of help:

si non aurea sunt iuvenum simulacra per aedes
lampadas igniferas manibus retinentia dextris,
lumina nocturnis epulis ut suppeditentur
nec domus argento fulget auroque renidet
nec citharae reboant laqueata aurataque templa,
cum tamen inter se prostrati in gramine molli
propter aquae rivum sub ramis arboris altae
non magnis opibus iucunde corpora curant,
praesertim cum tempestas adridet et anni
tempora conspergunt viridantis floribus herbas.

('[Nature does not complain] if there are no golden images of youths about the house, holding flaming torches in their right hands to illumine banquets prolonged into the night. What matter if the hall does not sparkle with silver and gleam with gold, and no carved and gilded rafters ring to the music of the lute? Nature does not miss these luxuries when men recline in company on the soft grass by a running stream under the branches of a tall tree and refresh their bodies pleasurably at small expense. Better still if the weather smiles on them, and the season of the year bedecks the green grass with flowers.')

Luxury is of course anathema to an Epicurean and here the contrast is between the natural ornaments of the flowers and the unnatural luxuries of the revellers. So also in Catullus the contrast implied is between the humdrum unnamed life with its humble vines, rakes, ploughshares etc and the exotic opulent scene of the wedding feast. Does this scene spell divine happiness or the sort of felicity which invites divine *phthonos* (resentment) – or the sort of indignation we associate with a Cato or an Epicurus?

Catullus therefore seems to be using the language of the moralist without necessarily wishing to moralise. The idyll of happy idleness is linked to the kind of luxury which other rural idealists see as a foil: Vergil's farmer (*Georgics* 2. 458-74) is happy because he does not have the counterfeit blessings of the rich city-dweller, just as Lucretius' happy man would sooner have peace in the grass than anxiety in the palace. Catullus' peasants appear to enjoy the luxury and to feel no guilt whatsoever, the poet apparently playing with stock themes from literature in a disquieting way: we end up questioning the pastoral idealism as not enough in itself to guarantee happiness – and anyway that age of rural peace is long gone.

LOVE

If we examine the treatment of love in the two poets we find a much greater measure of congruence. Lucretius is about as pessimistic about Romantic Love as he is about politics or wealth as potential givers of happiness. Love is seen as the futile pursuit of something which cannot be ingested and atttained, his language making this quite clear in 4. 1091-1104.

For the wretched lover is left with nothing but *simulacra* to enjoy – which are themselves as flimsy as it is logically possible for anything to be (4.110-115) – unlike the objects of our hunger and thirst which at least occupy fixed places in the body (4.1092) and this give real, if temporary, satisfaction. Sexual desire is simply the result of an excess of seed in the body (4.1037-57. cf. Plato *Timaeus* 86c) and so is a mechanical operation akin to excretion; notice the way Lucretius introduces the topic of sexual activity by passing from bedwetting straight to the nocturnal emission of semen, as if the two are equivalent phenomena, and then on to sexual love. This is partly satirical, of course: the very idea of getting so excited about a form of mechanical excretion is absurd, and the purpose of the juxtaposition is to strip love of its glamour and render it comic – just as he does later on (4.1185-9) in describing the *grandes dames* of Roman society with their ineffective personal hygiene. The simile of the dreamer (4.1097-1100) is no idle analogy either. Dreams are not real life, and it therefore fits Lucretius' case admirably to argue that the lover is a dreamer who is not seeing the world as it really is. This, after all, is the thread linking the different sections of the fourth book: all perceptions are true and the evidence of the senses is valid – except where the subject is deluded into misinterpreting the evidence with which his senses present him. The sceptic, who believes nothing, is one extreme, the lover the opposite extreme in that he believes anything about his beloved. The most memorable example of this last point is the famous catalogue of euphemisms (4.1160-70) used by lovers to 're-interpret' the obvious blemishes of their beloved, where the analysis of hallucinations (as used earlier of optical illusions at 4.324-468) becomes material for satire, the lover being somehow to blame for his wilful self-deception in a way that (e.g.) the jaundiced man (4.332-6) is not.

When we turn to Catullus we see an equally bleak view of love as both blind and futile. Ariadne most obviously, whose plight and lament take up a large part of poem 64, evinces this attitude: at line 54 her love is described as 'untamed frenzy' (*indomitos furores*), her passion is madness. She can not believe her eyes in line 55 and we see the Lucretian theme of disillusionment in 175-6:

nec malus hic celans dulci crudelia forma

consilia, in nostris requiesset sedibus hospes

She *thought* he was a good man but his cruelty lay hidden within him just as the word *crudelia* is sandwiched inside *dulci..forma*. Ariadne is *caeca (197)*, and

Theseus himself is *caeca mentem caligine...consitus* (207) when he forgets his father's instructions.

Love in Catullus 64 is futile, as is stressed again and again (e.g. 59, 142). The gender rôles which we find in Lucretius are reversed here as the male is the cavalier partner while the female repines in anguish, but the anguish is the same. Look also at the unheroic realism of lines 63-7:

> non flavo retinens subtilem vertice mitram
> non contecta levi velatum pectus amictu
> non tereti strophio lactentis vincta papillas,
> omnia quae toto delapsa e corpore passim
> ipsius ante pedes fluctus salis alludebant...

The poet's eye looks down the body from head to foot, focussing on what appears to be her futile sexual signalling to an absent lover, the futility stressed in *omnia...toto...passim*. *Mitra* and *strophium* are Greek words; the garments are erotically described as flimsy and smoothly rounded (*subtilem...tereti*), *tereti* implying the contents of the *strophion* in the shape it delineates. There is also an ironic pointer to the inappropriately 'motherly' breasts – *lactentis papillas* – giving further the sense of waste, futility and sterility. The scene is charged with sensuality which can in the present situation only ever be sterile; furthermore the waves *alludebant*, a most inappropriately cheerful, playful, even sexual (cf. OLD s.v. 'ludus' 1d, 'ludo' 4) word to use of the waves lapping at the feet of a deserted woman.

Love is also wretched. *miser* is Lucretius' word for the love-sickness which he contrasts with the *sani* who escape the passion of romantic love (cf. 8.1, 64.94, 76.12, Propertius 1.1.1). Ariadne fell in love at first sight (86ff) just as Peleus and Thetis did (19ff). Here again Catullus dwells on Ariadne's safe chaste happy *lectulus*, sweet-smelling *in molli complexu matris*. This contrasts with the very unsafe *cubile* – ironically like the one on which all this is being depicted – just as the luxurious comfort of her life (86-93) is contrasted sentimentally with the grim reality she is now facing as the truth of love overtakes the dreaming of a young girl; she is if anything leaving a life of *ataraxia** at home for the perilous seas of romantic love. When the contrast is drawn again at 117ff all has been abandoned for love, with the sense of waste prominent in *misera...deperdita* and the bitter loss of the safe embrace of her mother and sister so fondly depicted at 88. The word *dulcem* is savagely ironic; love for Theseus was sweet – but only for the moment.

The clearest expression of this is in the apostrophe* to Cupid (94ff). *misere* suggests the wretched lover; love is a form of madness (*furores*) and the god drives us relentlessly (*inmiti corde*) to suffering. Catullus draws on earlier literature such as Apollonius Rhodius 4. 445-7, where:

'Wicked Eros, great source of pain, hateful to mankind; it is from you that deadly strife comes, along with laments and groaning and countless pains..'

The notion of Cupid mixing joys and sorrows is also of course reminiscent of Zeus mixing good and bad fortunes of men into the pots (Homer *Iliad* 24.527-40), where Peleus is singled out by the poet for his felicity:

'There are two urns on the floor of Zeus, urns of gifts which he gives, one of bad things, the other of good. Anyone to whom Zeus who delights in the thunderbolt gives a mixture will meet now with bad fortune, now with good; but the man to whom he gives only grievous things he has made reviled, and evil madness drives him over the godlike earth, and he wanders honoured neither by men nor by gods. The gods gave Peleus glorious gifts from his birth – for he exceeded all men in wealth and property and ruled over the Myrmidons, and although he was only mortal they gave him a goddess for a wife. Yet the gods gave even Peleus evils since he had no offspring of strong sons in his halls, but he produced only one son and he was ill-fated...'

Peleus is here held up as a paradigm of felicity in all except his son, whose character and exploits are to be the centre of attention later in the poem. How appropriate here in Catullus to find good and evil being given out not by Zeus but by Cupid: it is love which drives Peleus to marry Thetis and produce Achilles who expresses the grim view of human life presented in Homer. Catullus presumably expects his learned audience to pick up the reference here, especially in view of the predominance of Achilles later in the poem, and also in view of the contrast and parallel between Aegeus' mourning for his son (215ff) and Priam's mourning over his son Hector in *Iliad* 24 – the contrast being in the fact that of course Theseus is not dead and so his father's love and suicide is as fatuous as the feelings of Ariadne. Once again, the romantic love of Peleus and Thetis, just like the love of Ariadne for Theseus, can never produce lasting happiness.

Nor is it solely love between the sexes which is doomed and blind. Theseus fails to carry out his father's instructions because he is 'blind' and Aegeus is wrong in thinking that the ship brings bad news. We can then compare and contrast the lament of Aegeus for Theseus with the lament of Ariadne: his loss is just as plaintive as hers, but his admiration for Theseus' *virtus* (218) is sincere, whereas Ariadne's is bitterly sarcastic. The searing irony is brought home at 247ff: Theseus is *morte ferox* but here he kills his own father. Theseus is sad, Aegeus commits suicide in despair and Ariadne is waiting to die. No love, it seems, is free from pain, illusion and suffering – neither romantic love nor parental/ filial love. If further evidence is needed, look at the delightful offspring of the love of Peleus and Thetis and watch his homicidal mania at Troy.

The parallels with Lucretius' view of love are striking. Ariadne has learnt the hard way what Lucretius tells us in his poem, even showing herself ready to be the slave (161-3) of her beloved as mentioned also in Lucretius (4.1122) and developed in the later elegists' concept of *servitium amoris* (on which see Lyne (1979) *passim*). Ariadne also, however, expected Theseus to love her in return for what she had done for him (149-50) but her only reward is desertion without even the honour of burial.

The wedding of Peleus and Thetis is told in overblown colours throughout; when it is pleasant it is idyllic, when it is not it is bizarre. Their falling in love and the supreme felicity of a man being loved by a goddess, their warm love-making (330-2) reminding us closely of the love-making of Venus and Mars at Lucretius 1. 33-40. Even here, however, there are dark shadows looming ahead, the future for their cosy family being that their son will one day wreak slaughter at Troy such as never before, slaughter to make the mothers beat their aged breasts with feeble hands as they mourn the death of their sons slain by this hero of the Greeks (349-51). The bizarre nature of the wedding is shown especially in the Parcae singing the wedding song, their song a pastiche of lyricism and a scenario of carnage and misery culminating in the rhetorical climax that this hero will be able to slaughter innocent non-combatants such as Polyxena even when he is dead.

HUMAN SACRIFICE

The theme of human sacrifice is developed throughout poem 64. Early on we are told that the reason for Theseus' journey was to kill the Minotaur who was being fed with human beings (76-83), and Ariadne's help was also bitterly ironic for her in that it saved the lives of the unnamed youths of Athens but only at the cost of her own abandonment. She takes their place, just as Theseus the saviour and deliverer from the monster (her 'brother') becomes in her eyes worse than the monster itself. The theme then recurs in the extended and garish description (362-70) of the slaughter of Polyxena at the tomb of the dead Achilles where again, like Ariadne, the victim is young, female and innocent. The passage is rich in associations. The word *praeda* reminds us of the 'prize' of Achilles in the *Iliad* (again a girl) and the parallel with the Minotaur is uncomfortable. At least the Minotaur ate his victims and derived some benefit from the sacrifice – Achilles' corpse will get little benefit from this act of futile brutality. The poet dwells on the savagery with unswerving gaze: her limbs are snow-white, she is unmarried, and her collapse is described with the word *succumbens* as she is struck down (*perculsae*). The scene is pictorial in quality, portraying the end-result immediately in the tomb wet with blood (cf. 359-60, where the river is warmed up with blood) followed by a replay of the killing itself; note the detail of the two-edged sword before which she collapses, her knees giving way in graphic style and leaving her without a head (*truncum*). The last word sums up the whole scene leaving her a dead body (*corpus*).

   This scene is certainly parallel to the sacrifice of Iphigeneia in Lucretius 1. 84-101. Lucretius is far more explicit than Catullus in driving home the 'moral' point. The bitter 'funeral marriage' idea which Catullus could well have brought out to good effect since the Parcae are singing at a wedding is amplified in Lucretius into a sharp stinging jibe at the indecency (*inceste*) of the act. She is also a wretched lover (*miserae*) calling in vain on the claims of paternal love – just as Ariadne calls on the claim of Theseus' love in vain. Agamemnon is also mourning (*maestum*) just as

Aegeus does in Catullus, but again to no effect. The description of the sacrifice has obvious verbal correspondences, some of which may be coincidental. Both girls kneel down (*summisso poplite* – *genibus summissa*). More significantly, the end result of the sacrifice in both cases is that the next stage should be *felix* – the fleet's journey to Troy in Lucretius and the wedding union in Catullus (372-5). The same tone of outrage is detectable in both writers, but the contexts are different. Lucretius is concerned at this point to persuade us that the pursuit of philosophy does not lead the student into a life of wickedness, but rather that it is religion which has caused more cruelty than philosophy. It cannot be proven that Catullus is inspired by the same idea: his poem has taken the theme of human sacrifice and developed it from the Minotaur through Ariadne to the slaughter of Polyxena, the 'monsters' being respectively Minotaur, Theseus and Achilles. It has one more appearance to make, in the epilogue. As part of the catalogue of wickedness (397-408) which explains the gods' refusal to visit us any more, he singles out bloodshed in general and innocent bloodshed in particular – the son whose only crime is that he is in the way when his father is marrying again – a human sacrifice to the god of Romantic Love.

Opinions will vary about the ending of poem 64, whether it is moralistic or not. In any case, as argued below *ad loc.*, the epilogue is not a mere afterthought but a recapitulation of themes from the rest of the poem. The brother's blood suggesting the killing of the Minotaur, the lamentation over parents recalling the mourning of Theseus over his father, the execution of the innocent son another human sacrifice, the sexual union of the mother and son bringing back the Lucretian image of love as blind (*ignaro*) and reckless, polluting the house and destroying the livelihood (4.1123ff). The word *furor* evokes the murderous, futile and mad passion of love which we have seen cause both the suffering of Ariadne and also cause the deaths wreaked by Achilles in the Trojan War – both because he was the son of the love of Peleus and Thetis and also because it was Paris' love for Helen which caused the Trojan war in the first place.

    Similar conclusions may be drawn about the ending of the *de rerum natura*. The plague shows us a cosmic and human catastrophe which renders all the moral and social order hollow and which brings out the degradation of the human being under extreme pressure. Only Epicurus has the 'answer', Lucretius may be arguing – the Epicurean wise man should be capable of happiness even when being roasted in the bronze bull of Phalaris, let alone when faced with disease. Alternatively, the poet of Epicureanism may be leaving us with the collapse of society and ethics to show us that the only form of goodness which outlasts everything is artistic goodness, and that the rendering of suffering into poetry (as in Homer and Greek tragedy) produces not merely pleasure but also good. The epilogue to Catullus 64 brings the *Kulturpessimismus* latent in the exploration of human wickedness up to date and involves ourselves (*nobis* 406). We may be only looking at a picture for much of the poem, but it is also, Catullus now tells us, a mirror in which we see ourselves reflected as well as a window into the past. The heroic age is addressed as better than we are now (22-4), but it too was filled with suffering, deception, pain. Heroism, love and duty are all shown to be flawed and powerless against the inevitability of wickedness. In this he agrees with the attitude of Lucretius, for whom all the enterprises with which man seeks to give his life meaning and purpose – warfare, politics, love, religion – are all empty dreams incapable of making us happy and doomed to disappointment. Love is a form of madness, striving for political power is a labour of Sisyphus, the gods will not hear our prayers in their oblivious serenity, and warfare is certain death with no afterlife save a hollow glory. What is there left but poetry? What values are remaining except aesthetic ones? Both poets leave us with these questions ringing in our ears, and it is unlikely that the similarities are pure coincidence.

THE METRES

Latin poetry is based on a fairly rigid system of metres, all of which in turn rely on the 'quantity' of each vowel as being either long or short. A syllable is reckoned to be a single vowel sound, followed either by nothing (an 'open' syllable) or by a consonant (a 'closed' syllable): usually a single consonant following a vowel is reckoned to be the first consonant of the following syllable (e.g. *ca-li-gi-ne*) and does not affect the length of the vowel: where two or more consonants follow a vowel, the first one is included in the first syllable (*men-sa*) which is thus 'closed' and becomes lengthened – the exceptions being combinations of mute and liquid consonants (*b, c, g, p, t* followed by *r,; t,* followed by *l*) are considered as belonging to the following syllable (*pa-tris*) and need not lengthen the vowel. Diphthongs (*ae, eu, au,* etc.) are always long by nature: single vowels may be long or short by nature and may vary with inflection (e.g. the final *-a* of *mensa* is long by nature in the ablative case, short in the nominative) or they may be lengthened by position when followed by two or more consonants as indicated above (e.g. 64.8 *quibus retinens* where the final *us* of *quibus* is followed by *r* and so lengthened). In cases where a word ending with a vowel (or a vowel + *m* such as *iustam*) is followed by a word beginning with a vowel or *h*, the two syllables usually merge ('elide') into a single syllable, as at 64. 190 *iustam a* is scanned as *iust(am) a*.

This collection of eight poems employs four different metres: hexameters (62, 64), elegiac couplets (65, 66, 67,68), Galliambics (63) and Glyconics/pherecrateans (61).

Hexameters

This is the 'epic' metre used by Homer and all later epic poets. The line is divided into six 'feet', each of which is either a dactyl (a long syllable followed by two short syllables (– ∪∪ in conventional notation)) or a spondee (two long syllables (– –)). The last foot is always dissyllabic, the last syllable of all being either long or short. Thus a 'typical' hexameter line will run:

– ∪∪ / – – / – // – / – – / – ∪∪ / – –

Pélia/có quon/dám // pro/gnátae/ vértice/ pínus

where ∪ indicates a short syllable, and – a long syllable, the ´ sign indicates the stressed syllable at the beginning of a foot and the // sign shows the 'caesura' – the word-break in the middle of a foot – usually the third.

Latin also had a stress accent, whereby most words were stressed on the penultimate syllable, or on the antepenultimate if the penultimate were a short vowel. Thus the first line of poem 66 would be spoken:

ómnia quí mágni dispéxit lúmina múndi

but 'scanned' metrically as:

ómnia quí magní dispéxit lúmina múndi.

Quite how the two ways of reading Latin verse blended or competed is unclear: one notes that in hexameters there is a tendency for the stress accent and the metrical beat (*ictus*) to collide in the earlier and middle parts of the line but to coincide at the end – a tendency which is however abruptly broken when the line ends with a monosyllable as at 66.63.

The hexameter had been used already in Latin before Catullus: Ennius (*c*.239-169 BC) had composed his *Annales* in the metre, and Catullus' contemporary Lucretius composed his didactic epic *de rerum natura* in hexameters. Catullus' use of the metre is distinguished most obviously by his liking for fifth-foot spondees – the penultimate foot in a hexameter is almost always a dactyl – a practice which was apparently common among the Neoteric poets, as noted by Cicero (*Letters to Atticus* 7.2.1). The amount of elision in Catullus' verses is also greatly in excess of that allowed by later poets such as Vergil and Ovid.

Elegiac couplets
This metre, as its name suggests, composes lines in pairs: the first line of the couplet is always a hexameter (exactly as above), while the second is a pentameter. The name tells us that there are five feet, but the line is conventionally composed in two halves, each of two dactylic/spondaic feet followed by a single syllable. The second half of the pentameter is in the overwhelming majority of cases dactylic (i.e. two dactyls followed by a single syllable). The pentameter thus runs:

    – ∪∪ / – – /– // – ∪∪ / – ∪∪/ ∪
    sévocat á doctís// Órtale vírginibús.

Elegiac couplets tend to be complete sense-making units; enjambement* from the hexameter to the following pentameter is common (cf. e.g. 66. 89-90) but only rarely do we find enjambement* from the pentameter into the next hexameter (66. 24-5 and 66. 80-81 are examples).

Galliambics

This is a very unusual metre, rarely attempted in either Greek or Latin: it is especially difficult in Latin owing to its need for a lot of short syllables to be juxtaposed when the language has a natural tendency towards long syllables. The rhythm is made up of two anacreontics, the first halves of which are the same: first a simple anacreontic

    ∪∪– ∪/ – ∪– –,

and then an anacreontic with resolution (two short syllables replacing a long syllable) and catalexis (the suppression of the final syllable), the last syllable of the line being *anceps* (the symbol for this is 'x': denoting that the syllable is either long or short at the poet's discretion):

    ∪∪– ∪/ ∪∪ ∪x
The whole line thus scans:

∪∪– ∪– ∪– – //∪∪– ∪∪∪∪x

Flexibility is secured by the use of 'resolution': each of the long syllables may be 'resolved' into by two short syllables, and two short syllables may be merged into a single long syllable. The shortest line in poem 63 is thus:

– – ∪–∪ – – // – –∪ –∪∪

iam iam dolet quod egi//iam iamque paenitet (73)

while the longest is:

∪∪ ∪∪∪ ∪ ∪ ∪ – – // ∪ ∪– ∪ ∪∪ ∪

ego mulier eg(o) adulescens// eg(o) ephebus, ego puer (63).

Poem 63 is a virtuoso performance in the application of this difficult metre without loss of either sense or poetic feeling.

Glyconics/Pherecrateans

This is the metre used in the Marriage Song 61 and the hymn to Diana in 34. The basic colon is the choriamb (– ∪ ∪ –), found in both the glyconic and the pherecratean, metres very similar in form as follows:

Glyconic: – x – ∪ ∪ – ∪ –

Pherecratean: – x – ∪ ∪ – –

In practice, the second syllable in this poem (unlike in 34) of both metres is virtually always short, although there are exceptions (e.g. 61.175). So for instance, poem 61 begins:

– ∪ – ∪∪–∪–   (glyconic)

Collis O Heliconii...

– ∪ – ∪ ∪ – –   (pherecratean).

O Hymen Hymenaee

Catullus – like his predecessor Anacreon but unlike Horace later on – observes strict synaphea both in 61 and 34 – i.e. the stanza is the metrical unit, with no hiatus between lines except at the ending of a stanza, lines ending with a vowel eliding into the next line within the stanza (e.g. 61. 135-6); the few occasions where synaphea is not observed make one wonder whether the text is sound. There is even one example of a word split across two lines (46-7).

THE TRANSMISSION OF THE TEXT

We have no certain knowledge of the form of Catullus' original text. He describes his work as a 'little book' (1.1) which rather suggests that the text we have was originally divided up into books – most obviously into three sections: 1-60 (polymetric poems), 61-64 (long poems) and then 65-116 (elegiacs). Any one of these groups would make a 'little book' (*libellus*) while the whole collection would be far too big to deserve the name.

This presupposes that the poet himself 'edited' and 'published' his work – another assumption in need of evidence. There is ample evidence of care in the ordering of these poems, but of course that ordering need not have been carried out by the poet himself. The eight poems published here have a coherence as a collection which is far from coincidental – the themes of marriage and adultery, the parallels between the mutilation of Attis in 63 and that of the lock in 66, the contrast between the happy married love of Manlius in 61 and the happy adulterous love in 68, the conventional lines about marriage in 62 contrasted with the highly unconventional lines about it in 67, all creating an overarching symmetry which leaves 64 in central splendour as the poet's masterpiece. That Catullus intended these eight poems to stand alone as a single volume is highly questionable: but there is no doubt that they do form a pleasing unity when so published.

Our texts of Latin and Greek literature have in many cases survived only by near-miracles. The original written texts of the poet were copied laboriously by hand by scribes in the Roman world. When the West entered what we now call the Dark Ages the copying of texts became the job of monasteries. Some authors survived comfortably with large numbers of manuscripts still extant: others only made it by the skin of their teeth. Catullus was one of the latter.

Poem 62 was very lucky: there is one manuscript surviving from the ninth century which contains it, the *codex Thuaneus* (*T*) now kept in Paris. This was an anthology of passages from Catullus, Martial, Juvenal and Seneca belonging to a certain Jacques-Auguste de Thou. For the rest we are indebted to a single manuscript of the poems which came to the poet's home town of Verona at the start of the fourteenth century. This manuscript, now known as *Codex Veronensis* or *V*, contained everything we have of Catullus. It was copied by a scholar (manuscript A) but this too was lost – as was the copy of A known as manuscript X. (For the existence of A see McKie (1977) 38-95) V, A and X did not survive, but A was copied again in the second half of the fourteenth century and this copy is kept in the Bodleian Library in Oxford, from which it derives its name *Codex Oxoniensis* ('the Oxford Manuscript') or *O*. X was then copied twice: the first copy (*G*) being kept in

Paris, the second (*R*) in Rome. So far, then, the descent is as follows:

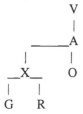

O, G and R are the basis of all modern texts: from a close comparison of their similarities and differences we can be reasonably sure of the text of V: and the much earlier testimony of T agrees with V sufficiently to make us fairly sure that T and V derive from a common ancestor. O, G and R were themselves copied many times, and there are occasions where these humanists' copies have an inspired correction of the tradition of V (e.g. 68.11, 66.18), but their emendations are based on no other knowledge of the textual tradition than is available to ourselves. There are over 100 of these later manuscripts before 1472 when the first printed edition appeared in Venice, an edition based on one single manuscript – with all its imperfections – out of the many, and destined to fix the printed text of Catullus for a long time to come. It has been estimated that V contained at least 1000 errors (Goold (1983) 11): renaissance humanists managed to rectify about half of them (460) before 1472: and since then scholars have continued to worry at the remaining half. Some of these emendations involve no change of reading but merely one of orthography (most famously, A.E. Housman's reading of V's *Emathiae tutamen opis, carissime nato* as the eminently sensible *Emathiae tutamen, Opis carissime nato* (64. 324)), while some of them reflect palaeographic confusions in the distant past (e.g. confusion of 'f' and 's' in V's reading *fundanti* for *sudanti* at 64.106; or *fragrantem* for *flagrantem* at 68.139) or a failure to recognise a proper name (e.g. *cuma est gravis* for *Cinna est Gaius* at 10.30). Nor have we finished this task: the text still contains what are called *cruces* – passages such as 68. 157 where the tradition is certainly wrong but where no convincing emendation has yet been thought up, and which are conventionally bracketed with a symbol of a cross (*crux*, †), as well as a whole range of passages where the received text has excellent credentials but still raises problems of meaning (e.g. 68.10), of inconsistency (e.g. the name-changing from 68.11 to 68.41), or of identity (who is *Amarunsia virgo* at 64.395?). Where the difference of opinion is far from obvious and the difference matters I have printed the various readings at the foot of the page in the *apparatus criticus* – for a fuller account of the readings see the *apparatus* in Mynors' Oxford Text. Throughout this edition I have printed what I consider to be the most convincing readings – some of which were suggested in the fourteenth century within a few years of V, some of which (e.g. 68.39) were suggested as recently as 1978. Work continues to be done on the history of the text (see e.g. McKie (1977)); and there is still ample scope for the reader of

Catullus to continue the long process of cleaning up what was in 1350 a hideously corrupted text and try to discover what the poet himself wrote. The skills of the textual critic are often seen as 'scientific' and arid, when in fact the ultimate arbiter of the printed text is our historical imagination and our sensitivity to the poetry being transmitted.

SIGLA

CODICES:
V= archetypum (codex Veronensis s. xii: fons communis O et X)
O= Oxoniensis Canonicianus
X= fons communis G et R
G= Parisianus lat. 14137 anni MCCCLXXV
R= Vaticanus Ottobonianus lat. 1829 s. xiv ex.
T= Parisinus lat. 8071 s. ix (*continet carmen lxii*)

FONTES CONIECTURARUM MANU SCRIPTI:

r = corrector(es) cod. R
g = corrector(es) cod. G
f = corrector anno MCCCCLVII
ζ = nescio quis ante annum MCCCCLX
i = corrector anno MCCCCLXV

POEMS 61-8

LXI

collis o Heliconii
cultor, Uraniae genus,
qui rapis teneram ad virum
virginem, o Hymenaee Hymen,
    o Hymen Hymenaee: 5

cinge tempora floribus
suave olentis amaraci,
flammeum cape laetus, huc
huc veni, niveo gerens
    luteum pede soccum;   10

excitusque hilari die,
nuptialia concinens
voce carmina tinnula,
pelle humum pedibus, manu
    pineam quate taedam.   15

namque Iunia Manlio,
qualis Idalium colens
venit ad Phrygium Venus
iudicem, bona cum bona
    nubet alite virgo.   20

floridis velut enitens
myrtus Asia ramulis
quos Hamadryades deae
ludicrum sibi roscido
    nutriunt umore.   25

---

16 Iunia *V*: Vinia *D (1463)*: Vibia *Syme*   25 nutriunt umore *V*: nutriuntur honore *Maehly*

61

O dweller on Mount Helicon,
son of Urania,
you who take by force to go to her husband the tender
virgin, O Hymeneal Hymen,
O Hymen Hymeneal: 5

wreath your temples with the flowers
of the sweet smelling marjoram,
take up the bridal veil joyfully and come here,
come here, wearing on your snow-white
foot the yellow slipper ;   10

and aroused by this happy day,
singing the marriage
hymns with your high-pitched voice,
beat the ground with your feet, with your hand
shake the pine torch.   15

For Junia is marrying Manlius,
just like she who dwells on Idalium,
Venus when she went to her Phrygian
judge, a virgin of goodness
with good auspices.   20

Just like the Asian myrtle,
brilliant with its flowery little branches,
which the divine wood-nymphs
nurture with the moisture of dew
to be their plaything.   25

quare age, huc aditum ferens,
perge linquere Thespiae
rupis Aonios specus,
nympha quos super irrigat
      frigerans Aganippe.   30

ac domum dominam voca
coniugis cupidam novi,
mentem amore revinciens,
ut tenax hedera huc et huc
      arborem implicat errans.   35

vosque item simul, integrae
virgines, quibus advenit
par dies, agite in modum
dicite, o Hymenaee Hymen,
      o Hymen Hymenaee.   40

ut libentius, audiens
se citarier ad suum
munus, huc aditum ferat
dux bonae Veneris, boni
      coniugator amoris.   45

quis deus magis est ama-
tis petendus amantibus?
quem colent homines magis
caelitum, o Hymenaee Hymen,
      o Hymen Hymenaee?   50

te suis tremulus parens
invocat, tibi virgines
zonula solvunt sinus,
te timens cupida novus
      captat aure maritus.   55

---

46 est amatis *Bergk:* amatis est *V:* anxiis est *Haupt*

Come then, approach this way,
set about leaving behind the Aonian
caverns of the Thespian rock,
caverns which the nymph Aganippe
showers with cooling waters from above.

Call your mistress home,
she who is longing for her new husband,
binding her mind with the fetters of love,
just like the unyielding ivy ties up
the tree as it creeps here and there.

You too, unwed maidens,
to whom is coming
a day like this, come, in accord with me,
sing, O Hymeneal Hymen,
O Hymen Hymeneal.

so that all the more willingly, hearing
himself summoned to his task,
he may come to us here,
the bringer of favourable Venus, the one
who brings favourable love together.

Which god is more to be sought
after by beloved lovers?
Which of the heavenly ones will men
honour more, O Hymeneal Hymen,
O Hymen Hymeneal?

The trembling parent calls upon you
in prayer for his family, it is for you that virgins
untie the girdle of their dresses,
you that the novice husband listens out for
in fear with eager ear.

tu fero iuveni in manus
floridam ipse puellulam
dedis a gremio suae
matris, o Hymenaee Hymen,
    o Hymen Hymenaee.   60

nil potest sine te Venus
fama quod bona comprobet
commodi capere, at potest
te volente. quis huic deo
    comparier ausit?   65

nulla quit sine te domus
liberos dare, nec parens
stirpe nitier; at potest
te volente. quis huic deo
    comparier ausit?   70

quae tuis careat sacris,
non queat dare praesides
terra finibus: at queat
te volente. quis huic deo
    comparier ausit?   75

claustra pandite ianuae.
virgo adest. viden ut faces
splendidas quatiunt comas?
    .   .   .   .
        .   .   .

    .   .   .   .
        .   .   .

tardet ingenuus pudor.
quem tamen magis audiens,   80
    fles quod ire necesse est.

---

77 adest V: ades *Schrader*
post versum 78 *lacunam indicavit Ellis.*   81 fles *Goold*: flet V

you hand over into the hands of the savage youth
the young girl in the flower of youth,
taking her from the bosom of her
mother,   O Hymeneal Hymen,
O Hymen Hymeneal.   60

without you Venus can seize no
benefit of which good renown would
approve, but she can do such a thing
with your approval. Who would dare
to be compared to this god?   65

without you no house can
bring forth children, nor can any parent
rely on his offspring – but they can
with your approval. Who would dare
to be compared with this god?   70

The land which is lacking your sacred rites
would not be able to provide guardians
for its borders: but it could do so
with your approval. Who would dare
to be compared with this god?   75

Open up the bolts of the door.
The bride is here. Do you see how the torches
shake their shining hair? ...
.   .   .   .
.   .   .   .

.   .   .   .
.   .   .   .
... be slowed by free-born modesty.
Heeding this all the more,   80
you weep because you must go.

flere desine.   non tibi, Au-
runculeia, periculum est,
ne qua femina pulcrior
clarum ab Oceano diem   85
            viderit venientem.

talis in vario solet
divitis domini hortulo
stare flos hyacinthus.
sed moraris, abit dies.   90
            <prodeas nova nupta.>

prodeas nova nupta, si
iam videtur, et audias
nostra verba.   viden? faces
aureas quatiunt comas: 95
            prodeas nova nupta.

non tuus levis in mala
deditus vir adultera,
probra turpia persequens,
a tuis teneris volet   100
            secubare papillis,

lenta sed velut adsitas
vitis implicat arbores,
implicabitur in tuum
complexum. sed abit dies: 105
            prodeas nova nupta.

o cubile, quod omnibus
  .   .   .   .

  .   .   .   .

  .   .   .

            candido pede lecti,

_____

post versum 107 *lacunam trium versuum indicavit Guarinus.*

Stop weeping. In your case, Au-
runculeia, there is no danger
that any woman more beautiful than you
has watched the bright day coming   85
from out of the Ocean.

This is how in the many-coloured
garden of a rich master
the hyacinth flower tends to stand.
But you delay and the day is passing.   90
<come forth, new bride>

Come forth, new bride, if
by now you have decided to do so, and hear
our words. Do you see? the torches
shake their golden tresses.   95
Come forth, new bride.

your husband is not fickle and
abandoned in the clutches of some evil adulteress,
following a life of filthy scandal;
he will not wish to sleep apart from   100
your tender breasts,

but rather, just as the pliant vine
entwines the trees planted alongside it,
so will he be entwined into your
embrace. But the day is passing: 105
come forth new bride.

O bed, which ... all ...
.   .   .   .   .
.   .   .   .   .
.   .   .   .   .
bed's white foot,

quae tuo veniunt ero,
quanta gaudia, quae vaga   110
nocte, quae medio die
gaudeat! sed abit dies:
            prodeas nova nupta.

tollite, <o> pueri, faces:
flammeum video venire.   115
ite concinite in modum
'io Hymen Hymenaee io
            io Hymen Hymenaee.'

ne diu taceat procax
Fescennina iocatio,   120
nec nuces pueris neget
desertum domini audiens
            concubinus amorem.

da nuces pueris, iners
concubine! satis diu   125
lusisti: nucibus libet
iam servire Talassio.
            concubine, nuces da.

sordebant tibi vilicae,
concubine, hodie atque heri: 130
nunc tuum cinerarius
tondet os. miser a miser
            concubine, nuces da.

diceris male te a tuis
unguentate glabris marite   135
abstinere, sed abstine.
io Hymen Hymenaee io
            <io Hymen Hymenaee.>

_____

114 o *addidit* r

61   33

what pleasures are coming for your master,
and how great are the pleasures which in the wayward   110
night, and at midday also,
he is to enjoy! But the day is passing:
come forth, new bride.

Boys, raise up the torches:
I can see the bridal veil approaching.   115
Come sing in unison:
O Hymeneal Hymen,
O Hymen Hymeneal.

Let not the unrestrained Fescennine
jesting keep silent for long,   120
nor may the pretty boy refuse to give nuts to the boys
when he hears of the master's
abandoned love.

Give nuts to the boys, sluggish
pretty-boy! You have played   125
for long enough; now it is time
to serve Talassius with nuts.
Pretty-boy, give out the nuts.

The farm women were beneath your contempt,
yesterday and today, pretty-boy: 130
but now the barber
shaves your cheek. Wretched, ah wretched
pretty boy, give out nuts.

You are said to be finding it difficult,
O perfumed bridegroom, to keep away from   135
the smooth-skinned boys, but keep away from them.
O Hymeneal Hymen,
O Hymen Hymeneal.

scimus haec tibi quae licent
soli cognita, sed marito 140
ista non eadem licent.
io Hymen Hymenaee io,
    io Hymen Hymenaee.

nupta, tu quoque quae tuus
vir petet cave ne neges, 145
ni petitum aliunde eat.
io Hymen Hymenaee io,
    io Hymen Hymenaee.

en tibi domus ut potens
et beata viri tui! 150
quae tibi sine serviat
(io Hymen Hymenaee io,
    io Hymen Hymenaee)

usque dum tremulum movens
cana tempus anilitas 155
omnia omnibus annuit.
io Hymen Hymenaee io,
    io Hymen Hymenaee.

transfer omine cum bono
limen aureolos pedes, 160
rasilemque subi forem.
io Hymen Hymenaee io,
    io Hymen Hymenaee.

aspice intus ut accubans
vir tuus Tyrio in toro 165
totus immineat tibi.
io Hymen Hymenaee io,
    io Hymen Hymenaee.

___

140 soli *i*: sola *V*

We know well that you are familiar
with the pleasures allowed a single man – but   140
those same pleasures are not allowed a husband.
O Hymeneal Hymen,
O Hymen Hymeneal.

Bride, you too must beware of refusing
what your husband will seek of you,   145
in case he goes off to seek it elsewhere.
O Hymeneal Hymen,
O Hymen Hymeneal.

Look, see how powerful
and prosperous is the house of your husband!   150
Let it be your slave
(O Hymeneal Hymen,
O Hymen Hymeneal)

until white-haired old-age keeps
moving your trembling head and   155
makes you agree with everybody in everything.
O Hymeneal Hymen,
O Hymen Hymeneal.

Bring with a good omen
your golden little feet across the threshold,   160
go under the planed doorway.
O Hymeneal Hymen,
O Hymen Hymeneal.

Look inside and see how your husband,
lying on a Tyrian couch,   165
is intent totally on you.
O Hymeneal Hymen,
O Hymen Hymeneal.

illi non minus ac tibi
pectore uritur intimo   170
flamma, sed penite magis.
io Hymen Hymenaee io,
        io Hymen Hymenaee.

mitte bracchiolum teres,
praetextate, puellulae: 175
iam cubile adeat viri.
io Hymen Hymenaee io,
        io Hymen Hymenaee.

vos bonae senibus viris
cognitae bene feminae,   180
collocate puellulam.
io Hymen Hymenaee io,
        io Hymen Hymenaee.

iam licet venias, marite:
uxor in thalamo tibi est,   185
ore floridulo nitens,
alba parthenice velut
        luteumve papaver.

at, marite, ita me iuvent
caelites, nihilo minus   190
pulcer es, neque te Venus
neglegit. sed abit dies:
        perge, ne remorare.

non diu remoratus es:
iam venis. bona te Venus   195
iuverit, quoniam palam
quod cupis cupis, et bonum
        non abscondis amorem.

---

170 uritur *V*: urit in *Goold*

In his case no less than in yours
in the depth of his breast is burning   170
the flame, but deeper within.
O Hymeneal Hymen,
O Hymen Hymeneal.

You page-boy wearing a purple toga, let go of the
delicate little arm of the young girl.   175
She is now to approach her husband's bed.
O Hymeneal Hymen,
O Hymen Hymeneal.

You, good women well known
to your aged husbands,   180
set the girl in her place.
O Hymeneal Hymen,
O Hymen Hymeneal.

Now, husband, you may approach:
your wife is in your bedroom,   185
shining with her flowery little face,
like to the white camomile
or the yellow poppy.

And yet, husband, you – so help me
the gods who dwell in the heavens – are no less   190
beautiful, nor does Venus
forget you. But the day is passing:
come on, do not delay.

You have not delayed long:
you are now on your way. May favourable Venus   195
assist you, since you make no secret
of your desires and do not
hide away an honourable love.

ille pulveris Africi
siderumque micantium   200
subducat numerum prius,
qui vestri numerare vult
        multa milia ludi.

ludite ut lubet, et brevi
liberos date. non decet   205
tam vetus sine liberis
nomen esse, sed indidem
        semper ingenerari.

Torquatus volo parvulus
matris e gremio suae   210
porrigens teneras manus
dulce rideat ad patrem
        semihiante labello.

sit suo similis patri
Manlio ut facie omnibus   215
noscitetur ab insciis,
et pudicitiam suae
        matris indicet ore.

talis illius a bona
matre laus genus approbet,   220
qualis unica ab optima
matre Telemacho manet
        fama Penelopeo.

claudite ostia, virgines:
lusimus satis. at, boni   225
coniuges, bene vivite et
munere assiduo valentem
        exercete iuventam.

215/6 ut *Bergk*: et *V*   facie *Burman*: facile *V*   omnibus noscitetur ab insciis *Dawes*:
insciens noscitetur ab omnibus *V*

Let him first reckon up the numbers
of the dust in Africa or   200
the stars that gleam above,
who wishes to count the many
thousands of your sports.

Play as you please, and
produce children soon. It is not right   205
for so ancient a name to
be lacking in children, but rather it should always
be reproduced from the same stock.

I would like to see a miniature Torquatus
from the bosom of his mother   210
reaching out his fresh young hands
smiling sweetly at his father
with his little lips half open.

Let him look like his father
Manlius, so that he can be recognised by   215
everyone, even people who do not know him,
and so by his facial features show forth
his mother's chaste fidelity.

Let this sort of praise of him
confirm his descent from a good mother,   220
just as the unique reputation abides
for Telemachus son of Penelope,
born of the best of mothers.

Maidens, close the doors:
we have played enough.   Good   225
wedded people, live well and
keep your youth fit and strong in constant
exercise of its function.

LXII

Vesper adest, iuvenes, consurgite: Vesper Olympo
exspectata diu vix tandem lumina tollit.
surgere iam tempus, iam pingues linquere mensas,
iam veniet virgo, iam dicetur hymenaeus.
Hymen o Hymenaee, Hymen ades o Hymenaee! 5

Cernitis, innuptae, iuvenes? consurgite contra;
nimirum Oetaeos ostendit Noctifer ignes.
sic certest; viden ut perniciter exsiluere?
non temere exsiluere: canent quod vincere par est.
Hymen o Hymenaee, Hymen ades o Hymenaee! 10

non facilis nobis, aequales, palma parata est;
aspicite, innuptae secum ut meditata requirunt.
non frustra meditantur: habent memorabile quod sit;
nec mirum, penitus quae tota mente laborant.
nos alio mentes, alio divisimus aures: 15
iure igitur vincemur: amat victoria curam.
quare nunc animos saltem convertite vestros;
dicere iam incipient, iam respondere decebit.
Hymen o Hymenaee, Hymen ades o Hymenaee!

Hespere, quis caelo fertur crudelior ignis? 20
qui natam possis complexu avellere matris,
complexu matris retinentem avellere natam,
et iuveni ardenti castam donare puellam.
quid faciunt hostes capta crudelius urbe?
Hymen o Hymenaee, Hymen ades o Hymenaee! 25

---

9 vincere *Guarinus*: visere *TV*

62

The Evening star is here – rise up, young men; the evening star
now at last is just about lifting up his long-awaited light on Olympus.
Now is the time to arise, now the time to leave the full tables:
now the bride will come, now the Hymenaeus will be sung.
O Hymenaeus Hymen, come, O Hymenaeus Hymen!   5

Unmarried girls, do you see the young men? Rise up to meet them.
Obviously the bringer of night must be showing his fires over Oeta.
Yes, for sure. Do you see how quickly they have leapt up?
Not for nothing have they leapt up – they will sing a song which is worth

      defeating.
O Hymenaeus Hymen, come, O Hymenaeus Hymen!   10

Not easy is the palm prepared for us, my comrades.
Look how the unwed girls are reminding themselves of their practised song:
not in vain are they reminding themselves – for they have something which
      is worth remembering.
No wonder, either, since they are working on it with full concentration.
As for us, we have split our attention and our ears in different directions. 15
We will deserve to be beaten – victory loves effort.
Therefore now for once turn your minds to business:
they will soon begin to sing, we shall soon be expected to reply.
O Hymenaeus Hymen, come, O Hymenaeus Hymen!

Evening Star, what fire which moves in the sky is more heartless than
      you? 20
You could rip a daughter from her mother's embrace,
from her mother's embrace rip the daughter as she clings on,
and hand over a pure girl to a youth burning with desire.
What do enemies do which is more heartless than this, when they capture a
      city?
O Hymenaeus Hymen, come, O Hymenaeus Hymen!   25

Hespere, quis caelo lucet iucundior ignis?
qui desponsa tua firmes conubia flamma,
quae pepigere viri, pepigerunt ante parentes,
nec iunxere prius quam se tuus extulit ardor.
quid datur a divis felici optatius hora?   30
Hymen o Hymenaee, Hymen ades o Hymenaee!

Hesperus e nobis, aequales, abstulit unam:
·   ·   ·   ·   ·   ·   ·   ·   ·
·   ·   ·   ·   ·   ·   ·   ·   ·
namque tuo adventu vigilat custodia semper,
nocte latent fures, quos idem saepe revertens,
Hespere, mutato comprendis nomine Eous.   35
at libet innuptis ficto te carpere questu.
quid tum, si carpunt, tacita quem mente requirunt?
Hymen o Hymenaee, Hymen ades o Hymenaee!

ut flos in saeptis secretus nascitur hortis,
ignotus pecori, nullo convulsus aratro,   40
quem mulcent aurae, firmat sol, educat imber;
multi illum pueri, multae optavere puellae:
idem cum tenui carptus defloruit ungui,
nulli illum pueri, nullae optavere puellae:
sic virgo, dum intacta manet, dum cara suis est;   45
cum castum amisit polluto corpore florem,
nec pueris iucunda manet, nec cara puellis.
Hymen o Hymenaee, Hymen ades o Hymenaee!
ut vidua in nudo vitis quae nascitur arvo,
numquam se extollit, numquam mitem educat uvam,   50
sed tenerum prono deflectens pondere corpus
iam iam contingit summum radice flagellum;
hanc nulli agricolae, nulli coluere iuvenci:
at si forte eadem est ulmo coniuncta marito,
multi illam agricolae, multi coluere iuvenci: 55

32/3 *lacunam statuit Avantius*
35 Eous *Sc̹. der*: eosdem *V*

Evening Star, what fire glows more pleasant than you in the sky?
For you with your flame confirm the wedding vows;
the pledges were made by husbands, made by parents,
but no union takes place until your fire blazes forth.
What is given to us by the Gods which is more desirable than the happy
                                                                    hour?   30
O Hymenaeus Hymen, come, O Hymenaeus Hymen!

Comrades, the Evening Star has stolen one of us...
.   .   .   .
for at your coming night-watchmen always keep guard.
Thieves lie hidden in the night, thieves whom you often catch,
Evening Star, when returning with the changed name of Eous.   35
Unmarried girls love to pick at you with invented complaints.
What does it matter that they pick at the one whom they in the silence of
                                              their heart are really looking for?
O Hymenaeus Hymen, come, O Hymenaeus Hymen!

Just as a flower grows hidden away in an enclosed garden,
a stranger to the flock, torn by no plough,   40
a flower which the breezes caress, the sun strengthens, the showers bring
                                                                         out:
many boys have desired that flower, as have many girls.
The same flower, when it has shed its petals, plucked by a slender fingernail,
has been desired by no boys, nor any girls either.
Thus it is with a girl: while she remains untouched, she is dear to her
                                                              people; 45
when she has dirtied her body and lost the flower of her purity,
she remains neither welcome to boys nor dear to girls.
O Hymenaeus Hymen, come, O Hymenaeus Hymen!

Just like the single vine which comes into being on a bare patch of land
never grows high, never brings forth the pleasant grape,   50
but rather drooping its skinny body downwards under its own flattening
                                                              weight
is all but touching her root with the topmost tendril:
this is a vine which no farmers have tended, nor any bullocks.
But if perhaps she is joined in wedlock to an elm,
then many farmers, many bullocks have tended her.   55

sic virgo dum intacta manet, dum inculta senescit;
cum par conubium maturo tempore adepta est,
cara viro magis et minus est invisa parenti.
<Hymen o Hymenaee, Hymen ades o Hymenaee!>   58b

et tu ne pugna cum tali coniuge, virgo.
non aequum est pugnare, pater cui tradidit ipse.   60
ipse pater cum matre, quibus parere necesse est.
virginitas non tota tua est, ex parte parentum est,
tertia pars patris est, pars est data tertia matri,
tertia sola tua est: noli pugnare duobus,
qui genero sua iura simul cum dote dederunt.   65
Hymen o Hymenaee, Hymen ades o Hymenaee!

58b *addidit Muretus*

So it is with a girl – while she remains untouched she grows old neglected.
When in the fullness of time she has obtained a favourable marriage,
then is she more dear to her husband and less resented by her father.
<O Hymenaeus Hymen, come, O Hymenaeus Hymen!>   58b

As for you, girl, do not fight against such a husband.
It is not fair to fight against him to whom your father himself gave you,   60
your father himself with your mother, both of whom you must obey.
Your virginity is not all your own, but partly your parents';
one third belongs to your father, a third is given to your mother,
you yourself only have a third share.   Do not fight against the two
who have given their son-in-law their own rights along with the dowry.   65
            O Hymenaeus Hymen, come, O Hymenaeus Hymen!

LXIII

super alta vectus Attis celeri rate maria,
Phrygium ut nemus citato cupide pede tetigit,
adiitque opaca silvis redimita loca deae,
stimulatus ibi furenti rabie, vagus animi,
devolsit ili acuto sibi pondera silice.   5
itaque ut relicta sensit sibi membra sine viro,
etiam recente terrae sola sanguine maculans,
niveis citata cepit manibus leve typanum,
typanum tuum, Cybebe, tua, mater, initia,
quatiensque terga tauri teneris cava digitis,   10
canere haec suis adorta est tremebunda comitibus.
'agite ite ad alta, Gallae, Cybeles nemora simul,
simul ite, Dindymenae dominae vaga pecora,
aliena quae petentes velut exules loca,
sectam meam secutae duce me mihi comites,   15
rapidum salum tulistis truculentaque pelagi,
et corpus evirastis Veneris nimio odio;
hilarate erae citatis erroribus animum.
mora tarda mente cedat: simul ite, sequimini
Phrygiam ad domum Cybebes, Phrygia ad nemora deae,   20
ubi cymbalum sonat vox, ubi tympana reboant,
tibicen ubi canit Phryx curvo grave calamo,
ubi capita Maenades vi iaciunt hederigerae,
ubi sacra sancta acutis ululatibus agitant,
ubi suevit illa divae volitare vaga cohors,   25
quo nos decet citatis celerare tripudiis.'
simul haec comitibus Attis cecinit, notha mulier,
thiasus repente linguis trepidantibus ululat,

---

4   animi *Parthenius*: animis *Lachmann*: amnis *V*
5   devolsit *Haupt*: devolvit *V*   ili...pondera silice *Bergk*:   iletas...pondere silices *V*
9   tuum *Lachmann*: tubam *V*   Cybebe *Sillig*: cibeles *V*
15 secutae *Bergk*: exsecutae *V*

63

Carried over the high seas in a swift boat, Attis,
when he touched the grove in Phrygia greedily with his speedy foot
and approached the gloomy woodland-crowned precinct of the goddess,
he was there goaded by an insane rage, his mind wandering,
and hacked off the weights of his groin with a sharp flint.   5
So, realising how the limbs left him were lacking in manhood,
still staining the soil of the ground with fresh blood,
she swiftly took up the light tambourine in her snowy hands,
your tambourine, Cybebe, your initiation, o mother:
and making the hollow bull's-hide to tremble with her delicate fingers,   10
she rose up shaking to sing this song to her companions.
'Gallae, come to the heights, make your way together to the groves of
                                                            Cybele,
come together, wandering flocks of the mistress of Dindymus:
like exiles seeking foreign lands,
following my lead and under my guidance, comrades,   15
you have borne the raging salt sea and the roughness of the ocean,
and you have unmanned your bodies out of too much hatred towards Venus.
With your hasty wanderings gladden the heart of your mistress.
Let slow sluggishness fall away from your mind: come together, follow me
to the Phrygian home of Cybebe, to the Phrygian groves of the goddess,   20
where the voice of cymbals sounds, where the tambourines resound,
where the Phrygian piper plays low on his curved reed,
where the ivy-wearing Maenads toss their heads violently,
where they set up holy rites with their sharp shrieks,
where the roaming coterie of the goddess is accustomed to race around – 25
that is where we ought to hasten with impetuous leaping dances.'
As soon as the fake female Attis has sung this to her comrades,
the throng suddenly shrieks with quivering tongues,

leve tympanum remugit, cava cymbala recrepant,
viridem citus adit Idam properante pede chorus.   30
furibunda simul anhelans vaga vadit, animam agens,
comitata tympano Attis per opaca nemora dux,
veluti iuvenca vitans onus indomita iugi:
rapidae ducem sequuntur Gallae properipedem.
itaque, ut domum Cybebes tetigere lassulae,   35
nimio e labore somnum capiunt sine Cerere.
piger his labante languore oculos sopor operit:
abit in quiete molli rabidus furor animi.
sed ubi oris aurei Sol radiantibus oculis
lustravit aethera album, sola dura, mare ferum,   40
pepulitque noctis umbras vegetis sonipedibus,
ibi Somnus excitam Attin fugiens citus abiit:
trepidante eum recepit dea Pasithea sinu.
ita de quiete molli rapida sine rabie
simul ipsa pectore Attis sua facta recoluit,   45
liquidaque mente vidit sine quis ubique foret,
animo aestuante rursus reditum ad vada tetulit.
ibi maria vasta visens lacrimantibus oculis,
patriam allocuta maestast ita voce miseriter.
'patria o mei creatrix, patria o mea genetrix,   50
ego quam miser relinquens, dominos ut erifugae
famuli solent, ad Idae tetuli nemora pedem,
ut aput nivem et ferarum gelida stabula forem,
et earum operta adirem furibunda latibula,
ubinam aut quibus locis te positam, patria, reor?   55
cupit ipsa pupula ad te sibi derigere aciem,
rabie fera carens dum breve tempus animus est.
egone a mea remota haec ferar in nemora domo?
patria, bonis, amicis, genitoribus abero?
abero foro, palaestra, stadio et gyminasiis?   60

---

42 excitam *Lachmann:* excitum V
45 ipsa *Guarinus:* ipse V
54 operta *Müller:* omnia V
60 gyminasiis *Ellis:* gummasiis O

the light tambourine beats, the hollow cymbals resound,
the swift chorus makes for green Ida on hurrying feet.   30
At the same time, out of her mind, gasping and panting for breath,
Attis wanders, accompanied by the drum, leading through the gloomy groves
like a heifer that has not been broken in and avoids the burden of the yoke:
the hastening Gallae follow their quick-footed leader.
When, therefore, the tired little women touched upon the dwelling of
                                                            Cybebe   35
they fall asleep thanks to their excessive efforts without the sustenance of
                                                            Ceres.
Lazy sleep covers their eyes with drooping sluggishness,
the furious madness of their mind departs in gentle restfulness.
But when the golden-faced Sun with his sparkling eyes
cleansed the white aether, the hard earth and the raging sea   40
and drove away the shades of night with his sprightly sounding hooves:
then did Sleep hurry swiftly away from wakened Attis,
and the Goddess Pasithea embraced him in her quivering bosom.
And so, rising from her gentle slumber and now free of her rabid ravings,
when Attis recalled her doings in her heart   45
and saw with a limpid mind what she now lacked and where she was,
she then bore her steps back to the shore with her heart swelling up.
There, seeing the wide expanse of sea with weeping eyes
she wretchedly spoke thus to her fatherland in a sad voice:
'O country that gave me life, o country that gave me birth,   50
country which I left to my cost, running away as fugitive slaves
flee their masters, bearing my steps to the groves of Ida
to spend my life amid snow and the icy lairs of wild beasts,
drawing near in my madness to their concealed hideouts –
where now, in what place do I think that you lie, O my country?   55
Even the pupil of my eye longs to direct its gaze at you,
while just for a short time my heart is free from savage madness.
Am I to take myself into these glades, far removed from my home?
To be away from my homeland, property, friends, parents?
Away from the Forum, the wrestling-school, the stadium, the gymnasia? 60

miser a miser, querendum est etiam atque etiam, anime.
quod enim genus figuraest, ego non quod obierim?
ego mulier, ego adulescens, ego ephebus, ego puer,
ego gymnasi fui flos, ego eram decus olei:
mihi ianuae frequentes, mihi limina tepida,   65
mihi floridis corollis redimita domus erat,
linquendum ubi esset orto mihi sole cubiculum.
ego nunc deum ministra et Cybeles famula ferar?
ego Maenas, ego mei pars, ego vir sterilis ero?
ego viridis algida Idae nive amicta loca colam?   70
ego vitam agam sub altis Phrygiae columinibus,
ubi cerva silvicultrix, ubi aper nemorivagus?
iam iam dolet quod egi, iam iamque paenitet.'
roseis ut huic labellis sonitus citus abiit,
geminas deorum ad aures nova nuntia referens,   75
ibi iuncta iuga resolvens Cybele leonibus
laevumque pecoris hostem stimulans ita loquitur.
'agedum' inquit 'age ferox i, fac ut hanc furor agitet,
fac uti furoris ictu reditum in nemora ferat,
mea libere nimis qui fugere imperia cupit.   80
age caede terga cauda, tua verbera patere,
fac cuncta mugienti fremitu loca retonent,
rutilam ferox torosa cervice quate iubam.'
ait haec minax Cybebe religatque iuga manu.
ferus ipse sese adhortans rabidum incitat animum,   85
vadit, fremit, refringit virgulta pede vago.
at ubi umida albicantis loca litoris adiit,
teneramque vidit Attin prope marmora pelagi,
facit impetum: illa demens fugit in nemora fera:
ibi semper omne vitae spatium famula fuit.   90
dea, magna dea, Cybebe, dea, domina Dindymi,
procul a mea tuus sit furor omnis, era, domo:
alios age incitatos, alios age rabidos.

---

64 fui *V*: sui *X:* suus *Nisbet*
75 deorum *V*: deae *Munro* tum *Goold*
85 rabidum *Schwabe:* rapidum *V*   animum *Baehrens:* animo *V*
88 teneramque *Lachmann*: tenerumque *V*
89 illa *Lachmann* ille *V*

Pathetic, ah pathetic – again and again you must lament thus, O my heart.
For what species of shape is there that I have not taken on?
I a woman, I a young man, I a youth, I a boy,
I have been the flower of the gymnasium, I used to be the glory of the
                                              wrestler's oil:
my doors were thronged, my threshold warm,   65
my house garlanded with flowery wreaths
when at sunrise I had to leave my bedroom.
Am I now going to be called a handmaid of the gods and the servant girl of
                                              Cybele?
Shall I be a Maenad, a mere part of myself, a sexless man?
Shall I haunt the cold, snow-clad regions of green Ida?   70
Shall I pass my life under the high columns of Phrygia,
where the forest-haunting deer and the grove-roaming boar are?
Now I suffer for what I have done, now I regret it.'
When the impetuous sound came forth from this woman's rosy lips,
bearing new tidings to the twin ears of the gods,   75
then Cybele, untying the yoke which was lashed to her lions
and goading on the flock's foe on the left side, spoke thus:
'Go' she said 'make your way, fierce one, make madness stir her on,
make her return to the groves with the lash of madness –
she who desires too freely to flee my commands.   80
Come now, beat your back with your tail, endure your own strokes,
see that everywhere thunders with your bellowing roar.
Fierce one, toss the ruddy mane on your muscular neck.'
Cybebe said this threateningly and untied the yoke with her hand.
The savage beast bestirred himself and awoke his furious spirit;   85
he rushes forward, he roars, he flattens the undergrowth with his straying
                                              paw.
But when he has approached the wet region of the whitening seashore
and has there seen delicate Attis beside the smooth marble of the ocean,
he pounces. She, out of her mind, flees into the savage groves,
and there for the whole expanse of her life was a handmaid for ever. 90
Goddess, great goddess, Cybebe, goddess, mistress of Dindymus,
may all that madness of yours stay far from my house, my lady.
Drive other people with your goads, drive other people into frenzy.

LXIV

Peliaco quondam prognatae vertice pinus
dicuntur liquidas Neptuni nasse per undas
Phasidos ad fluctus et fines Aeetaeos,
cum lecti iuvenes, Argivae robora pubis,
auratam optantes Colchis avertere pellem   5
ausi sunt vada salsa cita decurrere puppi,
caerula verrentes abiegnis aequora palmis.
diva quibus retinens in summis urbibus arces,
ipsa levi fecit volitantem flamine currum,
pinea coniungens inflexae texta carinae.   .   10
illa rudem cursu prima imbuit Amphitriten.
quae simul ac rostro ventosum proscidit aequor,
tortaque remigio spumis incanuit unda,
emersere freti candenti e gurgite vultus
aequoreae monstrum Nereides admirantes.   15
illa, atque haud alia, viderunt luce marinas
mortales oculi nudato corpore Nymphas
nutricum tenus exstantes e gurgite cano.
tum Thetidis Peleus incensus fertur amore,
tum Thetis humanos non despexit hymenaeos,   20
tum Thetidi pater ipse iugandum Pelea sensit.
o nimis optato saeclorum tempore nati
heroes, salvete, deum genus! o bona matrum
progenies, salvete iter*um, salvete, bonarum!*   23b
vos ego saepe meo vos carmine compellabo.
teque adeo eximie taedis felicibus aucte,   25
Thessaliae columen Peleu, cui Iuppiter ipse,
ipse suos divum genitor concessit amores,
tene Thetis tenuit pulcherrima Nereine?
tene suam Tethys concessit ducere neptem,
Oceanusque, mari totum qui amplectitur orbem?   30

---

14 freti *Schrader*: feri *V*   16 atque haud *Bergk*: atque *V*: haud ante alia *Goold*
23b *om. V: ex scholiis huc revocavit Orioli. Lacunam implevit Peerlkamp.*

64

Once upon a time, pine-trees grown on the peak of Mount Pelion
swam, they say, through the liquid waves of Neptune
to the streams of Phasis and the territory of Aeetes.
This was when chosen young men, the strength of the Argive youth,
wishing to take back from Colchis the golden fleece,   5
had the nerve to run through the salt straits in a swift ship,
sweeping the sky-blue plains with palms of fir-wood.
The goddess who keeps hold of the citadels on the tops of cities,
she herself made the chariot for them which flew before the light breeze,
by joining together the pinewood web to a curving keel.   10
That ship was the first to baptise the unskilled Amphitrite with sailing.
As soon as she ploughed through the windy plain with her beak
and the wave, curled with the rowing, spun white foam,
then from the white torrent of the strait the watery
Nereids lifted their faces in astonishment at the prodigy.   15
On that day and no other, did mortals see
with their eyes the sea-nymphs bare of body,
standing out of the white torrent up to their breasts.
Then Peleus is said to have been inflamed with love of Thetis,
then Thetis did not despise a human wedding,   20
then even the father himself realised that Peleus must be joined to Thetis.
O heroes, born in an age of time all too desirable –
hail, race of gods! O goodly offspring of good mothers, hail again!
You will I often address with my song.
You also, blessed beyond others in the good fortune of your wedding,   25
Peleus, mainstay of Thessaly, to whom Jupiter himself,
the father of the gods himself, resigned the object of his own love,
was it you whom Thetis, the most beautiful of the daughters of Nereus, held?
Was it you whom Tethys and Oceanus – who embraces
the whole world with sea – granted to marry their own grand-daughter? 30

quae simul optatae finito tempore luces
advenere, domum conventu tota frequentat
Thessalia, oppletur laetanti regia coetu:
dona ferunt prae se, declarant gaudia vultu.
deseritur Cieros, linquunt Phthiotica Tempe,   35
Crannonisque domos ac moenia Larisaea,
Pharsalum coeunt, Pharsalia tecta frequentant.
rura colit nemo, mollescunt colla iuvencis,
non humilis curvis purgatur vinea rastris,
non glebam prono convellit vomere taurus, ·   40
non falx attenuat frondatorum arboris umbram,
squalida desertis robigo infertur aratris.
ipsius at sedes, quacumque opulenta recessit
regia, fulgenti splendent auro atque argento.
candet ebur soliis, collucent pocula mensae,   45
tota domus gaudet regali splendida gaza.
pulvinar vero divae geniale locatur
sedibus in mediis, Indo quod dente politum
tincta tegit roseo conchyli purpura fuco.
     haec vestis priscis hominum variata figuris   50
heroum mira virtutes indicat arte.
namque fluentisono prospectans litore Diae,
Thesea cedentem celeri cum classe tuetur
indomitos in corde gerens Ariadna furores,
necdum etiam sese quae visit visere credit,   55
utpote fallaci quae tum primum excita somno
desertam in sola miseram se cernat harena.
immemor at iuvenis fugiens pellit vada remis,
irrita ventosae linquens promissa procellae.
quem procul ex alga maestis Minois ocellis,   60
saxea ut effigies bacchantis, prospicit, eheu,
prospicit et magnis curarum fluctuat undis,
non flavo retinens subtilem vertice mitram,
non contecta levi velatum pectus amictu,

---

35 Cieros *Meineke*: siros V
37 Pharsalum *Pontanus:* farsaliam V
64 velatum V: *fortasse* variatum *Nisbet*

When once the longed-for days arrived after the passage of time,
then the whole of Thessaly throngs the house in a gathering,
and the palace is swarming with a joyous crowd.
They bear gifts in front of them, they state their joy on their faces.
Cieros is abandoned, they leave behind Phthiotic Tempe, 35
the homes of Crannon and the city-walls of Larissa:
they gather at Pharsalus, they throng the houses of Pharsalus.
Nobody tends the countryside, the bullocks' necks grow soft,
the low-growing vine is not cleared with curved rakes,
the bull does not turn over the clod of earth with the downward-pointing
ploughshare, 40
the pruners' hook does not thin out the shade of the tree,
and a scale of rust spreads over the abandoned ploughs.
The master's house, however, as far as the rich palace
spread, is brilliant with gleaming gold and silver.
Ivory is white on the thrones, the cups on the table shine, 45
the whole house rejoices, blazing bright with princely treasure.
The sacred wedding-couch of the goddess is positioned
in the middle of the palace: it is polished with Indian tooth
and covered with purple dyed with the crimson stain of the seashell.
This coverlet, tricked out with the antique figures of people, 50
shows forth the heroisms of great men with wonderful skill.
For there gazing forward on the wave-sounding shore of Dia,
Ariadne watches Theseus departing with his swift fleet,
bearing uncontrolled madness in her heart:
nor does she yet believe that she sees what she is seeing, 55
since she has only just been awakened from a deceitful sleep
to see her poor self abandoned on the lonely sand.
But the young man flees beating the waves with his oars oblivious,
leaving behind his empty promises to the windy storm.
The daughter of Minos gazes out at him from the seaweed afar off with sad
little eyes, 60
just like a stone statue of a Bacchant she gazes, alas,
gazes and tosses on huge waves of emotions,
not keeping the delicate headband on her blonde head,
not keeping her breast veiled and concealed with the light robe,

non tereti strophio lactentis vincta papillas,   65
omnia quae toto delapsa e corpore passim
ipsius ante pedes fluctus salis alludebant.
sed neque tum mitrae neque tum fluitantis amictus
illa vicem curans toto ex te pectore, Theseu,
toto animo, tota pendebat perdita mente.   70
a misera, assiduis quam luctibus externavit
spinosas Erycina serens in pectore curas,
illa ex tempestate, ferox quo ex tempore Theseus
egressus curvis e litoribus Piraei
attigit iniusti regis Gortynia templa.   75
nam perhibent olim crudeli peste coactam
Androgeoneae poenas exsolvere caedis
electos iuvenes simul et decus innuptarum
Cecropiam solitam esse dapem dare Minotauro.
quis angusta malis cum moenia vexarentur,   80
ipse suum Theseus pro caris corpus Athenis
proicere optavit potius quam talia Cretam
funera Cecropiae nec funera portarentur.
atque ita nave levi nitens ac lenibus auris
magnanimum ad Minoa venit sedesque superbas.   85
hunc simul ac cupido conspexit lumine virgo
regia, quam suavis exspirans castus odores
lectulus in molli complexu matris alebat,
quales Eurotae progignunt flumina myrtus,
aurave distinctos educit verna colores,   90
non prius ex illo flagrantia declinavit
lumina, quam cuncto concepit corpore flammam
funditus atque imis exarsit tota medullis.
heu misere exagitans immiti corde furores
sancte puer, curis hominum qui gaudia misces,   95
quaeque regis Golgos quaeque Idalium frondosum,
qualibus incensam iactastis mente puellam
fluctibus, in flavo saepe hospite suspirantem!

---

73   ex *addidit Baehrens*
75   templa *nescio quis ante annum 1450:* tempta *V:* tecta *Parthenius.*

not binding her milky breasts with the flimsy brassière -   65
all of which slipped right off her entire body in all directions
and the waves of the brine played with them in front of her feet.
But at that time she cared nothing for what happened to a headband
nor for a fluttering robe, she cared with all her breast for you, Theseus,
with all her spirit, with all her mind she clung on, lost in love.   70
Oh love-sick girl – whom Erycina, sowing thorny cares in her heart,
drove mad with constant grief
from the time when savage Theseus,
leaving the curving shores of Piraeus,
reached the Cretan palaces of the unjust king.   75
For they say that once, forced by a cruel plague
to pay the penalty for the murder of Androgeon,
the land of Cecrops had grown used to giving chosen young
men and the flower of the unwed maidens to the Minotaur as his feast.
When the narrow walls were being sorely tried by these evils,   80
Theseus himself chose to risk his own body on behalf of his
dear Athens, rather than have such undead deaths carried
to Crete from the land of Cecrops.
In this way, therefore, carried on a light ship and the gentle breezes
he came to great-hearted Minos and his haughty palace.   85
As soon as the unwed princess saw this man with her lustful eye –
she whom, in the soft embrace of her mother,
the pure little bed, breathing forth pleasant odours, used to nurse,
odours such as those of the myrtles which the streams of Eurotas bring forth
or of the flowers which the spring breeze brings out in all their colours – 90
she did not turn her blazing eyes away from
him until she had conceived a flame deep in her entire body
and was totally on fire in the depths of the marrow of her bones.
Alas, divine boy who stir up madness so sadly with your
ruthless heart, who mix together human joys with human cares, 95
and you lady who rule over Golgi and leafy Idalium –
on what streams did you toss the girl, aflame in her mind,
sighing frequently over the fair-haired foreigner!

quantos illa tulit languenti corde timores!
quanto saepe magis fulgore expalluit auri!   100
cum saevum cupiens contra contendere monstrum
aut mortem appeteret Theseus aut praemia laudis.
non ingrata tamen frustra munuscula divis
promittens tacito succendit vota labello.
nam velut in summo quatientem brachia Tauro   105
quercum, aut conigeram sudanti cortice pinum,
indomitus turbo contorquens flamine robur,
eruit (illa procul radicitus exturbata
prona cadit, late quaeviscumque obvia frangens),
sic domito saevum prostravit corpore Theseus   110
nequiquam vanis iactantem cornua ventis.
inde pedem sospes multa cum laude reflexit
errabunda regens tenui vestigia filo,
ne labyrintheis e flexibus egredientem
tecti frustraretur inobservabilis error.   115
sed quid ego a primo digressus carmine plura
commemorem, ut linquens genitoris filia vultum,
ut consanguineae complexum, ut denique matris
quae misera in nata deperdita lamentata est,
omnibus his Thesei dulcem praeoptarit amorem: 120
aut ut vecta rati spumosa ad litora Diae,
venerit, aut ut eam devinctam lumina somno
liquerit immemori discedens pectore coniunx?
saepe illam perhibent ardenti corde furentem
clarisonas imo fudisse e pectore voces,   125
ac tum praeruptos tristem conscendere montes,
unde aciem in pelagi vastos protenderet aestus,
tum tremuli salis adversas procurrere in undas
mollia nudatae tollentem tegmina surae,
atque haec extremis maestam dixisse querellis,   130
frigidulos udo singultus ore cientem.
'sicine me patriis avectam, perfide, ab aris,
perfide, deserto liquisti in litore, Theseu?

---

109   late quaeviscumque *Ellis*: lateque cum eius *V*: late quaecumque habet *Baehrens*
119   lamentata est *Conington*: laetabatur *Lachmann*: leta *V*.

64

59

What great fears did she bear in her slow-beating heart!
How much paler than the gleam of gold did her complexion often turn,   100
when Theseus longing to set out against the wild monster
went looking for either death or the rewards of praise!
Not, however, unwelcome or futile were the small gifts
which she promised the gods as she undertook her vow with silent lips.
For just as an oak tree shaking its arms on the top of Mount Taurus   105
or a cone-bearing pine tree with its resinous bark are ripped out
by a relentless hurricane which unscrews the tree-trunk with its
blast – the tree then falls flat afar off, torn out
by the roots, shattering whatever lies in its path –
in this way Theseus laid flat the wild monster with its body overcome,   110
tossing its horns in vain at the empty winds.
From there he unwound his steps safely with abundant praise,
controlling his fallible footsteps with a thin thread
to prevent his exit from the labyrinthine contortions
being thwarted by the palace's undiscoverable maze.   115
But I have digressed from where I began my song. Why should I make
mention of any more – how the daughter leaving behind the face of her
                                   father,
the embrace of her sister, even that of her mother,
who grieved in despair over her love-sick daughter,
all of which she placed second to the sweet love of Theseus: 120
or then how she came, carried on a ship to the foamy shores of Naxos,
and how her husband in his forgetfulness of heart departed leaving
her as she lay with her eyes bound in sleep?
Often, they say, she was raging with a blazing heart
and poured out piercing voices from the bottom of her heart;   125
now in her grief she climbed the sheer mountains
so as to be able to stretch forth her gaze over the endless swellings of the
                                   ocean,
then would run out into the oncoming waves of the trembling salt-water,
lifting the soft coverings of her bared calf
and, sad, said these things in her final laments,   130
stirring up icy little sobs on her soaking face:
'Is this the way you carried me off, traitor, from my father's altars,
traitor, only to abandon me on this deserted shore, Theseus?

sicine discedens neglecto numine divum,
immemor - a! - devota domum periuria portas? 135
nullane res potuit crudelis flectere mentis
consilium? tibi nulla fuit clementia praesto,
immite ut nostri vellet miserescere pectus?
at non haec quondam blanda promissa dedisti
voce: mihi non haec miserae sperare iubebas, 140
sed conubia laeta, sed optatos hymenaeos,
quae cuncta aerii discerpunt irrita venti.
tum iam nulla viro iuranti femina credat,
nulla viri speret sermones esse fideles;
quis dum aliquid cupiens animus praegestit apisci, 145
nil metuunt iurare, nihil promittere parcunt:
sed simul ac cupidae mentis satiata libido est,
dicta nihil metuere, nihil periuria curant.
certe ego te in medio versantem turbine leti
eripui, et potius germanum amittere crevi, 150
quam tibi fallaci supremo in tempore dessem.
pro quo dilaceranda feris dabor alitibusque
praeda, neque iniacta tumulabor mortua terra.
quaenam te genuit sola sub rupe leaena,
quod mare conceptum spumantibus exspuit undis, 155
quae Syrtis, quae Scylla rapax, quae vasta Charybdis,
talia qui reddis pro dulci praemia vita?
si tibi non cordi fuerant conubia nostra,
saeva quod horrebas prisci praecepta parentis,
at tamen in vestras potuisti ducere sedes, 160
quae tibi iucundo famularer serva labore,
candida permulcens liquidis vestigia lymphis,
purpureave tuum consternens veste cubile.
sed quid ego ignaris nequiquam conquerar auris,
externata malo, quae nullis sensibus auctae 165
nec missas audire queunt nec reddere voces?
ille autem prope iam mediis versatur in undis,
nec quisquam apparet vacua mortalis in alga.
sic nimis insultans extremo tempore saeva

---

148 metuere V: meminere Czwalina

Is this the way you ignore the power of the gods   134
and depart, mindless – ah! – as you carry home your cursed broken oaths?
Was nothing capable of turning your mind's unfeeling
purpose?   Did you have no mercy in you,
to make your cruel heart prepared to pity me?
These were not the promises which you once gave me with your flattering
voice, these were not the hopes you bade this love-sick woman to have, 140
but rather joyful marriage, the wedding-songs I longed for –
all of which the winds of the air scatter for nothing.
From now on let no woman believe a man's oath,
let no woman expect a man's words to be reliable:
with men, as long as their lustful heart is ardent to obtain something,   145
then there is nothing that they are afraid to swear, no promise that they hold
                                               back from making.
Once the urge of their lustful mind has been slaked, however,
then they show no fear of their words, no concern for their broken oaths.
You cannot deny that you were tossing in the middle of the whirlpool of
                                               death
when I saved you, and I decided to lose my brother   150
rather than to fail you in your hour of crisis, you cheat.
As thanks for all this I shall be given over to the wild beasts to be torn apart,
as carrion to the birds, nor will I have a mound heaped over me with earth
thrown upon me when I am dead.
What lioness gave birth to you under a lonely rock?
What sea conceived you and vomited you out of its foaming waters?   155
What Syrtes, what voracious Scylla, what devouring Charybdis –
seeing that you give back returns such as this for your sweet life?
Even if your heart had gone against marriage with me,
because you shrank back from the unflinching commands of an aged father,
all the same you could have taken me to your home   160
to be a household slave in a labour of love,
soothing your white feet with liquid waters
and strewing your bed with a garment of crimson.
But why am I complaining in vain to the ignorant breezes,
out of my mind with sorrow speaking to winds which are endowed with no
                                               senses   165
and cannot hear the voices uttered to them nor return them?
By now he is almost in the middle of the waves in his course,
nor does any human being appear on the empty seaweed.
This is how spiteful fate – all too exultant in my last hour –

fors etiam nostris invidit questibus auris.   170
Iuppiter omnipotens, utinam ne tempore primo
Gnosia Cecropiae tetigissent litora puppes,
indomito nec dira ferens stipendia tauro,
perfidus in Creta religasset navita funem,
nec malus hic celans dulci crudelia forma   175
consilia in nostris requiesset sedibus hospes!
nam quo me referam? quali spe perdita nitor?
Idaeosne petam montes? at gurgite lato
discernens ponti truculentum dividit aequor.
an patris auxilium sperem? quemne ipsa reliqui   180
respersum iuvenem fraterna caede secuta?
coniugis an fido consoler memet amore?
quine fugit lentos incurvans gurgite remos?
praeterea nullo colitur sola insula tecto,
nec patet egressus pelagi cingentibus undis: 185
nulla fugae ratio, nulla spes: omnia muta,
omnia sunt deserta, ostentant omnia letum.
non tamen ante mihi languescent lumina morte,
nec prius a fesso secedent corpore sensus,
quam iustam a divis exposcam prodita multam,   190
caelestumque fidem postrema comprecer hora.
quare facta virum multantes vindice poena,
Eumenides, quibus anguino redimita capillo
frons exspirantis praeportat pectoris iras,
huc huc adventate, meas audite querellas,   195
quas ego, vae misera, extremis proferre medullis
cogor inops, ardens, amenti caeca furore.
quae quoniam verae nascuntur pectore ab imo,
vos nolite pati nostrum vanescere luctum,
sed quali solam Theseus me mente reliquit,   200
tali mente, deae, funestet seque suosque.'
has postquam maesto profudit pectore voces,
supplicium saevis exposcens anxia factis,
annuit invicto caelestum numine rector.

---

178 at *Muretus*: a! *Guarinus*: a V
184 colitur *Palmer*: litus V

has begrudged me even ears to hear my complaints.   170
Almighty Jupiter, would that the Athenian ships had never
touched the Cretan shores in the first place
and that, bearing the dreadful wages to the untamed bull,
the treacherous sailor had never tied up his cable onto Crete:
would that this wicked man, hiding his heartless plans in a sweet   175
appearance, had never rested as a guest in our home!
For where shall I go to? What hope may I depend on in my helplessness?
Shall I seek the mountains of Ida? But the rough plain
of the sea divides and separates us with its wide gulf.
Or shall I hope for the help of my father – whom I left behind   180
when I followed after a young man who was spattered with my brother's
                                                              blood?
Or should I console myself with the faithful love of my husband –
who is running away from me, bending his pliant oars over the sea?
What is more, the island is lonely, tended by no dwelling,
and no means of escape lies open to me with the waves of the ocean
surrounding it all round. Of flight there is no method, no hope: all is 185
                                                              silent,
all is abandoned, all things show doom.
Yet my eyes will not droop in death,
nor will my senses withdraw from my exhausted body,
before I demand a fair punishment from the gods in my betrayal   190
and pray for the faith of the heavenly ones in my final hour.
Wherefore, you who punish the deeds of men with vengeful penalty,
Kindly Ones, whose forehead, bound with snakes for hair,
carries forward the snorting anger of your breast –
come here, come here, hear my laments   195
which I – wretch that I am – am compelled to express from the furthest
marrow of my bones helpless, blazing, blind with mindless madness.
Since these laments are sincerely born from the bottom of my heart,
do not suffer my grief to evaporate,
but see to it that Theseus shall bring destruction to himself and his people 200
with the same state of mind, goddesses, with which he abandoned me all
                                                              alone.'
After she poured these utterances from her sad breast,
anxiously demanding retribution for the savage deeds,
the ruler of the gods nodded assent with his invincible nod.

quo motu tellus atque horrida contremuerunt 205
aequora concussitque micantia sidera mundus.
ipse autem caeca mentem caligine Theseus
consitus oblito dimisit pectore cuncta,
quae mandata prius constanti mente tenebat,
dulcia nec maesto sustollens signa parenti 210
sospitem Erechtheum se ostendit visere portum.
namque ferunt olim, classi cum moenia divae
linquentem natum ventis concrederet Aegeus,
talia complexum iuveni mandata dedisse.
'nate mihi longa iucundior unice vita, 215
nate, ego quem in dubios cogor dimittere casus,
reddite in extrema nuper mihi fine senectae,
quandoquidem fortuna mea ac tua fervida virtus
eripit invito mihi te, cui languida nondum
lumina sunt nati cara saturata figura, 220
non ego te gaudens laetanti pectore mittam,
nec te ferre sinam fortunae signa secundae,
sed primum multas expromam mente querellas,
canitiem terra atque infuso pulvere foedans,
inde infecta vago suspendam lintea malo, 225
nostros ut luctus nostraeque incendia mentis
carbasus obscurata dicet ferrugine Hibera.
quod tibi si sancti concesserit incola Itoni,
quae nostrum genus, has sedes defendere Erechthi
annuit, ut tauri respergas sanguine dextram, 230
tum vero facito ut memori tibi condita corde
haec vigeant mandata, nec ulla oblitteret aetas;
ut simul ac nostros invisent lumina collis,
funestam antennae deponant undique vestem,
candidaque intorti sustollant vela rudentes, 235
quam primum cernens ut laeta gaudia mente
agnoscam, cum te reducem aetas prospera sistet.'
haec mandata prius constanti mente tenentem
Thesea ceu pulsae ventorum flamine nubes
aereum nivei montis liquere cacumen. 240

---

237 aetas *V*: fors *Dousa*

At this movement the earth and the bristling plains   205
of the sea trembled and the firmament rattled its gleaming stars.
Theseus himself, however, with his mind planted with unseeing darkness,
put everything out of his forgetful heart –
all the instructions which he was previously holding on to in constancy of
purpose;
he did not raise up the welcome sails to his sad parent   210
and thus show that he was seeing the port of Athens safe and sound.
For they say that once, when he was leaving the city walls of the goddess
in his fleet and Aegeus was entrusting his son to the winds,
he had embraced him and given him the following instructions:
'My only son, sweeter to me than long life,   215
son, whom I am compelled to send away into uncertain chance,
when you have just recently been given to me on the furthest edge of old
age,
seeing that my fortune and your boiling courage
snatches you away from me against my will – when my drooping eyes
are not yet satisfied with the beloved shape of my son.   220
I shall not send you away rejoicing with a glad heart,
nor shall I allow you to bear the ensigns of good fortune,
but first of all I will express many laments from my soul,
defiling my white hair with earth and dust poured on it,
and then I will hang dyed sails on your wandering mast,   225
so that the darkened canvas may proclaim my grief
and the fire of my mind with its Iberian purple.
But if the one who dwells in divine Itonus, the one
who consents to defend our race and the abodes of Erechtheus,
if she grants that you may spatter your right hand with the blood of the
bull,   230
then see to it that these instructions be buried in your unforgetting mind
and be kept fresh, and that no passage of time should blot them out.
As soon as your eyes see our hills,
so that your yard-arms everywhere may lower the cloth of death
and let the twisted sheets hoist white sails,   235
so that I may see my joys with a glad heart as soon as possible and
recognise the moment when favourable time will restore you after your
journey.'
Theseus had held on to these instructions up to that time with fixed purpose.
Now they left him, as clouds beaten by the blast of the winds
leave the airy peak of a snowy mountain.   240

at pater, ut summa prospectum ex arce petebat,
anxia in assiduos absumens lumina fletus,
cum primum inflati conspexit lintea veli,
praecipitem sese scopulorum e vertice iecit,
amissum credens immiti Thesea fato. 245
sic funesta domus ingressus tecta paterna
morte ferox Theseus, qualem Minoidi luctum
obtulerat mente immemori talem ipse recepit.
quae tamen aspectans cedentem maesta carinam
multiplices animo volvebat saucia curas. 250
at parte ex alia florens volitabat Iacchus
cum thiaso Satyrorum et Nysigenis Silenis,
te quaerens, Ariadna, tuoque incensus amore.
quae tum alacres passim lymphata mente furebant
euhoe bacchantes euhoe capita inflectentes. 255
harum pars tecta quatiebant cuspide thyrsos,
pars e divulso iactabant membra iuvenco,
pars sese tortis serpentibus incingebant,
pars obscura cavis celebrabant orgia cistis,
orgia, quae frustra cupiunt audire profani, 260
plangebant aliae proceris tympana palmis,
aut tereti tenuis tinnitus aere ciebant,
multis raucisonos efflabant cornua bombos
barbaraque horribili stridebat tibia cantu.
    talibus amplifice vestis decorata figuris 265
pulvinar complexa suo velabat amictu.
quae postquam cupide spectando Thessala pubes
expleta est, sanctis coepit decedere divis.
hic, qualis flatu placidum mare matutino
horrificans Zephyrus proclivas incitat undas, 270
aurora exoriente vagi sub limina Solis:
quae tarde primum clementi flamine pulsae
procedunt, leni et resonant plangore cachinni,
post vento crescente magis magis increbrescunt,
purpureaque procul nantes ab luce refulgent: 275

---

243 inflati V: *fortasse* infecti Sabellicus
254 quae Bergk: qui tum alacres V: cui Thyades O. Skutsch:

But the father, when he looked for a sighting from the top of his citadel,
wasting away his fearful eyes in constant weeping,
when first he caught sight of the canvas of the billowing sail,
he threw himself headlong from the peak of the rocks,
believing that Theseus had been taken away by cruel fortune.   245
In this way, entering the dwelling of his home which was mourning for his
                                                                    father's
death, fierce Theseus received the sort of grief which
in his forgetfulness of mind he had inflicted on the daughter of Minos.
She meanwhile, gazing sadly out at the departing ship,
was turning layer upon layer of feelings over in her mind, stricken.   250
And yet, from elsewhere, flowery Iacchus was flying
with his group of Satyrs and Sileni born on Mount Nysa,
looking for you, Ariadne, and on fire with passion for you.
They were then raging keenly everywhere with distracted mind,
shouting 'Evoe' in tumult, 'Evoe' as they bent their heads back.   255
Some of them were shaking their bacchic wands with covered tip,
some were tossing around the limbs from a heifer torn apart,
some were encircling themselves with twisted snakes,
some were thronging in worship of the ritual objects concealed in their
                                                              deep baskets
– rites which the uninitiated long in vain to hear;   260
other women beat drums with uplifted palms,
or produced gentle tinklings on their cymbals of rounded bronze.
In many cases horns blasted out rough-sounding boomings
and the foreign pipe wailed with its distressing song.
      The coverlet was generously decorated with shapes such as this,   265
and in its embrace covered the bed with its cloth.
When once the young of Thessaly had been satisfied with eager
gazing on this, they began to make way for the awesome gods.
At this, just as the Zephyr ruffles the placid sea with his morning breath
and arouses waves which tumble forwards   270
as the dawn rises up to the threshold of the wandering sun;
the waves move slowly at first, beaten by the gentle wind,
and sound lightly with a splash as laughter:
later on as the wind increases they grow more and more frequent
and swimming far from the crimson glow they reflect it back.   275

     sic tum vestibulo linquentes regia tecta
     ad se quisque vago passim pede discedebant.
     quorum post abitum princeps e vertice Peli
     advenit Chiron portans silvestria dona:
     nam quoscumque ferunt campi, quos Thessala magnis   280
     montibus ora creat, quos propter fluminis undas
     aura aperit flores tepidi fecunda Favoni,
     hos indistinctis plexos tulit ipse corollis,
     quo permulsa domus iucundo risit odore.
     confestim Peneus adest, viridantia Tempe,   285
     Tempe, quae silvae cingunt super impendentes,
     Haemonisin linquens crebris celebranda choreis,
     non vacuus: namque ille tulit radicitus altas
     fagos ac recto proceras stipite laurus,
     non sine nutanti platano lentaque sorore   290
     flammati Phaethontis et aerea cupressu.
     haec circum sedes late contexta locavit,
     vestibulum ut molli velatum fronde vireret.
     post hunc consequitur sollerti corde Prometheus,
     extenuata gerens veteris vestigia poenae,   295
     quam quondam silici restrictus membra catena
     persolvit pendens e verticibus praeruptis.
     inde pater divum sancta cum coniuge natisque
     advenit caelo, te solum, Phoebe, relinquens,
     unigenamque simul cultricem montibus Idri: 300
     Pelea nam tecum pariter soror aspernata est,
     nec Thetidis taedas voluit celebrare iugalis.
     qui postquam niveis flexerunt sedibus artus,
     large multiplici constructae sunt dape mensae,
     cum interea infirmo quatientes corpora motu   305
     veridicos Parcae coeperunt edere cantus.
     his corpus tremulum complectens undique vestis
     candida purpurea talos incinxerat ora,

---

276 vestibulo *Schrader*: vestibuli *V*
282 aperit *Housman*: perit *V*: parit *g*.
287 Haemonisin *Heinsius:* minosim *V*.   crebris *Lachmann*: doris *V*

That is how the people, leaving the royal household by the forecourt,
all departed home in all directions with wandering steps.
After their departure the first to arrive, from the peak of Pelion,
was Chiron bearing gifts from the woodland;
for whatever flowers which the fields bear, all that the land of Thessaly   280
produces on its great mountains, all those which the fertile breeze
of the warm Favonius opens up by the waves of the river –
all these he brought woven together in mingled garlands,
and the house laughed, caressed by the pleasant odour.
Immediately after him was Peneus, leaving green Tempe,   285
Tempe which the overhanging woods encircle,
for the daughters of Thessaly to celebrate with frequent dances.
He was not empty-handed – for he brought high trees – roots and all -
beeches and tall laurels straight of stem,
complete with the nodding plane tree, and the pliant sister   290
of Phaethon who was devoured in flames, and the lofty cypress.
He placed these, woven together, far and wide around the house,
so that the forecourt might be covered and green with soft foliage.
After him there follows intelligent Prometheus,
bearing faint traces of the old punishment   295
which he had undergone once, his limbs tied by a chain
to a rock and hanging from craggy cliffs.
Then the father of the gods with his divine wife and sons came,
leaving in heaven only you, Phoebus,
and the dweller of the mountains of Idrus, your twin sister;   300
for you and your sister both equally rejected Peleus
and refused to celebrate the bridal torches of Thetis.
After they had bent their limbs on the snow-white chairs,
tables were generously erected with a many-layered feast,
when in the meantime the Fates, shaking their bodies with uncertain   305
 movement, began to utter truth-telling song.
These women had their trembling bodies completely hugged by
a white garment which surrounded their ankles with a crimson border,

at roseae niveo residebant vertice vittae,
aeternumque manus carpebant rite laborem.   310
laeva colum molli lana retinebat amictum,
dextera tum leviter deducens fila supinis
formabat digitis, tum prono in pollice torquens
libratum tereti versabat turbine fusum,
atque ita decerpens aequabat semper opus dens,   315
laneaque aridulis haerebant morsa labellis,
quae prius in levi fuerant exstantia filo:
ante pedes autem candentis mollia lanae
vellera virgati custodibant calathisci.
haec tum clarisona vellentes vellera voce   320
talia divino fuderunt carmine fata,
carmine, perfidiae quod post nulla arguet aetas.

o decus eximium magnis virtutibus augens,
Emathiae tutamen, Opis carissime nato,
accipe, quod laeta tibi pandunt luce sorores,   325
veridicum oraclum: sed vos, quae fata sequuntur,
    currite ducentes subtegmina, currite, fusi.

adveniet tibi iam portans optata maritis
Hesperus, adveniet fausto cum sidere coniunx,
quae tibi flexanimo mentem perfundat amore,   330
languidulosque paret tecum coniungere somnos,
levia substernens robusto brachia collo.
    currite ducentes subtegmina, currite, fusi.

nulla domus tales umquam contexit amores,
nullus amor tali coniunxit foedere amantes,   335
qualis adest Thetidi, qualis concordia Peleo.
    currite ducentes subtegmina, currite, fusi.
nascetur vobis expers terroris Achilles,
hostibus haud tergo, sed forti pectore notus,
qui persaepe vago victor certamine cursus   340
flammea praevertet celeris vestigia cervae.

---

320 vellentes *Fruterius*: pellentes *V*

and chaplets of rose sat on their snow-white head,
as their hands ritually plucked away at their everlasting task. 310
The left hand held a distaff covered in soft wool,
the right hand drawing down the threads gently, with fingers facing
upwards shaped them and then twisting it on downward-facing thumb
spun the spindle poised on its circular wheel,
and then their tooth constantly kept plucking their work clean and even, 315
and sticking to their dry little lips were bitten fragments of wool
which had previously been rough on the smooth thread;
before their feet wicker baskets looked
after the soft fleeces of white wool.
Carding these fleeces then they poured out with a clear-sounding voice 320
these fates in godly song,
song which no later generation will ever convict of mendacity.
'You who enrich your outstanding glory with your great acts of courage,
fortress of Thessaly, most beloved to the son of Ops,
receive the truth-telling oracle which the sisters reveal to you 325
on this happy day; but you, drawing the woof-threads which
the fates follow, run spindles, run.

The Evening Star will come to you soon, bringing what husbands long for,
 your wife will come to you with a star of good omen,
your wife who is to soak your heart with soul-twisting love 330
and to prepare to join her languid little sleeps with you,
putting her smooth arms under your strong neck.
Drawing the woof-threads, run spindles, run.

No home has ever covered love such as this, 335
no love has joined together lovers in such a bond,
as there is with Thetis or as is the harmony with Peleus.
Drawing the woof-threads, run spindles, run.

Achilles will be born to you, a man knowing no fear,
a man known to the enemy not by his back but by his strong front,
who very often as victor in the wide-ranging running race 340
will outstrip the steps of the swift stag, fast as fire.

currite ducentes subtegmina, currite, fusi.
non illi quisquam bello se conferet heros,
cum Phrygii Teucro manabunt sanguine campi,
Troicaque obsidens longinquo moenia bello,   345
periuri Pelopis vastabit tertius heres.
currite ducentes subtegmina, currite, fusi.

illius egregias virtutes claraque facta
saepe fatebuntur natorum in funere matres,
cum incultum cano solvent a vertice crinem,   350
putridaque infirmis variabunt pectora palmis.
currite ducentes subtegmina, currite, fusi.

namque velut densas praecerpens cultor aristas
sole sub ardenti flaventia demetit arva,
Troiugenum infesto prosternet corpora ferro.   355
currite ducentes subtegmina, currite, fusi.

testis erit magnis virtutibus unda Scamandri,
quae passim rapido diffunditur Hellesponto,
cuius iter caesis angustans corporum acervis
alta tepefaciet permixta flumina caede.   360
currite ducentes subtegmina, currite, fusi.

denique testis erit morti quoque reddita praeda,
cum teres excelso coacervatum aggere bustum
excipiet niveos perculsae virginis artus.
currite ducentes subtegmina, currite, fusi.   365
nam simul ac fessis dederit fors copiam Achivis
urbis Dardaniae Neptunia solvere vincla,
alta Polyxenia madefient caede sepulcra:
quae, velut ancipiti succumbens victima ferro,
proiciet truncum summisso poplite corpus.   370
currite ducentes subtegmina, currite, fusi.

---

359 caesis *V*: *fortasse* celsis *Baehrens*

Drawing the woof-threads, run spindles, run.
No hero will compare himself in war with this man,
when the Phrygian plains will drip with Trojan blood,
and he, besieging the Trojan fortress in a drawn-out war,   345
the third heir of perjured Pelops, will despoil it.
Drawing the woof-threads, run spindles, run.

That man's outstanding heroism and famous deeds
will often be spoken of by mothers at their sons' funeral,
when they will loosen their unkempt hair from their hoary head   350
and will bruise their decaying breasts with feeble hands.
Drawing the woof-threads, run spindles, run.

For just as the harvester cutting down the thick ears of corn
under the blazing sun mows down the gleaming yellow fields,
so will he strew the bodies of the sons of Troy with his offensive steel.   355
Drawing the woof-spindles, run spindles, run.

The wave of Scamander will testify to his immense heroism,
Scamander which flows broadly into the engulfing Hellespont,
whose stream he will choke with heaps of bodies, slaughtered,
warming the deep river with mingled blood.   360
Drawing the woof-threads, run spindles, run.

Final witness will be the sacrifice given to to him even when he is dead,
when a rounded barrow heaped up with a lofty mound
will receive the snowy limbs of a virgin struck dead.
Drawing the woof-threads, run spindles, run.   365
For as soon as fate will have given the tired Greeks the power
to untie the Neptunian bonds of the Dardan city,
then will the lofty tomb be soaked with Polyxena's blood;
Polyxena, who, falling like a beast-victim to the two-edged steel,
will buckle at the knees and throw her headless body forward.   370
Drawing the woof-threads, run spindles, run.

quare agite optatos animi coniungite amores.
accipiat coniunx felici foedere divam,
dedatur cupido iam dudum nupta marito.
    currite ducentes subtegmina, currite, fusi.   375

non illam nutrix orienti luce revisens
hesterno collum poterit circumdare filo,
[currite ducentes subtegmina, currite, fusi]
anxia nec mater discordis maesta puellae
secubitu caros mittet sperare nepotes.   380
    currite ducentes subtegmina, currite, fusi.

talia praefantes quondam felicia Pelei
carmina divino cecinerunt pectore Parcae.
praesentes namque ante domos invisere castas
heroum, et sese mortali ostendere coetu,   385
caelicolae nondum spreta pietate solebant.
saepe pater divum templo in fulgente revisens,
annua cum festis venissent sacra diebus,
conspexit terra centum procumbere tauros.
saepe vagus Liber Parnasi vertice summo   390
Thyadas effusis euantis crinibus egit,
cum Delphi tota certatim ex urbe ruentes
acciperent laeti divum fumantibus aris.
saepe in letifero belli certamine Mavors
aut rapidi Tritonis hera aut Amarynthia virgo   395
armatas hominum est praesens hortata catervas.
sed postquam tellus scelere est imbuta nefando,
iustitiamque omnes cupida de mente fugarunt,
perfudere manus fraterno sanguine fratres,
destitit extinctos natus lugere parentes,   400
optavit genitor primaevi funera nati,
liber uti nuptae poteretur flore novellae,
ignaro mater substernens se impia nato

---

378 *seclusit Bergk*
402 uti nuptae *Maehly:* ut innuptae *V.* novellae *Baehrens:* novercae *V*

And so come now, join together the longed for love of your heart.
Let the husband receive his goddess in a bond of bliss,
let the bride be handed over now at last to her eager bridegroom.
Drawing the woof-threads, run spindles, run. 375

When the nurse sees her again at the rising of the light she will not
be able to wind her neck all around with the thread of yesterday,
[Drawing the woof-threads, run, spindles, run]
nor will the fearful mother, sad at the sleeping apart of her
estranged girl, give up hoping for beloved grandsons. 380
Drawing the woof-threads, run spindles, run.

Such were once the prophetic songs, portending happy things
for Peleus, which the Fates sang from their divine breast.
For in earlier times the heaven-dwellers used to visit
the pure homes of heroes in person, and show themselves 385
to human gathering since religion had not yet been spurned.
Often the father of the gods visited his gleaming temple
when the annual rites had come around on festival days
and saw a hundred bulls crash to the ground.
Often the roaming Bacchus drove his whooping Thyiads 390
on the topmost summit of Parnassus with their hair flowing,
when the people of Delphi rushed in competition with each other out of the
                                                                                whole town
to receive the god on their smoking altars in gladness.
Often in the death-delivering clash of war Mars
or the mistress of the racing Triton or the Amarynthian maid 395
urged on their armed battalions of men in person.
But after the earth was soaked with evil crime
and everybody scattered justice from their lustful minds,
brothers wet their hands with brothers' blood,
the son stopped grieving for his deceased parents, 400
the father longed for the death of his first-born son
so that he might be able freely to enjoy the flower of a new young wife:
the wicked mother laying herself underneath her unwitting son,

impia non verita est divos scelerare penates,
omnia fanda nefanda malo permixta furore   405
iustificam nobis mentem avertere deorum.
quare nec talis dignantur visere coetus,
nec se contingi patiuntur lumine claro.

---

404 penates *nescio quis ante annum 1450:* parentes V

wickedly showed no fear of adulterating her family gods.
Everything both speakable and unspeakable, mingled together in wicked
madness,   405
has turned the righteous mind of the gods away from us.
That is why they do not deem our gatherings worthy of visiting,
nor do they allow themselves to be touched with the clear light of day.

LXV

etsi me assiduo confectum cura dolore
    sevocat a doctis, Hortale, virginibus,
nec potis est dulcis Musarum expromere fetus
    mens animi, tantis fluctuat ipsa malis -
namque mei nuper Lethaeo gurgite fratris   5
    pallidulum manans alluit unda pedem,
Troia Rhoeteo quem subter litore tellus
    ereptum nostris obterit ex oculis -

.   .   .   .   .   .

numquam ego te, vita frater amabilior,   10
aspiciam posthac? at certe semper amabo,
    semper maesta tua carmina morte canam,
qualia sub densis ramorum concinit umbris
    Daulias, absumpti fata gemens Ityli -
sed tamen in tantis maeroribus, Hortale, mitto   15
    haec expressa tibi carmina Battiadae
ne tua dicta vagis nequiquam credita ventis
    effluxisse meo forte putes animo,
ut missum sponsi furtivo munere malum
    procurrit casto virginis e gremio,   20
quod miserae oblitae molli sub veste locatum,
    dum adventu matris prosilit, excutitur,
atque illud prono praeceps agitur decursu,
    huic manat tristi conscius ore rubor.

65

I am exhausted by constant grief, and care
calls me away from the Learned Maidens, Hortalus,
nor can my mind produce the sweet offspring of the Muses,
for so great are the ills on which it is tossing;
for not long ago a wave spreading from the flood of Lethe   5
washed over the poor little pale foot of my brother.
The land of Troy now presses him down under the Rhoetean shore,
stolen away as he is from our eyes.
.   .   .   .   .
Shall I never see you again, O brother more lovable than life itself?   10
I will always love you certainly,
always sing sad songs over your death –
the sort of songs which beneath the thick shades of the branches,
the Daulian bird sings moaning for the fate of her murdered Itylus.
And yet, Hortalus, despite such sorrows, I am still sending   15
you these songs of Battiades which I have rendered for you:
just in case you may think that your words have been entrusted in vain
to the wandering winds and have poured clean out of my mind;
like an apple, sent to a girl by her betrothed as a secret gift,
which rolls out of her virginal lap;   20
the poor girl had put it under her soft clothes and forgotten it,
and it is shaken out when she leaps up at the arrival of her mother.
The apple falls right down and rolls along the floor,
and a guilty blush spreads over her sad face.

80

LXVI

Omnia qui magni dispexit lumina mundi,
    qui stellarum ortus comperit atque obitus,
flammeus ut rapidi solis nitor obscuretur,
    ut cedant certis sidera temporibus,
ut Triviam furtim sub Latmia saxa relegans   5
    dulcis amor gyro devocet aereo:
idem me ille Conon caelesti in limine vidit,
    e Bereniceo vertice caesariem,
fulgentem clare, quam cunctis illa deorum
    levia protendens bracchia pollicita est,   10
qua rex tempestate novo auctus hymenaeo
    vastatum finis iverat Assyrios,
dulcia nocturnae portans vestigia rixae,
    quam de virgineis gesserat exuviis.
estne novis nuptis odio Venus? an quod aventum   15
    frustrantur falsis gaudia lacrimulis,
ubertim thalami quas intra limina fundunt?
    non, ita me divi, vera gemunt, iverint.
id mea me multis docuit regina querellis
    invisente novo proelia torva viro.   20
et tu non orbum luxti deserta cubile,
    sed fratris cari flebile discidium?
quam penitus maestas exedit cura medullas!
    ut tibi tunc toto pectore sollicitae
sensibus ereptis mens excidit! at <te> ego certe   25
    cognoram a parva virgine magnanimam.

---

7 limine *Heinsius*: numine *V*: in lumine *Vossius*
9 cunctis..deorum *Haupt*: multis...dearum *V*
11 auctus *V*: auctatus *Goold*
15 an quod aventum *Munro*: atque parentum *V*

66

The man who saw all the lights of the great firmament,
    who calculated the risings and the settings of the stars,
how the flaming brilliance of the scorching sun is darkened,
    how the stars withdraw at fixed times,
how sweet love, banishing Trivia in secret under the Latmian rocks   5
    seduces her from her heavenly rotation:
that same Conon saw me on the floor of heaven,
    me, a lock from the head of Berenice,
shining brightly: I am the one whom she promised to all of the gods,
    as she stretched out her smooth arms   10
at the time when the king, increased by a new marriage,
    had gone out to ravage the Assyrian borders,
carrying on him the sweet evidence of his nightly grappling
    which he had carried on for the prize of her virginity.
Do new brides hate Venus? Or do they foil the pleasures   15
    of the randy men with fake little tears,
tears which they pour out by the bucket inside the doorway of the bedroom?
    May the gods help me, they do not groan true.
This my queen taught me with many a lamentation
    when her new husband went to see savage battles.   20
Did you weep not as an abandoned woman for her bereft bed
    but for the lamentable separation from your dear brother?
How deep did emotion eat out the sad marrow of your bones!
    How then when you were troubled with all your heart
you lost your senses and fell unconscious! And yet I knew you   25
    to be brave-hearted right from when you were a little girl.

anne bonum oblita es facinus, quo regium adepta es
　　　coniugium, quo non fortius ausit alis?
sed tum maesta virum mittens quae verba locuta es!
　　　Iuppiter, ut tristi lumina saepe manu!　　　　　　　30

quis te mutavit tantus deus?　an quod amantes
　　　non longe a caro corpore abesse volunt?
atque ibi me cunctis pro dulci coniuge divis
　　　non sine taurino sanguine pollicita es,
si reditum tetulisset.　is haud in tempore longo　　　35
　　　captam Asiam Aegypti finibus addiderat.
quis ego pro factis caelesti reddita coetu
　　　pristina vota novo munere dissoluo.
invita, o regina, tuo de vertice cessi,
　　　invita:　adiuro teque tuumque caput,　　　　　　40
digna ferat quod si quis inaniter adiurarit:
　　　sed qui se ferro postulet esse parem?
ille quoque eversus mons est, quem maximum in oris
　　　progenies Thiae clara supervehitur,
cum Medi peperere novum mare, cumque iuventus　　　45
　　　per medium classi barbara navit Athon.
quid facient crines, cum ferro talia cedant?
　　　Iuppiter, ut Chalybon omne genus pereat,
et qui principio sub terra quaerere venas
　　　institit ac ferri stringere, duritiem!　　　　　　50
abiunctae paulo ante comae mea fata sorores
　　　lugebant, cum se Memnonis Aethiopis
unigena impellens nutantibus aera pennis
　　　obtulit Arsinoes Locridos ales equus,
isque per aetherias me tollens avolat umbras　　　　55
　　　et Veneris casto collocat in gremio:
ipsa suum Zephyritis eo famulum legarat,
　　　Graia Canopitis incola litoribus.
hic liquidi vario ne solum in limine caeli
　　　ex Ariadnaeis aurea temporibus　　　　　　　60

---

25 te *addidit Avantius*
28 quo *g*: quod *V*   fortius *Muretus*: fortior *V*
59 hic liquidi *Friedrich*: hi dii ven ibi *V*: *alii alia*

Or have you forgotten the brave deed with which you obtained a royal
    marriage – no braver deed than this could another dare to do.
Then, when sending off your man, what words you spoke sadly!
    Jupiter, how often you wiped your eyes with your hand!   30

Which god is so great as to have changed you? Or is it that lovers
    do not want to be far away from their beloved's body?
There and then you promised me – complete with bull's blood -
    to all the gods for your sweet husband's sake,
if he brought about his return. In no long space of time he   35
    had added captured Asia to the boundaries of Egypt.
For these deeds I, given to the company of heaven,
    pay old vows with a new offering.
O queen, it was against my will that I left your head,
    against my will: I swear by you and by your head.   40
Let anyone who swears frivolously get his just deserts -
    but who could expect to be equal to a blade?
Even that mountain was overturned, the largest on dry land
    over which the brilliant offspring of Thia travels,
when the Medes gave birth to a new sea, when the youth   45
    of the Orient sailed through the middle of Athos with their fleet.
What could mere hair do, when such things as this yield to steel?
    Jupiter, may the entire race of Chalybes perish,
and he who first set about seeking veins of metal underground
    and to harden the toughness of iron!   50
My sister locks of hair were bewailing my fate as I was
    just cut off from them, when there presented himself the sibling
of Ethiopian Memnon, striking the air with his nodding wings,
    the winged horse of Locrian Arsinoe;
and he then raising me up through the shades of air flies away   55
    and places me in the chaste lap of Venus.
The mistress of Zephyrium had despatched her servant there,
    the Greek inhabitant of the shores of Canopus.
Here, so that not only the golden crown from the temples of Ariadne
    might be planted in the varied floor of   60

fixa corona foret, sed nos quoque‿fulgeremus
　　　devotae flavi verticis exuviae,
uvidulam a fluctu cedentem ad templa deum me
　　　sidus in antiquis diva novum posuit.
Virginis et saevi contingens namque Leonis　　　　　　　65
　　　lumina, Callisto iuncta Lycaoniae,
vertor in occasum, tardum dux ante Booten,
　　　qui vix sero alto mergitur Oceano;
sed quamquam me nocte premunt vestigia divum,
　　　lux autem canae Tethyi restituit.　　　　　　　　　　70
pace tua fari hic liceat, Ramnusia virgo,
　　　namque ego non ullo vera timore tegam -
nec si me infestis discerpent sidera dictis -
　　　condita quin veri pectoris evoluam:
non his tam laetor rebus, quam me afore semper,　　　75
　　　afore me a dominae vertice discrucior.
quicum ego, dum virgo quondam fuit, omnibus expers
　　　unguentis, una vilia multa bibi.
nunc vos, optato quas iunxit lumine taeda,
　　　non prius unanimis corpora coniugibus　　　　　80
tradite nudantes reiecta veste papillas,
　　　quam iucunda mihi munera libet onyx -
vester onyx, casto colitis quae iura cubili.
　　　sed quae se impuro dedit adulterio,
illius - a! - mala dona levis bibat irrita pulvis:　　　85
　　　namque ego ab indignis praemia nulla peto;
sed magis, o nuptae, semper concordia vestras,
　　　semper amor sedes incolat assiduus.
tu vero, regina, tuens cum sidera divam
　　　placabis festis luminibus Venerem,　　　　　　　90
unguinis expertem non siris esse tuam me,
　　　sed potius largis affice muneribus,
sidera corruerint utinam! coma regia fiam!
　　　proximus Hydrochoi fulgeret Oarion!

78　vilia *Lobel*: milia *V*
91　siris *Lachmann*: vestris *V*
93　corruerint *Lachmann*: cur iterent *V*

the transparent heaven, but that I tc᛫ might shine
    as the dedicated spoil from a blonde head,
the goddess placed me, wet from the stream, as I went to the temples
    of the gods, and put me among the ancient stars as a new star.
Touching the lights of Virgo, of the savage Leo   65
    joined to Callisto child of Lycaon;
I turn towards my setting point leading the way before the sluggish Bootes
    who only just manages to sink, late, in the depths of the sea.
Yet although at night the footsteps of gods press hard on me,
    still the dawn restores me to white-haired Tethys;   70
may I have permission by your leave, O Rhamnusian maiden, to say this,
    for I shall not conceal the truth out of any fear;
and not even the stars, if they tear me apart with hostile words,
    will stop me from unfolding the truth buried in my heart.
I am not happy at these circumstances but rather am tormented always   75
    that I shall be away, away always from my mistress' head –
She with whom I, while she was once a maiden, ignorant of all
    perfumes, I drank up many a cheap scent.
You, whom the wedding-torch has joined with its longed-for light,
    do not now hand over your bodies to your affectionate spouses   80
casting aside your clothes and baring your breasts,
    before the onyx pours pleasing gifts to me,
the onyx belonging to you who cultivate the laws in chaste marriage.
    But as for the woman who has given herself to filthy adultery,
let the powdery dust drink up her evil gifts – ah! – and render them futile;
    for I seek no rewards from the unworthy.   86
Rather, O brides, may harmony always, may constant
    love always inhabit your homes.
But you, O queen, when you gaze at the stars and
    appease the goddess Venus on festival days   90
do not allow me (who am yours) to go without perfume
    but rather treat me with generous gifts.
Would that the stars would perish! Could I but become a royal lock of hair,
    then Orion could shine next to Aquarius!

LXVII

O dulci iucunda viro, iucunda parenti,
    salve teque bona Iuppiter auctet ope,
ianua, quam Balbo dicunt servisse benigne
    olim, cum sedes ipse senex tenuit,
quamque ferunt rursus nato servisse maligne,   5
    postquam es porrecto facta marita sene.
dic agedum nobis, quare mutata feraris
    in dominum veterem deseruisse fidem.

'Non (ita Caecilio placeam, cui tradita nunc sum)
    culpa mea est, quamquam dicitur esse mea,   10
nec peccatum a me quisquam pote dicere quicquam:
    verum istuc populi lingua quiete tegit,
qui, quacumque aliquid reperitur non bene factum,
    ad me omnes clamant: 'ianua, culpa tua est.'

non istuc satis est uno te dicere verbo,   15
    sed facere ut quivis sentiat et videat.

'qui possum? nemo quaerit nec scire laborat.'

    nos volumus: nobis dicere ne dubita.

'primum igitur, virgo quod fertur tradita nobis,
    falsum est. non illam vir prior attigerat,   20
languidior tenera cui pendens sicula beta
    numquam se mediam sustulit ad tunicam;
sed pater illusi nati violasse cubile

---

5 nato *Froehlich*: voto *V*
12 istuc *Heyse*: istius *V*: est ius *Munro*   lingua quiete tegit *Palmer*: ianua qui te facit *V:*
ianua quicque facit *Munro*
20 attigerat *g*: attigerit *V*
23 illusi *Baehrens*: illius *V*

67

POET: Pleasing to the beloved husband, pleasing to the parent,
hail, and may Jupiter enrich you with a favourable blessing,
O door, who they say served Balbus generously
once, when the old man himself held the house;
but who on the other hand they say served his son meanly   5
after the old man was laid out and you were made a bridal door.
Come now, tell us why people say that you have changed
and abandoned your long-standing loyalty to your master.

DOOR: May it please Caecilius, to whom I have by now been entrusted,
it is not my fault, even though it is said to be mine;   10
nor can anyone tell of anything wrong done by me:
of course that is something which the popular tongue covers in
                                        silence;
and yet whenever anything is uncovered which is not right,
then they all shout at me: 'Door, you are to blame!'.

POET: It will not do simply to state that in a single word -   15
you have to ensure that everyone feels and sees it.

DOOR: How can I do that? Nobody asks or makes any effort to find out.

POET: Well I do, for one. Tell me at once.

DOOR: In the first place, that tale that she was handed over to us a virgin
is untrue. Not that her husband had been the first to touch her –   20
his sword hung floppier than a young beet and
never raised itself to the middle of his tunic –
but rather the sick fool's father is said to have stained

dicitur et miseram conscelerasse domum,
sive quod impia mens caeco flagrabat amore,   25
    seu quod iners sterili semine natus erat,
ut quaerendum unde <unde> foret nervosius illud,
    quod posset zonam solvere virgineam.'

egregium narras mira pietate parentem,
    qui ipse sui nati minxerit in gremium.   30
'atqui non solum hoc dicit se cognitum habere
    Brixia Cycneae supposita speculae,
flavus quam molli praecurrit flumine Mella,
    Brixia Veronae mater amata meae,
sed de Postumio et Corneli narrat amore,   35
    cum quibus illa malum fecit adulterium.
dixerit hic aliquis: qui tu istaec, ianua, nosti,
    cui numquam domini limine abesse licet,
nec populum auscultare, sed hic suffixa tigillo
    tantum operire soles aut aperire domum?   40
saepe illam audivi furtiva voce loquentem
    solam cum ancillis haec sua flagitia,
nomine dicentem quos diximus, utpote quae mi
    speraret nec linguam esse nec auriculam.
praeterea addebat quendam, quem dicere nolo   45
    nomine, ne tollat rubra supercilia.
longus homo est, magnas cui lites intulit olim
    falsum mendaci ventre puerperium.'

---

27 quaerendum unde unde *Statius*: quaerendus unde *V*
44 speraret *Calphurnius*: sperent *V*

his son's bed and to have incriminated the wretched household;
either because his unscrupulous mind was ablaze with blind lust, 25
or else because his son was impotent with barren seed
and so they had to look elsewhere to find something stiffer
to be able to untie her virgin's belt.

POET: An outstanding example of wonderful loyalty, this parent you tell of,
      a man who pissed in his own son's lap.   30

DOOR: But that is not the only thing which Brixia claims to know for a fact -
      Brixia seated below the Cycnean watch-tower,
      with golden Mella flowing past it with her soft stream,
      and beloved mother-city of my own Verona.
      It also tells the tale of Postumius and the love of Cornelius,   35
      men with whom that woman committed shameful adultery.
      At this someone might say: 'How do you know that, door,
      since you are never allowed to be away from the master's threshold,
      never allowed to listen in to people but fastened here to the lintel,
      just keep constantly opening and shutting the house?'   40
      I have often heard her talking – just her with her maidservants –
      of these misdeeds of hers in a secretive voice,
      naming the men I have spoken about, as if she
      expected me to have no tongue and no little ear.
      She also mentioned somebody else, whom I do not want   45
      to name in case he raises his blazing red eyebrows.
      He is a tall man: once he was landed in a big courtcase
      by a fake childbirth with a lying belly.'

LXVIII

quod mihi fortuna casuque oppressus acerbo
    conscriptum hoc lacrimis mittis epistolium,
naufragum ut eiectum spumantibus aequoris undis
    sublevem et a mortis limine restituam,
quem neque sancta Venus molli requiescere somno   5
    desertum in lecto caelibe perpetitur,
nec veterum dulci scriptorum carmine Musae
    oblectant, cum mens anxia pervigilat:
id gratum est mihi, me quoniam tibi dicis amicum,
    muneraque et Musarum hinc petis et Veneris.   10
sed tibi ne mea sint ignota incommoda, mi Alli,
    neu me odisse putes hospitis officium,
accipe, quis merser fortunae fluctibus ipse,
    ne amplius a misero dona beata petas.
tempore quo primum vestis mihi tradita pura est,   15
    iucundum cum aetas florida ver ageret,
multa satis lusi: non est dea nescia nostri,
    quae dulcem curis miscet amaritiem.
sed totum hoc studium luctu fraterna mihi mors
    abstulit. o misero frater adempte mihi,   20
tu mea tu moriens fregisti commoda, frater,
    tecum una tota est nostra sepulta domus,
omnia tecum una perierunt gaudia nostra,
    quae tuus in vita dulcis alebat amor.
cuius ego interitu tota de mente fugavi   25
    haec studia atque omnes delicias animi.
quare, quod scribis, 'Veronae turpe, Catulle,
    esse', quod hic quisquis de meliore nota
frigida deserto tepefactet membra cubili;
    id, mi Alli, non est turpe, magis miserum est.   30

11 mi Alli *Schöll*: Manli *f*: Mani *Lachmann*: Mali *V*
27 Catulle *V*: Catullo *g*
29 tepefactet *Bergk*: tepefacit *V*
30 mi Alli *Schöll*: Manli *f*: Mali *V*

68

The fact that you, ground down with misfortune and bitter mischance,
send me this letter written in tears,
like a shipwrecked man thrown up from the foaming waves of the sea
for me to rescue and bring back from the threshold of death,
a man whom neither holy Venus allows to rest in soft sleep,   5
abandoned on his bachelor bed,
nor do the Muses delight you with the sweet song of writers of old,
since your troubled mind can find no rest:
this is welcome to me, since you call me your friend
and you ask me for the gifts of the Muses and of Venus.   10
In case my own discomforts are not known to you, my Allius,
and in case you might think that I am spurning the duty of a friend,
hear what streams of misfortune I am sunk in myself and
cease to seek the gifts of good fortune from one who is himself pitiful.
When the white garment was first given to me,   15
when my flowery time of life was exercising a pleasurable spring,
then I sported quite enough. The goddess is not unaware of my existence,
the goddess who mingles sweet bitterness with passions.
But the death of my brother has removed all this enthusiasm with grief.
O brother, stolen from me in my misery,   20
dying you shattered my pleasures, brother,
our whole house is buried with you,
all our joys have perished along with you,
joys which your sweet love fed while you lived.
At his decease I have banished right out of my mind   25
these enthusiasms and all pleasures of the mind.
So, when you write "Catullus, it is a disgrace for you to be in Verona",
because here anyone of higher quality
warms up his cold limbs in a lonely bed –
it is not a disgrace, my Allius, it is more a pitiful state of affairs.   30

ignosces igitur si, quae mihi luctus ademit,
    haec tibi non tribuo munera, cum nequeo.
nam, quod scriptorum non magna est copia apud me,
    hoc fit, quod Romae vivimus: illa domus,
illa mihi sedes, illic mea carpitur aetas;   35
    huc una ex multis capsula me sequitur.
quod cum ita sit, nolim statuas nos mente maligna
    id facere aut animo non satis ingenuo,
quod tibi non hucusque petenti copia praesto est:
    ultro ego deferrem, copia siqua foret.   40
non possum reticere, deae, qua me Allius in re
    iuverit aut quantis foverit officiis,
ne fugiens saeclis obliviscentibus aetas
    illius hoc caeca nocte tegat studium:
sed dicam vobis, vos porro dicite multis   45
    milibus et facite haec carta loquatur anus.

    .   .   .   .   .   .

    notescatque magis mortuus atque magis,
nec tenuem texens sublimis aranea telam
    in deserto Alli nomine opus faciat.   50
nam, mihi quam dederit duplex Amathusia curam,
    scitis, et in quo me torruerit genere,
cum tantum arderem quantum Trinacria rupes
    lymphaque in Oetaeis Malia Thermopylis,
maesta neque assiduo tabescere lumina fletu   55
    cessarent tristique imbre madere genae,
qualis in aerii perlucens vertice montis
    rivus muscoso prosilit e lapide
(qui cum de prona praeceps est valle volutus,
    per medium densi transit iter populi,   60
dulce viatori lasso in sudore levamen,
    cum gravis exustos aestus hiulcat agros).
ac velut in nigro iactatis turbine nautis
    lenius aspirans aura secunda venit

---

39 hucusque *Nisbet*: utriusque *V*   praesto *Froehlich*: posta *V*
42 foverit *Cornelisson*: iuverit *V*
52 torruerit *Turnebus*: corruerit *V*
63 ac *Palladius*: hic *GR*: haec *O*

You will forgive me, therefore, if I do not send you these gifts
(of which grief has robbed me), since I am unable to send them.
The reason why I have no great abundance of writings with me
is that I live in Rome; that is my home,
that is my abode, there is my life spent – 35
only one out of many book-boxes follows me here.
That being so, I would hate you to deduce that I was doing this out of spite
or with a spirit which is less than generous
because you have up until now not received what you asked for:
if I had any sort of supply, I would give it you unasked. 40
Goddesses, I cannot keep silent about the matter in which Allius
assisted me, or the extent of the duties with which he fostered my cause,
in case time fleeing in its forgetful generations
should shroud this care of his in blind night:
but I shall tell you, and you then tell many thousands 45
and make this old page of mine speak out

. . . .

and being dead may yet grow more and more famous,
and also so that the spider weaving its slender web up on high
may not make the deserted name of Allius into her next task. 50
For you know the passion which the perfidious Amathusia gave to me,
and the way in which she scorched me
when I was burning as much as the Trinacrian crag
and the Malian water in Thermopylae of Oeta,
when my sad eyes did not cease to melt with constant weeping 55
and my cheeks to be soaked with a shower of sadness,
just as a gleaming stream on the summit of a high hill
leaps out from a mossy stone –
a stream which when it has rolled straight down the sloping valley
passes over the middle of the road thronged with people, 60
a sweet refreshment for the wayfarer in his tired sweat
when heavy heat cracks open the burnt fields:
and also like when sailors are tossed about in a black storm,
a favourable breeze comes with gentler breath,

iam prece Pollucis, iam Castoris implorata, 65
    tale fuit nobis Allius auxilium.
is clausum lato patefecit limite campum,
    isque domum nobis isque dedit dominam
ad quam communes exerceremus amores.
    quo mea se molli candida diva pede 70
intulit et trito fulgentem in limine plantam
    innixa arguta constituit solea,
coniugis ut quondam flagrans advenit amore
    Protesilaeam Laudamia domum
inceptam frustra, nondum cum sanguine sacro 75
    hostia caelestis pacificasset eros.
nil mihi tam valde placeat, Ramnusia virgo,
    quod temere invitis suscipiatur eris.
quam ieiuna pium desideret ara cruorem,
    docta est amisso Laudamia viro, 80
coniugis ante coacta novi dimittere collum,
    quam veniens una atque altera rursus hiems
noctibus in longis avidum saturasset amorem,
    posset ut abrupto vivere coniugio,
quod scibant Parcae non longo tempore abesse, 85
    si miles muros isset ad Iliacos.
nam tum Helenae raptu primores Argivorum
    coeperat ad sese Troia ciere viros,
Troia (nefas!) commune sepulcrum Asiae Europaeque,
    Troia virum et virtutum omnium acerba cinis, 90
quaene etiam nostro letum miserabile fratri
    attulit. ei misero frater adempte mihi,
ei misero fratri iucundum lumen ademptum,
    tecum una tota est nostra sepulta domus,
omnia tecum una perierunt gaudia nostra, 95
    quae tuus in vita dulcis alebat amor.

---

66 Allius *O*: Manlius *GR*: Manius *Lachmann*
68 dominam *V*: dominae *Froehlich*
91 quaene etiam *Heinsius*: que vetet id *V*

implored with prayers now to Pollux, now to Castor - 65
that was what Allius' help was like to me.
He opened up a closed field with a broad path,
he gave us a house, he gave a mistress,
where we might exercise our mutual love.
My gleaming goddess brought herself to it with delicate foot 70
and set her shining sole on the well-rubbed threshold,
standing there leaning on it with her sandal tapping on it,
just as once Laudamia, blazing with love for her husband,
came to the house of Protesilaus:
a house begun in vain, since the sacrificial victim had not yet 75
appeased the heavenly lords with its sacred blood.
May nothing please me so much, Maiden of Rhamnus,
as to be undertaken rashly against the will of the gods.
How much the hungry altar yearns for the holy blood,
this was Laudamia taught when she lost her man, 80
forced to send away the embrace of her new husband
before one winter and then again another winter
could have satisfied her greedy passion in its long nights,
to make her able to live with her marriage stolen from her –
a fact which the Fates knew was not far away 85
if he went as a soldier to the walls of Troy.
For at that time, with the stealing of Helen, Troy had begun
to draw to itself the leaders of the Greeks,
Troy (what wickedness!) the shared grave of Asia and of Europe,
Troy the bitter ashes of men and of all manly qualities, 90
Troy which also brought lamentable death to my brother.
 Alas, brother stolen from me in my pitiful state,
alas the pleasant light of life stolen from my pitiful brother;
our whole house is buried with you,
all our joys have perished along with you, 95
joys which your sweet love fed while you lived.

quem nunc tam longe non inter nota sepulcra
    nec prope cognatos compositum cineres,
sed Troia obscena, Troia infelice sepultum
    detinet extremo terra aliena solo.   100
ad quam tum properans fertur <lecta> undique pubes
    Graeca penetralis deseruisse focos,
ne Paris abducta gavisus libera moecha
    otia pacato degeret in thalamo.
quo tibi tum casu, pulcherrima Laudamia,   105
    ereptum est vita dulcius atque anima
coniugium: tanto te absorbens vertice amoris
    aestus in abruptum detulerat barathrum,
quale ferunt Grai Pheneum prope Cyllenaeum
    siccare emulsa pingue palude solum,   110
quod quondam caesis montis fodisse medullis
    audit falsiparens Amphitryoniades,
tempore quo certa Stymphalia monstra sagitta
    perculit imperio deterioris eri,
pluribus ut caeli tereretur ianua divis,   115
    Hebe nec longa virginitate foret.
sed tuus altus amor barathro fuit altior illo,
    qui tamen indomitam ferre iugum docuit.
nam nec tam carum confecto aetate parenti
    una caput seri nata nepotis alit,   120
qui, cum divitiis vix tandem inventus avitis
    nomen testatas intulit in tabulas,
impia derisi gentilis gaudia tollens,
    suscitat a cano volturium capiti;
nec tantum niveo gavisa est ulla columbo   125
    compar (quae multo dicitur improbius
oscula mordenti semper decerpere rostro,
    quam quae praecipue multivola est mulier).
sed tu horum magnos vicisti sola furores,
    ut semel es flavo conciliata viro.   130
aut nihil aut paulo cui tum concedere digna
    lux mea se nostrum contulit in gremium,

---

101 lecta *addidit Eldik*

Now so far away, not among the familiar tombs,
not laid to rest near the ashes of those known to you,
but held in filthy Troy, buried in unhappy Troy,
strange earth holds you on its furthest soil.   100
That was the place to which at that time <chosen> Greek youth
is said to have hurried from all sides, abandoning their homes and hearths,
to prevent Paris getting away with his stolen lover
and living a life of liberty and idleness in his war-free bedroom.
By that same misfortune, o most beautiful Laudamia,   105
your marriage was stolen from you, a marriage sweeter to you than your life
and your soul; the tide of love had sucked you in so great a whirlpool
and dropped you into a precipitous pit,
just like the one the Greeks say is near Cyllenaean Pheneus
and dries out the rich soil with a drained marsh.   110
The false-parented son of Amphitryon is said
once to have dug this out by cutting out the heart of the mountain,
at that time when he shot down the Stymphalian monsters with his unerring
arrow on the orders of a master inferior to himself,
so that the doorway of heaven might be trodden by more gods   115
and to prevent Hebe from enduring a long virginity.
But your deep love was deeper than that pit,
a love which taught you – although not broken in yet – to bear the yoke.
For not so dear to a parent worn out with age,
is the head of a late grandson being fed by his one and only daughter: 120
the child has been found for his grandfather's wealth in the nick of time
and has had his name entered into the witnessed will,
putting a stop to the wicked joys of the foiled next of kin,
and shooing away the vulture from his white head.
Nor has any dove found such great happiness with his snowy mate –   125
although the dove is said to be much more shameless
than the most outstandingly promiscuous woman
in constantly plucking kisses with her nibbling beak.
But you alone outdid the great passions of all these,
when once you were joined with your fair-haired husband.   130
Totally or all but totally comparable to this woman,
my darling brought herself into my embrace,

quam circumcursans hinc illinc saepe Cupido
    fulgebat crocina candidus in tunica.
quae tamen etsi uno non est contenta Catullo,   135
    rara verecundae furta feremus erae,
ne nimium simus stultorum more molesti.
    saepe etiam Iuno, maxima caelicolum,
coniugis in culpa flagrantem contudit iram,
    noscens omnivoli plurima furta Iovis.   140
atqui nec divis homines componier aequum est -   141

     *   *   *   *   *   *

    ingratum tremuli tolle parentis onus;   142
nec tamen illa mihi dextra deducta paterna
    flagrantem Assyrio venit odore domum,
sed furtiva dedit mira munuscula nocte,   145
    ipsius ex ipso dempta viri gremio.
quare illud satis est, si nobis is datur unis
    quem lapide illa diem candidiore notat.
hoc tibi, quod potui, confectum carmine munus
    pro multis, Alli, redditur officiis,   150
ne vestrum scabra tangat rubigine nomen
    haec atque illa dies atque alia atque alia.
huc addent divi quam plurima, quae Themis olim
    antiquis solita est munera ferre piis.
sitis felices et tu simul et tua vita,   155
    et domus <ipsa>, in qua lusimus, et domina,
et qui principio nobis te tradidit Afer,
    a quo sunt primo <mi> omnia nata bono,
et longe ante omnes mihi quae me carior ipso est,
    lux mea, qua viva vivere dulce mihi est.   160

---

139 contudit *Hertzberg:* concoquit iram *Lachmann:* cotidiana *V*
141-2 *lacunam indicavit Marcilius.*
145 mira *V*: muta *Heyse*
148 diem *editio Parmensis:* dies *V*
156 ipsa *addidit g*
157 te tradidit *Scaliger* Afer *Munro: alii alia* terram dedit aufert *V*
158 bono *V*: bona *ζ* mi *addidit Haupt*

with Cupid frequently darting around her, now here now there,
shining brilliantly in his saffron tunic.
She may not be content with Catullus alone,   135
but we will put up with the infrequent infidelities of my modest mistress,
to prevent us being too much of a nuisance in the manner of stupid men.
Often even Juno, the greatest of the heaven-dwellers,
swallowed up her anger blazing at the misbehaviour of her husband,
realising that all-desiring Jupiter's lapses were multitudinous.   140
And yet it is not fair to compare human with divine,
*   *   *   *   *   *   *
pick up the thankless burden of an aged parent.
But she was not led down to me by the hand of her parent,
coming to the house which burned with Assyrian scent,
but rather she gave me stolen little gifts in the wonderful night-time,   145
gifts taken right from the very embrace of her very own husband.
And so it is enough, if to me alone is given
the day which she marks out with a brighter stone.
This is the gift, Allius, such as I could manage, finished off in verse
and given to you in return for many kindnesses,   150
so that this day and then another, and then another and then another
may not touch your name with foul rust.
To this the gods will add as many as possible of the gifts which Themis once
was in the habit of bringing to good people of old.
May you be happy, both you and the love of your life,   155
and the house itself in which we sported, and my mistress too,
and Afer who first gave you to us,
the man from whose original goodness all I have now stems,
and far above all others she who is dearer to me than I am to myself,
my light, whose life makes living sweet.   160

Commentary

6 1

Words marked with an asterisk* will be found in the Glossary.

This is a poem to mark a wedding, combining the *Hymenaeus* (the song sung during the procession (*deductio*) of the bride from the house of her father to her new marital home) and the *epithalamium* (song sung outside the bridal chamber) with Fescennine verses (ribald address to the couple). Here we have the traditional features of the *Hymenaeus* (praise of the beauty and virtue of the bridal pair, invocation of the god, prayer for children, etc.) filled with Roman wedding traditions (e.g Talassius (127), the throwing of nuts, the formal *deductio* of the bride, the *matronae*) and also the very Roman Fescennine ribaldry. It is, however, unlikely that the poem was actually sung to accompany the wedding itself: attempts to match the words to the actions of the Roman wedding ceremony are unconvincing, if only because the poet would hardly have timed the text to synchronise with the actions. What we have instead is a literary artefact which incorporates the elements of a Roman wedding and comments on them in a mock-realistic manner.

The genre of the Wedding Song is apparently very old: we hear of a *hymenaios* being sung in a scene on the shield of Achilles (Homer *Iliad* 18. 493) and the lyric poetess Sappho wrote *Epithalamia* – some (like this poem) in lyric metre, some (like poem 62) in hexameters – of which fragments remain. The nearest we get to complete poems in Greek are in drama, either serious (e.g. Euripides *Phaethon* fr. 781 N) or satiric (Aristophanes *Peace* 1333-66) and in later Hellenistic literature (Theocritus *Idyll* 18). Roman literature mocks the genre in Plautus' *Casina* (798-814) before Catullus and his neoteric contemporaries took it up: there are fragments of lyric hymenaeals by Ticidas and Calvus, the lyric *epithalamium* having been pronounced dead by Catullus' contemporary the poet and critic Philodemus (*de.Mus.* 68K, Wiseman (1985) 115 n.78). In Catullus' long poems we find the marriage song treated in different ways: 61 is at least apparently composed for a real wedding, 62 is a freer composition combining the amoebean poetry of Greek pastoral with a very Roman flavour, while 64 contains a wedding song sung by the Fates in a mythological setting.

The poem is mostly auspicious and optimistic, as one expects of a wedding-hymn: today is a 'happy day' (*hilari die*) (11) for dancing (14), the bride is like the goddess Venus (17-19) or a flower (87-90) and is as keen as the bridegroom to get married (32-5); marriage is a source of health and safety for individual (61-5), family (66-70) and state (71-5); the bridegroom is clean-living (97-101) and devoted (102-6), and great joys await the couple by night and by day (109-112) as many as the stars in the sky or the grains of dust in Africa (199-203), out of which joys will emerge charming children (205-218). These sentiments could be paralleled at virtually any wedding anywhere in the world and do not tie the poem to Rome in the late republic.

Other features of the poem appear less bright and cheerful, however: right at the start
we see Hymen 'snatching a delicate girl for a man' (3-4) and when Venus appears(18-19)
she is cast before the judgement of Paris – where her beauty won through, but at enormous
cost to poor Paris, whose own subsequent marriage to Helen cost him his family and his
fatherland and was itself a sterile union. The 'tender girl' image is heightened at 56-60,
where the rhetoric sounds rather like 62.21-4 as the 'flower of a little girl' (*floridam ...
puellulam*) is snatched from her mother's lap and handed over to a 'wild young man' (*fero
iuveni*). The danger of infidelity by this devoted husband is denied – the bride is the most
beautiful woman in the world (82-6) – but dwelt upon, the implication of 97-101 being
that he will be content with the bride because of her 'tender breasts' (*teneris papillis*) and
only as long as they remain so. This husband is teased over his attachment to the
'hairless *concubinus*' (134-6), and his wife is darkly warned not to refuse her husband for
fear that the paragon of fidelity will seek affection elsewhere (144-6). 'Virtue, as
represented by the tender breasts of Vibia Aurunculeia, is an attractive proposition'
(Wiseman (1985) 115); but the poet also reminds us that the temptation to indulge 'in
wicked adultery' is always there as the other, darker side of this picture of the blissful
family of elderly women (154-6), happy couple and smiling baby (209-13).

A further source of ironic distance is provided by the debt of the poet to earlier Greek
literature: the hymn to Hymen owes more than a little to the *Hymns* of Callimachus in its
dramatic shape, its learned allusions (descriptions such as *Phrygius* for Paris, etc.) and its
literary tone, as it also owes something to the *epithalamia* of Sappho. The idealised
vision of the chaste and happy couple winning through to married bliss is redolent of the
popular Greek novel (Wiseman (1985) 118), whereas the rude Fescennine innuendo is
Roman satire. The mixture of genres is thoroughly Alexandrian (though Hutchinson (15-
16) doubts the extent and the importance of Hellenistic 'crossing of genres') and gives the
poem a flavour which is obviously artificial but none the less delicious for being so.
Once again, *ars est celare artem*, and the Wedding Hymn is all the more cleverly crafted for
looking so spontaneous.

The 'Manlius' and 'Junia' celebrating their wedding are commonly thought to have been
Manlius Torquatus and his bride Junia Aurunculeia. The bridegroom was probably the
Lucius Manlius Torquatus who was born in about 90 BC, a successful orator in the
lawcourts who prosecuted P. Cornelius Sulla for corruption in 66 BC and later became
praetor in 49 BC and died fighting for the Pompeian side against Caesar in the civil war:
he fought at Dyrrachium in 48 and took his own life after Thapsus. Cicero admired him

and made him one of the interlocutors in books 1 and 2 of his *de finibus*, where he is made to espouse the Epicurean philosophy. The name of the bride is surprising: both Junia and Aurunculeia are *nomina gentilicia* and there is no precedent for a double *gentilicium* in the republic. Fordyce suggests that she might have started life as a plebeian Aurunculeia and been adopted into the *gens Iunia*: Syme proposed that her real name was *Vibia*, a common first name (*praenomen*) in Central Italy, 'corrected' by a scribe ignorant of Oscan *praenomina* – a tempting but not compelling emendation.

In the surviving poems of Catullus the metre is found only here and in poem 34 (The Hymn to Diana): it consists of four lines of Glyconics ($-x-\cup\cup-\cup$) followed by a Pherecratean ($-x-\cup\cup-x$) to finish off the stanza: for further discussion see Introduction # 'The Metres'.

The general structure of the poem is as follows:
1-75   Invocation of the marriage god (hymenaeus)
76-81   Arrival of the bride
82-113   Address to the bride
114-83   Address to various people
184-98   Address to the bridegroom
199-223   Address to the couple (epithalamium)

1-75 INVOCATION TO THE MARRIAGE GOD
1-45 invokes the god, 46-75 sings his praises.

1-2   **Dweller ... Helicon:** The poem begins with a *hymnos kletikos*, a 'Prayer formula' in traditional style: the customary mention of the god's home and origin, the defining relative clause and then the imperative request; cf. Fedeli 18-22. Helicon is the mountain in Boeotia famous as the home of the nine Muses, goddesses of the Arts. One of the Muses was called Urania, and her child was the Marriage God Hymenaeus by an unknown father (addressed as such also in Callimachus *Aetia* frag. 2a.42-3 Pfeiffer, Nonnus 24.88) – a late addition to the ancient pantheon.

3-4   **who:** prayers usually pass from the naming of the god and his abode to a relative clause describing him: cf. (e.g.) Homer *Iliad* 3.277.
        force ... tender: the violence of the marriage act is stressed, as it is by the girls' chorus in 62.20-24. Note here the juxtaposition of *rapis teneram* and the jingle of *virum virginem*, the latter word being stressed by being placed last in the phrase.

4-5   **O Hymeneal ... :** the refrain occurs at the end of the stanza fifteen times in all and was standard in the Wedding Hymn: cf. Euripides *Trojan Women* 314, Theocritus 18.58, and Aristophanes' burlesque of the genre in *Birds* 1743, *Peace* 1342.

6-10   **wreath ... :** the god is to appear dressed like a Roman bride, who traditionally wore a wreath of flowers underneath her bridal veil (*flammeum*) and also bright yellow shoes. The whole description of the god is effeminate, both in dress and in voice (*tinnula*); and it is something of a surprise to have a Greek god instructed to appear dressed like a Roman woman.

7   **marjoram:** the fragrance with which the locked-out lover smears the doorway in Lucretius 4. 1179.

8   **bridal veil:** traditionally orange-yellow in colour (hence the name).

9-10 **snow-white ... yellow:** the colour contrast is fully in Catullus' manner.

11-15 Hymen is invited to share in the music (*nuptialia concinens voce carmina tinnula*) and the dancing (*pelle humum pedibus*) as well as the ritual (*pineam quate taedam*).

13   **high-pitched:** *tinnula* is a diminutive, suggesting that the singer is young and/or feminine.

14   **beat the ground:** for the dancing which went with celebrations, cf. Horace *Odes* 1. 37.1-2.

15   **pine torch:** a common feature of the marriage ceremony, so much so that *taedae* comes to mean 'marriage' by synecdoche* at 64. 25. In fact Roman sources tell us that the torch carried during the *deductio* of the bride was made of hawthorn (Festus, 282.22ff)

16   **For Junia:** The reason for the invocation is now given. *Iunia* is the reading of V: for discussion see introduction to this poem, and also Wiseman (1985) 112 n.70.

17-25 The beauty of the bride is compared first to that of Venus and then to that of myrtle flowers, a pair of similes customary in such wedding hymns: for the comparison of the bride or groom with a deity, cf. Sappho frag 111.5-6 (L-P), as well as the familiar 31.1 ('he seems to me to be like a god ... '). The comparison of human beauty with that of a flower was common in eulogistic poetry of this kind: compare 62.39-47.

17   **Idalium:** the modern Dali on the island of Cyprus and a familiar cult centre of Venus/Aphrodite. cf. 64.96, Theocritus 15.100.

18   **Phrygian judge:** i.e. the Trojan prince Paris who was chosen to judge which of the three goddesses Aphrodite/Venus, Athene/Minerva and Hera/Juno best deserved the golden apple (inscribed "for the fairest") thrown into the wedding of Peleus and Thetis by the mischievous Eris ("Discord"). Venus carried the day after she offered her judge the most beautiful woman in the world, Helen (married to Menelaus King of Sparta at the time), whose abduction brought about the Trojan War and all its attendant disasters both for the Greeks and especially for the family and city of Paris himself. The mention of Paris here is on one level to signify that Venus was indeed reckoned to be "the fairest"; at another level it ties the poem together with the description of the wedding of Peleus and Thetis and the Trojan slaughter of their child Achilles in 64, as well as the emotional jeremiad against Troy and the War to be found in 68.

19   **goodness ... good:** for the repetition of *bona* cf. 44, 195-7.

20   **auspices:** literally, "with good bird", recalling Hesiod Frag 240.11 (Merkelbach-West) 'with good birds'. The Romans foretold the future – at least in the negative way that 'bad omens' deterred them from undertaking a specific course of action – frequently from the flight and the groupings of birds: see Ogilvie (1969) 66-68. The bird-watching prophet (*auspex*) was a necessary witness of any marriage.

21 *enitens*: 'brilliant' is to be taken closely with *floridis*.

22 **myrtle:** often associated with Venus: see especially Vergil *Georgics* 1.28: Thomas (ad loc) suggests that the association may have arisen because both myrtle and Venus are associated with the seashore. More to the point here, it is suggested in at least one source (Nicander *Alexipharmaka* 618ff) that Venus was crowned with myrtle upon winning the judgement of Paris. The diminutive *ramulis* is expressive.

23 **wood-nymphs:** Hamadryads are properly spirits of trees whose lives ended when the tree died. The poet presents a playful picture of these spirits nurturing the myrtle as their toy, with the noun *deae* not strictly necessary but adding to the 'magic' of the scene being set.

25 **moisture:** the reading *nutriunt umore* is metrically difficult as there is no other example – in either poem 61 or 34 – of 2 long syllables replacing the dactyl in a Pherecratean (although similar substitution occurs in the hendecasyllabics of poem 55); but the meaning is better served by 'moisture' than by the rather feeble 'honour' suggested by Maehly.

26 **come ... approach:** we return to the invocation of the god Hymenaeus. *perge aditum ferens linquere* is a lengthy way of urging the god to 'come and leave ... '

27-8 **Aonian ... Thespian**: The Aones were a native people of Boeotia – see Pfeiffer on Callimachus fragment 572 – and Aonia is often mentioned in connection with the Muses and Mt Helicon (e.g. Vergil *Eclogue* 6.65, *Georgics* 3.11). Thespiae is at the foot of Mount Helicon, home of the Muses; cf. 1-2.

30 **Aganippe** indicates both the nymph and the spring which came to bear her name, in the manner of aetiological myths where the water is personified as a divine spirit.

31 **mistress home:** the jingle in the Latin – *domum dominam _* is striking.

32 **longing for:** a familiar theme in these poems; cf. the ardent young men of 62. 23, Ariadne in 64.86, Laudamia in 68.83. Unlike the coy protestations of the girls in 62, the poet here asserts the desire of the bride for the groom, *novi* adding the subtle hint that she might not find him so desirable when the novelty has worn off (cf. 68. 82-4). Alternatively, it is possible to punctuate after *voca* which would give the eager mind to the bridegroom rather than the bride.

33-5 **binding ... ivy:** the poet returns to the imagery of plants, ideal to represent the entwining of lovers' limbs, less obvious here in the case of love entwining the mind of the lover. Theocritus had also used the image (20.21ff).

36-40 Appeal to the unmarried girls to sing.

36 **unwed:** *integrae* really means 'whole' or 'untouched': for its significance 'virginal' cf. Plautus *Casina* 832. They will one day enjoy equal (*par*) ceremony.

38 **in accord:** *in modum* is rendered 'in tune' by Fordyce, 'in the right and proper way' by Quinn, 'in unison' by Goold: OLD however more plausibly reads it as 'rhythmically, in time' (s.v. '*modus*' 7b).

42 **summoned:** *citarier* is the archaic passive present infinitive, common in early verse (cf. 65, 70, 75, 68.141).

42-3 **his task:** i.e. uniting lovers in marriage.

44   **favourable ... favourable:**   the repetition *bonae ... boni* stresses the
      goodness of Venus, perhaps implying that Hymenaeus would not unite lovers
      whose love was not approvable – cf. the lock's distinction between married love
      and 'unclean adultery' in 66.79-85.

45   **the one who brings:** *coniugator* only occurs here.

46-75 The praise of the god, also customary in prayers designed to persuade the god to act
in a specific way. The series of rhetorical questions is paralleled in Callimachus' *Hymn to
Zeus* 92ff and *Hymn to Artemis* 113ff

47   **beloved lovers:**   *amatis est* is the reading of the MSS: the collocation of
      amatis ... amantibus reminds us of Acme and Septimius *amant amantur* (45.20):
      this past participle perhaps means 'loved before and still loving', neatly
      combining both the reciprocity of their affection and its permanence.   The
      inversion of the words is necessary to restore the metre, as first noted by Bergk –
      for the word broken over two lines cf. 82, 11.11-12. Haupt's *anxiis est* (adopted
      by Goold) is not necessary.

48   **men:** *homines* means 'people of both sexes' and not only males.

49   **the heavenly ones:**   *caelites* is archaic and solemn, an invention of Ennius
      on the analogy of *ouraniones* in Greek (Fedeli 49-50, citing Ennius *Scaen.* 316V^2)
      and used here to lend grandeur to the prayer.

51   **trembling:** old age traditionally makes one dodder and tremble; cf. 68.142.

52-3 **girdle:**   the restrictive girdle was part of the uniform and imagery of the
      unmarried girl, to be undone at marriage: cf. 67.28, 2b.13.

54   **fear ... eager:**   the mixture of anxiety and desire is well brought out by the
      juxtaposition *timens cupida*, though his eagerness at this point is confined to his
      ear (cf. Lucretius 4. 594). *captat* must here mean something like 'strains to hear'.

56-9 **savage:** the whole stanza takes the point of view of the girl-victim as expressed
      at 62. 20-24, emphasising the power of the god and reminding one of the
      primitive couplings described by Lucretius (5.964).   The ferocity of the
      bridegroom is well contrasted with the little flower of a girl (note the metaphor in
      floridam and the diminutive *puellulam*, and cf. 64.86–93) and the security of her
      parental home (*gremio ... matris*).

56   **hands:** *manus* is a term in Roman matrimony, as the bride passed into the *manus*
      of her husband; Roman women in the late Republic were more at liberty to be
      independent (*sui iuris*) or to remain under the *patria potestas* of their father, but of
      course Wedding hymns and ceremonies are the last things to respond to changes
      in social life. Treggiari (1991) 16-36 discusses the different forms of marriage and
      the degree of *manus*/control exercised by the husband: Fedeli suggests (52-3) that
      there is here a reference to the Roman custom of *raptio* where the procession of
      relatives pretend that they snatch the girl out of her mother's arms.

61-75 The following three stanzas examine the power of the god as shown in the benefits
of marriage for a) the individual, b) the household/family, c) the state.

61-4 This stanza appears to reject all extra-marital sex as unlikely to produce happiness:
but all that Catullus actually says is that extra-marital sex will produce no benefit of

which gossip would approve – on which compare his words elsewhere on the *rumores senum severiorum* (5. 2). The phrasing *sine te* followed by a delineation of an absurd or unacceptable situation is quite common in prayers and hymns: cf. Pindar *Nemean* 7.2-4, Aeschylus *Suppliants* 823-4, Lucretius 1.21-3.

66-9 Children can of course be born out of wedlock, but such offspring would form no legitimate part of the *domus* and would not grow into adults with rights which could support the (by then) aged parents. Furthermore, the culture of Rome tended to demand that its citizen girls be virgin before their (first) marriage (Treggiari (1991) 100-101), and such girls can therefore never have children if they never marry at all.

66   **without you:** *nulla quit sine te* picks up and echoes *nil potest sine te* of 61.

67   **children ... parent:** *liberos* and *parens* stand neatly at either end of the line.

68   **rely ... offspring:**   the metaphor is of the child(ren) as a prop or support holding up the household. Parents depend on their children to look after them in their old age and in fact such dependence was a major reason to have children in the first place – though such a consideration would not have applied to a man as wealthy as Torquatus: cf. Homer *Iliad* 24. 540, Euripides *Medea* 1033, Lucretius 4. 1255-6, Seneca *Cons. ad Marc.* 15.2, Plautus *Most.* 121.

71-3 The subject of the opening relative clause is not revealed until line 73.   The argument is presumably that marriage alone produces the legitimate children who will defend the state.

76-81 Arrival of the bride.
The opening instruction is addressed to the slaves, to allow the bride to come out and begin the formal *deductio* from her father's house to her new home.

78   **torches ... hair:**   the old metaphor of flames being like a shock of hair (cf. Aeschylus *Prometheus* 1044) here has added point in that one presumes that the bride has hair as brilliant as fire.

78/9   There is a lacuna of at least four lines: the mss have a six-line stanza with a break in sense after line 78, suggesting that the scribe omitted the last glyconic and the pherecratean from the stanza beginning 76 and also the first two glyconics from the next stanza as well. Pighi wrote the following verses (*exempli gratia*) to fill the gap:

   cur moraris? abit dies: /prodeas, nova nupta.// neve respicias domum/quae fuit tua, neu pedes ...
   (' Why do you delay? the day is passing/ come forward, new bride!//and do not look back at the home which was yours, nor let your feet ... ')

79   **free-born modesty:**   'the delicacy of feeling which comes from birth and breeding' (Fordyce). The assumption is made that the free-born citizen behaves in a more restrained and conventional manner than her non-citizen contemporaries.

80   **Heeding ... :**   *audiens* has the sense 'listening to (and obeying)'. If the bride heeds the considerations of modesty she will weep.

81   **you weep:** *fles* is the suggestion of Goold, fitting with the 2nd person address of *flere desine* in the next line.

82-113 ADDRESS TO THE BRIDE (I)

82-3   no danger ... : the audience imagine that the poet is reassuring the girl about the safety of getting married, when the 'danger' in fact turns out to be the risk of a more beautiful woman appearing.

85-6   has watched ... Ocean: a periphrastic way of saying 'alive'; the rising day is that of the wedding itself, and the phrasing allows the poet to juxtapose *pulcrior clarum* and to alliterate *viderit venientem*.

87-9   hyacinth: for the comparison of the bride with a flower cf. 21-5, 62.39-47: for the hyacinth cf. Homer *Odyssey* 6. 231. The flower is made more precious by being in a little garden (*hortulo* is a diminutive) belonging to a rich master (only rich men, perhaps, could afford to waste land growing flowers).

91   <come forth, new bride>: the first instance of the phrase was omitted due to haplography and has to be restored here to supply the missing pherecratean.

92-5   repeats ideas from earlier with perhaps a touch of impatience at the bride's delay.

93   decided: *videtur* is similar to the Greek *dokei* meaning 'it seems (good)'. Here is produces a pleasing combination of *videtur et audias* (seeing and hearing).

94-5   torches ... : imitated from 77-8 with the change of *splendidas* to *aureas*.

97-101 your husband: reassurance to the bride that her new husband will not be unfaithful to her. For the theme of adultery in these poems see e.g.68.135-48, 66.84-8 and the whole background to 67.

97   fickle: *levis* (fickle, irresponsible) is the opposite of *gravis* (a Roman virtue). The husband's misbehaviour is stressed by the juxtaposition of *levis ... mala.*

98-99   abandoned ... following: *deditus ... persequens* combine to create a picture of a man wholly given over (*deditus*) to the pursuit (*persequens*) of evil.

99-100 filthy ... tender: the poet loads the issue by the pejorative term *turpia* contrasted with the positive term *teneris.*

101   breasts: Catullus as often gives the specific detail; cf. 64.18, 66.81.

102-5 just as the ... vine: this looks forward to the image of the vine in 62.49-55. Here the words *lenta ... vitis* manage to entwine *adsitas ... arbores* just as the trees are entwined by the vine; the trees are planted beside the vines to allow the vines to grow upon them. Sappho compares the groom to a delicate twig (frag. 115 L-P), while Catullus, as in 62, uses the language of Roman viticulture to convey a traditionally Greek comparison between the human and the plant.

107-112 O bed: the apostrophe* to the marriage bed, unfortunately incomplete. For a similar address to a lovers' bed see Propertius 2.15. 1-2.

107/8 Guarinus noticed the lacuna here – obvious (as in 78-9) from the metrical irregularity. Wilamowitz composed a filler thus:

> *dignum amoribus instruit/ veste purpurea Tyros/ fulcit India eburnei*
> ('as worthy of all the ways of love Tyre has adorned you with crimson cloths
> and India shores you up with an ivory bed's white foot').

109-112 what pleasures: the exclamation is strengthened by the repetitions *quae ... quanta ... quae ... quae* and also *gaudia ... gaudeat*. The contrast of night and day is

108 CATULLUS

also striking; night as the time for love-making is conventional (cf. 68.83) but this young man will enjoy sex during the day also, as Catullus himself hopes to do in poem 32.

114-23 ADDRESS TO THE ATTENDANTS

119-20 **Fescennine jesting:** i.e. the improvised singing of racy verse as part of the wedding itself. The name derives possibly from the word *fascinum* ('the evil eye', cf. 7.12), the theory being that happy bridal partners must be mocked in case the evil eye, resenting their excessive good fortune, punishes them; Fordyce well compares the rude songs sung at the triumph of a victorious general. The ribald verses so essential to the setting are of course very much Catullus' own *métier*.

121 **nuts:** the Fescennine singing included the throwing of walnuts into the audience (see also Vergil *Eclogues* 8.30). The *concubinus* throws the nuts to boys, implying perhaps (as suggested by Fordyce) that he now has to give up the toys of youth and grow up.

121-2 **pretty-boy:** a favourite slave to whom the young man now marrying a woman has been attached. This sort of attachment of a man or a youth to a younger (or, if coeval, at least socially inferior) boy certainly finds a place in Rome (cf. e.g. Lucretius 4. 1053, Petronius *Satyricon* 64. 5-6, Griffin (1985) 25-6) though without the intensity one finds in Athens. Propertius recommends the love of a boy because it is without any emotional intensity (2.4.17-22), but Ovid the connoisseur finds it less rewarding because the boy (unlike a woman) does not share the pleasure (*Ars Am.* 2. 683-4, cited Lyne (1980) 174). Quinn suggests, however, that the servant was the valet of the older man, sleeping in his room as a kind of bodyguard and now obviously dismissed from the role: such a relationship can inspire good-humoured innuendo precisely because it is innocent and thus poses no real threat to the marriage (Quinn (1972) 252-3). For excellent discussion of the difficulties of applying modern terms of sexual orientation to Catullus and his society see Wiseman (1985) 10-14).

124-33 ADDRESS TO THE *CONCUBINUS*

124 **sluggish:** such boys were a byword for laziness – cf. Cicero *On the Nature of the Gods* 1.102.

125-6 **played ... long enough:** *ludo* often has a sexual sense (cf. 68.17, Cicero *Pro Caelio* 28, Adams 162f.).

127 **Talassius** became the Roman equivalent of Hymenaeus, a marriage god. For references see Martial 1.35.6-7, 3.93.25, 12.42.4. Livy (1.9.12) and Plutarch (*Rom.* 15.2ff, *Pomp.* 4.3) both ascribe the origin of the name and its ritual exclamation to an incident in the famous Rape of the Sabine Women: when a girl of superior beauty was being carried off to the house of Talassius, her abductors (who were servants of Talassius) replied to those asking where she was being taken 'To Talassius': the phrase thus combined the implied compliment to the beauty of the girl being taken and also the sense of 'abduction' still prominent in the language of this poem and also 62.

129 **farm women ... contempt:** the aloof young man in the city could turn his nose up at the boorish rustic women while he enjoyed his master's love, but now

that his master has deserted him (122) he might need them. The implication is
that this slave will practise adultery with the wives of bailiffs on country estates –
who would be also of servile status.

131   **barber shaves:**   the hairdresser (*cinerarius*) derives his name from *cinis* (ash)
because he heated his rollers in ash or because he used ash-like powder as a dye.
The point here is that the effete young man has had a hairdresser attend him for
years, but now he is not to cut his hair but rather to shave his face – a point
brought out by the positioning of *os* at the end of the sentence. Trimalchio has
kept his first beard as a souvenir in Petronius *Satyricon* 29.8 (cf. Suetonius *Nero*
12.4). The *concubinus* no longer qualifies as a 'smooth-skinned boy' (136).

134-43 ADDRESS TO THE BRIDEGROOM
134-6 **perfumed ... smooth-skinned:**   the bridegroom is mocked for his attraction
to the effeminate youths. Note the juxtaposition of *unguentate glabris*: for the
mockery implicit in 'perfumed' cf. the way in which Vergil's Turnus threatens
Aeneas and mocks him as a 'Phrygian half-man' and threatens to 'befoul his hair in
the dust, the hair which is curled with hot iron and wet with perfume' (*Aeneid* 12.
99-100).

140-2   The advice to the bridegroom continues: the point here is not that the young man
has misbehaved in the past, but that what did not count as misbehaviour in the
past would be misbehaviour now that he is married .

144-73 ADDRESS TO THE BRIDE (II)
144-6   **beware of refusing:**   salutary advice to the bride to preclude her husband's
adultery, surprising perhaps in the context of the marriage hymn, especially in
view of the confident assertion of the husband's fidelity at 97-101. The two
phrases together would amount to a claim that if the husband does seek love
elsewhere it must be the bride's fault. The phrasing is repetitive: *tu ... tuus; ne
neges.*

149   **look ... house:**   as Quinn observes, this is a touch of verisimilitude as the
bridal procession is now imagined reaching the home of the groom. The
attractiveness of the house is its opulence (*beata ... potens*).

152   The only place in the poem where the refrain interrupts a sentence.

154-7   **old age:**   a caricature portrait of the old woman, complete with the joke that the
old lady appears to agree with everybody because she keeps nodding her head. The
abstract noun *anilitas* (from *anus* = old woman) is only found here and its novelty
may also be part of the humour, reinforced by the adjectives *tremulum ... cana*).

159-61 Another stage-direction, as the bride is seen crossing the threshold. The double
accusative (*limen* and *aureolos pedes*) is perhaps to be explained as *transfer
aureolos pedes <trans> limen*, the preposition being implicit from the compound
verb. The adjective *aureolus* ('golden little') is appropriate here of a girl's dainty
feet in bright yellow slippers: cf. 2b.12, 68.70-72.

161   **planed doorway:**   *rasilis* refers either to the finely polished wood or metal of
the door, or else to the doorstep eroded by many feet, as in 68.71. For the
conventional epithet 'polished' of timber cf. e.g. Homer *Odyssey* 21. 44-5 ('the

threshold of oak, which the carpenter had skilfully planed ... '). *forem* here means the doorway rather than the door, if only because of the verb *subi* ('go under').

164   **look ... your husband:**   the groom has gone into the house and is there awaiting the bride.

165   **a Tyrian couch:**   either the groom is lying on the marriage-bed awaiting his bride, or else he is reclining at table (*accubare* often means that) enjoying a wedding feast. The second is made improbable by the fact that the wedding feast itself preceded the formal procession of the bride to her new home. The first is awkward because the marriage bed was (as one would expect) in an inner room of the house and not in the hallway; the only couch in the atrium is the *lectus genialis*, a symbolic couch upon which the tutelary deities were to recline, not the mortal couple. The language of 166 and then 169-71 is suggestive of passion: the wedding of Peleus and Thetis shows their bridal bed in copious detail, and it is difficult to imagine the reader not associating the 'Tyrian couch' with the bridal bed: one simply has to extend the sense of *aspice* and assume that it means 'go inside <the inner part of the house> and see'. For Tyrian as the exotic 'designer-label' couch covering cf. Tibullus 3.7.121, 3.8.11, Ovid *Ars Am.* 2. 297.

169-71   **the flame:**   the metaphor* of fire for love is very common in many languages (cf. e.g. 51.9-10, Vergil *Aeneid* 4. 68), but *flamma* as the subject is, as Fordyce notes, unparalleled. The phrase *uritur flamma* literally means 'the flame is being burned' and has caused anxiety: properly speaking a thing burns with flame, but the flame itself does not get burned; hence Goold's suggestion *urit in*.

174-6 ADDRESS TO AN ATTENDANT.

The boy is addressed as *praetextate*, literally 'having a toga with a purple border'; it was customary for boys up to the age of majority and also for senators to wear a toga with a purple border. The singular here is surprising as there were usually two attendants at a Roman wedding, with even a third one carrying a torch (Festus 282 L): Fedeli suggests (116) that Catullus 'may have been influenced by the Greek tradition that attached an important role to the *paranymphos* in the development of the ceremony'.

174   **delicate little:**   the bride once again is signified with diminutives *brachiolum ... puellulae* : cf. 160, 181.

176   The attendants of the bride are to be imagined as leaving her at the door of the bridal chamber.

179-81 ADDRESS TO THE MATRONS: these matrons are the *pronubae*, the married women of irreproachable record (*bonae*) who escorted the bride. They are traditionally *univirae*, i.e. only married to one man throughout their lives, an ideal aspired to even by the serially-polygamous Roman nobility (for more discussion of this concept see Treggiari (1991) chapter 8).

179/80   **well known:**   *cognitus* almost in the Biblical sense of 'know'. cf. Propertius 2.29.33, and the use of *nosse* in 72.1. Note also here the emphasis of *bonae ... bene*.

18'   **set in place:**   *collocare* is the right word for giving of a daughter in marriage: cf. Cicero *Pro Cluentio* 190, OLD s.v. '*colloco*' 9. Here it is used not of the father but of the matrons.

184-98 ADDRESS TO THE GROOM.
Here begins the *epithalamium* proper – i.e. the song sung outside the door of the bridal
chamber – and we no longer have the hymenaeal refrain.

186-8 flowery ... : for the flower simile cf. 21-5, 62. 39-47. The phrase begins as a
metaphor* ('flowery ... face') and then becomes a simile* ('like to ... '). The
colours of the flowers are fitting here: the white and yellow combination
recalling that of lines 9-10. The name for camomile is *parthenice*, recalling the
Greek word for 'virgin, unmarried woman'.

189-91 so help me ... : for the form of the oath cf. 66. 18. For the acquaintance
with Venus cf. 68. 17-8.

191-2 nor does Venus forget: a striking litotes*; cf. 68. 17.

194-5 delayed long: note the chiastic* response to *venias ... remorare* in *remoratus
... venis*. There is possibly a play here on *venis ... Venus*.

195 favourable Venus: cf. 44, 61-4.

199-203 count ... thousand: a familiar Catullan idea: cf. the amatory arithmetic of
5. 7-13 and also 7. For *ludus* of sex-play see 126n.

204-5 Play ... children: notice here the progression of sounds from *ludite* to *lubet*
to *liberos*. The bridal couple are encouraged to 'play', but the serious purpose of
their play is to produce children to maintain the family name.

208 reproduced: *ingenerare* means to breed from the same stock – reproduction
without recourse to adoption from outside the family.

209-13 miniature Torquatus: the mention of children raises this vision of a baby
reflecting the appearance of his father. It is also of course a nice way of bringing
the named addressee of the poem back into the text. The baby is described with
affecting, if not sentimental, detail, complete with telling adjectives (*teneras ...
dulce ... semihiante*, this last being an invention of Catullus).

215/6 There are major textual problems here. The sense is fairly clear: little Manlius
should look so much like the father that he proves that his mother conceived the
one by the other, and even people who have never seen the baby before will
recognise him from the similarity with the father. The MSS reading however is
faulty, *insciens* being particularly inept. Bergk's *ut* is better than the mss reading
et to explain the following subjunctive *noscitetur*. Dawes' emendation simply
inverts *insciens* and *omnibus* and then emends the former to a more plausible
insciis, for metrical reasons: the mss reading *omnibus/ et* breaks the rules of
synapheia as the final syllable of the line ought to be long and the following
vowel *et* will not lengthen the short vowel at the end of *omnibus*. Dawes'
transposition of *omnibus* and *insciis* achieves this purpose.

218 chaste fidelity: the resemblance to the father will prove that the mother
conceived by him alone.

219-23 An elliptical expression, neatly expressing the wish that his mother's good
name will be passed on to her son – as is likely since a woman as good as she will
bring him up to be virtuous. Penelope was the chaste and faithful wife of Odysseus
who spent the twenty years of her husband's absence bringing up their son

Telemachus and (for the last three years) putting off the many suitors who sought to
marry her.

224-8 Coda: not before time, the door is closed on the happy couple with a wish for their
future happiness and virtue, *bene vivite* conveying both the sense of 'live well' (i.e.
enjoy life) and also 'live a good life' (i.e. be faithful) – for the double meaning cf. the
final words of Plato's *Republic*. The wish for happiness is apparently conditional on
their virtue, just as is that of the lock at 66.79-88: similarly the constant love-making
is echoed in 66. 88.

227/8 **youth:** love is a young person's pursuit: cf. Horace *Odes* 4.1.1-8 and the wistful
nostalgia of 68.15-18.

6 2

The second of ιe two Wedding songs in the collecti⁊n – for the genre of the *epithalamium* see 'h⁊ introduction to poem 61. The differe⁊⁊es between the two poems are obvious: this ⁊oem is in hexameters, whereas 61 was in lyrics (glyconics/pherecrateans), '⁊is poem concerns marriage in general (and an anonymous *virgo*) and could be applied to any wedding, whereas 61 was tied to a specific named couple. The form of this marriage-hymn has two separate choruses of girls and boys seeking to defeat each other in their rival claims – a form of writing known as 'amoebean'; their words echo and 'cap' each other and the whole poem becomes a contest of wits and argument, something like the *agon* in a Greek cor⁊edy.

The beauty of this poem resides partly in its artificiality: Catullus puts the stage directions (e.g. 8-9) and the preparations before singing (1-19) into the finished poem which is thus a poem about (and containing) a performance rather than simply a record of the text performed; something in the manner of *A Mids⁊ nu⁊⁊r Night's Dream* or *Ariadne auf Naxos*. The 'stage-directions' do not, however, he p us place the poem in either a Greek or a Roman context: the time is evening (*vesⲅ⁊r adest* 1), *iam pinguis lincuere mensas* (3) suggests that the feast has finished, *iam veniet virgo* (4) that the bride is yet to arrive, although the final stanza assumes that she is (at least by then) within earshot. The feast, in both Greece and Rome, was held in the home of the bride's parents, with boys and girls carefully segregated in Greece but not in Rome, but the wedding feast in Greece always included the bridegroom: now Roman custom had the bridegroom leave the feast in order to await the *deductio* of his new wife into his house, which leads us to suppose that the feast is being held (in the bride's house) in advance of the procession of the bride (*iam veniet virgo* 4). Some commentators have made too much of line 3 2 ('Hesperus has stolen one of our number') and inferred from it that the bride is no longer present in the room – quite apart from the fact that line 32 is followed by several lines which we do not have, the words simply do not need to be made to bear so literal a significance. The fact that one of the girls is now a bride and so is no longer one of the unwed chorus would be quite sufficient to justify the phrase, and her presenc⁊ as the rival choruses quarrel over the rightness of her decision would add piquancy as well as inviting the personal apostrophe to the bride at lines 59-65. There seems little doubt that the poet has chosen the moment just after the feast but just before the *deductio* of the bride to set this song, the very last moment when such a poem could be sung before it would all be too late. The form of the contest (familiar from Greek pastoral poetry and imitated later by Horace (*Odes* 3.9)) is of Greek inspiration – so we have a Greek we⁊ding feast followed by a Roman *deductio*, a Greek genre employed with Roman content.

The content is decidedly Roman: from the wedding of vines to trees (49-55) to the sacking of cities (24), from the lively colloquialism of the language (*viden ... nec mirum ...*) to the *patria potestas* (60-1). This is not to say that Greeks never wedded vines (etc) – but simply that the poet's readers would have no cross-cultural shock in reading this poem as a Roman document and would not see it as anything other than what it is, a free composition. 'The reader is thereby relieved from the obligation to assimilate the poem

114 CATULLUS

to some occasion in real life which he should recognize.' (Williams (1968) 202. See also Fraenkel 6-8)

This poem has abundant literary interest. The girls have to lose their friend the bride, but they win the debate on emotional and poetic points. The contest is about the value of virginity versus marriage, and the girls pack quite a punch: note the strong verb *avellere* (21, repeated 22), the chiastic repetition of *natam ... matris ... matris ... natam* (21-2), the clash of *ardenti castam* (23) and the dismissive *donare* (give her away), rounded off with the savage comparison with the sacking of a city. 'The ancient world lived closer than we do to the reality of sacked cities and raping soldiers, and some parts of Italy had suffered that reality only thirty years before.' (Wiseman (1985) 119) The girls' third stanza similarly depicts the tender flower deflowered (*defloruit* 43), the precious and cherished being which has taken time to produce and takes up four lines in its creation being wrecked and spoiled in an instant (note the sudden two-word phrase *defloruit ungui*), the image of dirt and disgust in *polluto corpore* aided by the assonance of *corpore florem* (46). The depiction of the growth of the flower is masterly; line 39 'is almost entirely spondaic ... then the verse gathers momentum. Whereas the first line is a single indivisible unit, the second is broken into two phrases, and the third into three separate clauses. The effect of these lines is beautifully to convey a sense of expansion and growth ... ' (Jenkyns (1982) 51. The whole of his discussion of this poem merits serious study). The girls' allusion to the familiar 'double standard' whereby the virgin is sought by the ardent youths, but is less attractive to these same boys once she has become 'damaged goods' is accepted without contradiction by them.

All the boys can do is to respond with unemotional assertions of power: the girls have been betrothed and that is that (27-8), their reluctance is all feigned anyway (36) and the sturdy vine needs a husband/tree to produce offspring – for their husbands.

The words of Mercury are harsh after the songs of Apollo
(Shakespeare, *Love's Labours Lost*)

and their homespun male logic is inadequate to match what Wiseman well calls 'the beauty of innocence'. Their stanzas have rhetorical vigour (repetition of *pepigere ... pepigerunt* (28), the *para prosdokian** wit of the vine touching its root to its top, the arithmetical scoring of 62-4, even their studied casualness as they hear the girls rehearse (12)) but end up sounding like the famous verdict on Ovid's *Art of Love* – all art and no love. The final words addressed to the bride are counsels of caution advising her against trying to fight opponents who outnumber her and the last phrase in the audience's mind as the men clinch the argument, is that the girl's precious innocence has effectively been sold with money (65).

The structure of the poem is as follows:

1-5	Boys talk among themselves (5 lines)
6-10	Girls talk among themselves (5 lines)
11-19	Boys prepare to sing (9 lines)
20-25	Girls' first stanza (6 lines)
26-31	Boys' first stanza (6 lines)
32ff	Girls's second stanza (lacuna in ms- originally 7 lines))
33-38	Boys' second stanza (originally 7 lines)
39-48	Girls' third stanza (10 lines)

49-58   Boys' third stanza (10 lines + refrain)
59-66   Boys address the bride

As is obvious from the above, the poem is symmetrically written, with almost exactly equal parts for boys and girls until the boys press home their advantage at the end as (we imagine) the bride is about to begin the formal *deductio* which will surrender her virginity and give victory to the men.

1   **rise up:** the young men are reclining in typical Roman style on couches while enjoying the wedding feast. At the appearance of *vesper* they must stand up to greet the bride.
         on Olympus: this is something of a surprise: we expect 'in the heavens'. The usage is a complex metonymy* whereby the terrestrial abode of the gods stands for the celestial dwelling (cf. the parallel usage of *Olympos* in Greek). The usage is highly appropriate here as the sun and the stars seem to be rising from the tops of mountains (as e.g. at Lucretius 4. 404-407, Vergil *Georgics* 1.450) and also the word keeps the divine presence firmly in mind right from the start as we begin the wedding hymn.

2   **at last ... :** note the emphatic conjunction of *diu vix tandem*.

3-4   **now ... now ... :** the anaphora* of *iam* is effective in breaking the two lines into four almost equal parts.
         full: *pingues* may be at least partly a transferred epithet, as the diners are presumably as 'fat' – i.e. full of food – as their tables.

4   **the bride will come:** 'that is, she will leave her father's house and join the procession as she is summoned to do in 61.92-6' (Fordyce)
         Hymenaeus is the title of the formal wedding song. The final syllable of *dicetur* is lengthened before *hymenaeus*. exactly as in *despexit hymenaeos* (64. 20) The ritual cry 'Hymenaeus' was customary at Greek weddings: Hymen or Hymenaeus as the child of the Muse Urania (61.2, see Callimachus fr. 2a.42f Pfeiffer) and a personified god of marriage does not have a consistent character until Ovid and the attempts to invent a mythology to explain the ritual cry by personification are clearly late.

5   **O Hymenaeus ... :** a ritual cry repeated nine times in the poem. The poet varies the quantity of the first syllable of *Hymen*, whereby it is scanned long in the nominal form and short in the adjectival form (*Hymenaee*) – exactly as Theocritus does in *Idyll* 18.58 (in poem 61 it is always short): the second syllable is uniformly long here but varies in poem 61 between long in the short form *Hymen* but short in the adjectival *Hymenaee*. The poet has clearly adjusted the glyconic/pherecratean metre of 61 to fit the refrain into the hexameters of this poem.

6-10   The girls now rise to match the boys' song with their own in opposition (*contra*): they match the boys term for term, *Vesper* becoming *Noctifer*, *lumina tollit* becoming *ostendit ... ignes*, Olympus becoming Oeta.

7   **obviously:** the word *nimirum* is usually used to indicate an inference being drawn: here it indicates that the girls cannot see the evening star themselves from

deep within the dining hall, but that they infer the rising star from the behaviour of the boys.

Oeta: Hercules was famously cremated on Mount Oeta, and the mention of 'Oetean fires' would surely have elicited this 'implicit myth' memory in the reader (cf. 24n, and also 68.115-6, where Hercules' own marriage to Hebe is mentioned). Servius' explanation of Vergil *Eclogues* 8.30 ('Hesperus is leaving Oeta') is that there was a cult of Hesperus the Evening Star on Mount Oeta, and so that mountain would be seen as the abode of the god before and after his hours in the heavens.

bringer of night: *Noctifer* is a Catullan coinage on the model of *Lucifer*: it also makes for a pleasing oxymoron* as the bringer of darkness shows its fires.

8-9   **leapt up ... leapt up:**   the repetition of the word *exsiluere* is effective: the question form alternates with the assertion form almost like a catechism.

8   **Do you see:**   the contracted form *viden* (for *videsne*) is colloquial, both syllables being scanned short and the following verb indicative.   The verb is singular, although a plural group is being addressed.

9   **defeating:**   the mss read *visere*, defended by some (as meaning 'worth looking at') but not to be preferred to Guarinus' emendation *vincere*: 'The young women here, like the young men in 11, are not concerned with admiring their rivals, but with beating them' (Fordyce).   For this sense of *par* as 'fair, reasonable' see Lucretius 4.1184, OLD s.v. 14.

11   **palm:**   the palm was long used as a symbol of victory (see Nisbet and Hubbard on Horace *Odes* 1.1.5), its use in Rome being attested as early as 293 BC (Livy 10.47.3).

12   **Look how:**   picks up *viden ut* from 8.   *meditata* shows that the young women are rehearsed, unlike the extempore performance of the young men.

13   **not in vain:**   *non frustra* picks up *non temere* from line 9.

14   **with full concentration;**   *penitus ... tota* intensifies the girls' efforts.   Notice the e-i-u assonance of *nec mirum penitus.*

15   **split our attention:**   we have to imagine the young men hearing the girls practising their song (*meditata requirunt*): they only realise after hearing some of it how good it is (*habent memorabile quod sit*) and here they regret that they have not paid closer attention to the whole song, bemoaning the fact that they have been hearing but not taking note of what was sung (*alio mentes alio divisimus aures*).

16   **we shall deserve:**   a rare touch of honesty and sportsmanship as the men confess their inferiority to the girls with the gnomic utterance *amat victoria curam.*

17   **turn your minds:**   *animos convertite* responds to the charge of *mentes divisimus.*   The force of *saltem* is perhaps 'you do not usually take things seriously, but at least this once you can ... '

20-4   **Evening Star ... :**   here begins the performance of the girls' song proper, responded to almost word for word by the young men.   The girls' account of marriage is one of the plunder of the bride's virginity and security as she is handed over to a savage stranger.   The imagery of fire runs through the stanza: the star is an *ignis*, the youth is ablaze with passion, and the final image of the sacked – and presumably torched – city accords well with this.

21   **rip a daughter**: this image of the plunder of a child recalls e.g. the calf torn from the heifer at Lucretius 2. 352-66 as well as cases such as Iphigeneia or Polyxena, both maidens slaughtered for 'a greater good'.

21-2 **mother's embrace**:   note the epanalepsis* of *complexu avellere matris /complexu matris ... avellere* with the metrical variation of ictus, and the chiastic* repetition of *natam ... matris ... matris ... natam*. The poet focusses on the moment of plunder with the forceful juxtaposition of *retinentem avellere*.

23   **pure ... burning**:   the outrage is brought out by the juxtaposition of *ardenti castam* and by the simple verb *donare*, suggesting that this priceless child is just being given away to an unnamed youth of dishonourable intention.

24   **heartless**: the stanza is rounded off with *crudelius* picking up *crudelior* from line 20.

For the plunder of girls in the sacking of cities compare the sacking of Oechalia and capture of the beautiful Iole by Hercules (as in Sophocles' *Trachiniae*) – and see the introduction to this poem and also line 7n.

26   **Evening Star ... :** this line is as close as possible to line 20, the small changes indicating however a totally different stance. *iucundus* is not strictly antonymic to *crudelis*: what we have here is the same event (marriage) seen from the point of view first of the victims and now of the conquering males. The charge of cruelty is nowhere refuted in this stanza – the men focus simply on the agreement between the husband and the parents of the girl as later (49-58) they argue from the practical disadvantage suffered by the unwed girl. The poet's final advice to the girls (59-65) also makes no suggestion that the brides will enjoy their wedlock but rather that it is their duty to conform – contrast with this the unbridled desire of a Laudamia (68. 81-3).

fire: the stanza abounds in 'fire' imagery: *ignis – flamma – ardor*.

27-8 **wedding vows**:   the marriage has already been (*ante*) pledged at the betrothal stage, when the father and the prospective husband of the bride both undertake the commitment of marrying the bride to the groom. The consummation of the contract only takes place now that the Evening Star rises and the couple are joined.

28   **made by ... made by**: the repetition of *pepigere ... pepigerunt* underlines the formality of the betrothal ceremony.

29   **your fire**: a phrase just as appropriate in describing the young men's ardour as in referring to the star.

30   **desirable ... happy**:   note the emphasis of the juxtaposed *divis felici optatius*: the gods are a byword for happiness in general, from Homer's *makarioi theoi* onwards: Lucretius (often wrongly taken for an atheist) has the gods living a life of complete serenity and Epicurean *ataraxia* (3. 18-24).

32-3 The poem is, as we have seen, symmetrically composed with each of the two choruses having a roughly equal amount of space: the text here however jumps from the first line of a girls' stanza to the middle of a boys' stanza: there is clearly a lacuna (of at least the rest of the girls' stanza and the beginning of the boys', possibly more) in the mss at this point; presumably the eye of the copying scribe confused *Hesperus* in line 31 with a later line also beginning *Hesperus*. We can

infer the content of the lost stanza, however, from the wording of the 'reply' at
lines 33-7, and Goold suggests the following filler:

namque suo adventu fert omnibus ille pericla;
nocte timent cuncti, nisi quos aliena petentes,
Hespere, tu radiis properas accendere blandis.
at libet iniusta pueris te extollere laude.
quid tum, si laudant, sibi mox quem quisque timebunt?
Hymen o Hymenaee Hymen ades o Hymenaee!

Hespere, te innuptae nunc falso crimine laedunt:

('for at his coming he brings danger to everybody; by night everybody is
afraid, except those who are seeking to steal other people's property,
whom you, Evening Star, hasten to spur on with your soft beams. Boys
like to acclaim you with undeserved praise: what does their praise matter,
if soon they will all be fearing you? O Hymenaeus Hymen, come, O
Hymenaeus Hymen. Evening Star, the girls are stinging you with false
charges.')

34   **thieves:** there is a nice connection of thought here. The idea of the bride being
stolen by the groom from the safety of her parental home is linked with the
association of night-time with sex: hence the remark here about thieves in the
night. cf. also the *furtivos amores* of illicit sex in 7.8. The young men do not
rebut the charges of the girls beyond stating that in fact the Evening Star is the
signal for the night-watchmen to guard against thieves and accusing the girls of
making complaints which are not sincere as they actually desire the marriage
which they affect to fear.

34-5   **Evening Star ... Eous:** the two names for the same star neatly begin and end
line 35. The point of the phrase is a slight joke: the star which gives the go-
ahead to the burglar often changes his name to Eous and catches these same
burglars still burgling at dawn. 'To reject ... *Eous* and to swallow *eosdem* is a sign
of an iron digestion' (Fraenkel 3).

36   **invented:** cf. 66.16 for the common charge that girls only pretend coyly to be
averse to love and marriage.

39-47   'An exquisite, sensuously beautiful Homeric-type simile' (Quinn). 'This
passage displays a union of verbal beauty, perceptiveness and tenderness of feeling
which is found nowhere else in Catullus, nor in any other Latin poet except Vergil ... '
(Jenkyns (1982) 50-1) The point is crudely that the girl is only liked by her fellows or
desired by the boys when she is unwed: as soon as she has lost her 'flower' she will be
unwelcome to all. For the poetic conceit of the flower as the time of one's youthful best
cf. OLD s.v. 'flos' 8b and for the virgin as an unpicked flower cf. Sappho Fr. 105C LP.
The poet here manages to take a metaphor literally by converting it into a simile.

39-40   **hidden ... a stranger ... no:** the exclusivity of the flower is well stressed
with descriptive details such as the 'enclosed' garden and the point that it is
known to no animate thing but is well served by the sun, breezes and rains.
ignotus is a nice elliptical touch – if the flocks knew of the flower they would
chew it – and saves the violence of the flower's possible fate for the strong

COMMENTARY: 62   119

convulsus – from *convellere*, picking up *avellere* in lines 21-2. For the flower torn by the plough cf. 11.21-4, Homer *Iliad* 8. 306f, Vergil *Aeneid* 9. 435, 11.68f. The difference here is that this is no wild flower which chance has preserved, but rather a delicate and protected species.

39-42 The sequence – of a) a single indivisible line (39), b) a line in two phrases (40), c) three phrases of the form verb + subject and then d) two three-word phrases in the next line (42, imitated at 44) – has an expressive effect to convey the growth of the flower/child into the fullness of maturity. The three verbs are well chosen: *mulcent* suggests the comforting of an infant, *firmat* suggests the strengthening of the growing limbs, while *educat* brings the process to completion as the child/flower is brought to maturity. The comfort of a breeze in a hot climate is matched by the way the sun bakes things hard and the necessity of having rainfall to produce growth.

42   **many ... many:** a nice echoing line – complete with jingle of *pueri ... puellae* as below at lines 44 and 47 – imitated by Ovid in his description of the attractions of Narcissus at *Met.* 3. 353-5: 'many young men, many girls desired him, but in his delicate beauty there was such hard arrogance that no young men, no girls touched him'. *optavere* is in the so-called 'gnomic' perfect tense, expressing a general rule rather than a particular historic instance.

43   **plucked ... fingernail:** the fragility of the flower is well evoked in the way it is plucked with so insignificant a thing as a slender fingernail, the slenderness probably suggesting that it is a girl who does the plucking. The flower sheds its petals instantly on being plucked, as is shown by the juxtaposition of *carptus defloruit*.

45   **while:** this use of *dum* is a deliberate archaism – the second *dum* being correlative to the first, as at 56: 'while ... for so long ... ' (*quoad ... usque eo ...*) The phrase well evokes how in this case '*intacta = cara*', with the metrical clash of ictus and accent (on which see Introduction # 'Metres') in *cara suis est*, the strongest example of this usage in this poem.

46   **dirtied her body:** a hyperbolic* phrase and quite unnecessary in the context; the girls are clearly out to persuade the men by sheer rhetoric. The phrase also mixes the two metaphors* (of a) losing the flower of chastity and b) making the body dirty), as well as creating the pleasing assonance of *corpore florem*.

47   **welcome:** *iucunda* here means 'desirable' to men.

49-58 The men respond with a contrary interpretation of maidenhood. The language is partly that of the farmer 'marrying' the vine by making it to grow on and around a supporting tree; as with the 'flower' metaphor* above, this allows the chorus to take a metaphor and develop it into a simile complete with poetic and descriptive effects.

49   **single ... bare:** *vidua* usually is applied to people who are single but is frequently used as here of the unsupported vine (see OLD s.v. 3): *nudus* here means 'devoid of trees' but has the primary sense of 'naked' which reinforces the sexual imagery.

50   **never ... never:** note the repetition of *numquam* at the beginning of the line and immediately after the caesura. *educat* picks up line 41, and the line ends with pleasing assonance* of *educat uvam*.

51-2 drooping ... : the hapless plight of the limp vine unwedded to a tree is well brought out: *tener* though she is, her body still has too much weight (*pondere corpus* juxtaposed) to rise from the horizontal (*prono*). *iam iam contingit summum* is ironic here – the vine is stretching up and just manages to touch her topmost tendril to the root – again, the juxtaposition of *radice flagellum* shows in words the pathetic juxtaposition of vine's root and its topmost tendril. Line 51 is of the A-B-C-B-A pattern.

53 bullocks: used to break up the ground around the wild vine; cf. Vergil *Georgics* 2. 356.

54 wedlock: bringing the simile* firmly back to the marriage being undertaken. For the marital imagery used in vine-growing see Fordyce on 62.49

56 neglected: *inculta* comes from *colo* of the previous line; *senescit* looks forward to *maturo tempore* with the familiar consideration that the unwed girl quickly becomes an 'old maid'.

57 favourable: for *par* see 9n. The second syllable of *conubium* is usually scanned as long – a quantity only possible here if the *-i* is consonantal. More plausible is the theory that the *-u* can be scanned either as long or short: on the whole vexed question see Austin's magisterial note on Vergil *Aeneid* 4. 126. Scanning the word as three long syllables would have the effect of making the line very spondaic – appropriate perhaps for the stately marriage in the fullness of time.

58 more dear ... : it is easy to see why the bride is less resented by her father – who is anxious to marry her off his hands – but less easy to see the point of 'more dear to her husband' apart from the rhetorical antithesis of husband – father. If the girl was not known at all to her husband, and the marriage is happy, then there will be more affection after marriage than before – but there are too many imponderables here. More likely the young men are suggesting that if the girl weds earlier rather than later she will be more attractive to her husband and less of an expense to her father.

59-65 Advice to the bride; cf. 66. 79-88. We must imagine the contest as having ended at 58: this last section is presumably sung by the young men but is not an answer to the girls and is not responded to by them.

60-1 not fair: *aequum* in the simple sense of evenly-matched; the argument is that the poor girl is hopelessly outnumbered by the combined triple weight of her husband and both parents, and so she would be foolish to fight such odds.

62-5 one third ... : what Quinn calls 'the argument from arithmetic': for this sort of logical thinking applied to an emotional matter cf. Sophocles *Antigone* 905-912. The word *tertia* is used appropriately three times; the final remark leaves the girl's virginity sold off with a dowry.

6 3

This poem is one of the most unusual poetic creations of the Ancient World, a metrical *tour de force* and a text which has intrigued its readers ever since it was composed. It is also the one complete surviving example of the Galliambic metre, a genre used for hymns to the Phrygian goddess Cybele sung by her eunuch priests the Galli: for details of the metre see Introduction # 'The Metres'. The atmosphere of the tale is predominantly Greek (but see 26n), but Catullus may owe something to his contemporary Caecilius who also composed poetry on the subject (see poem 35).

Cybele, (or Cybebe, the Lydian form of her name (Herodotus 5. 102)), the Magna Mater (Great Mother) was worshipped in Rome from the third century BC, and was given a temple on the Palatine in 204 BC: in the late Republic the dancing of the priests was to be seen in the streets of Rome and inspired Lucretius to write a set-piece description of it (2. 610-643). The narrative of this poem is no homely aetiological Roman tale, however, but a retelling of the story of Attis, a Greek who rejects his former way of life and castrates himself in order to assimilate himself to the femininity of the Good Goddess. At the end of the poem he has changed his mind but must spend the rest of his life as the slave of the goddess in the forests of Phrygia. This is the version of the tale told here: other accounts have Attis as the Greek lover and husband of Cybele who was either unfaithful to her and castrated as a punishment (Lactantius *Divinae Institutiones* 1.17.7), or else castrated himself in despair when their marriage was abruptly ended (Pausanias 7.17). All agree on the castration of Attis as an aetiological myth to explain the eunuch priests of the cult. Many versions of the story see Attis as married to Cybele, even seeing him as a vegetation-god – a kind of male version of Demeter:

Catullus tells us very little about Attis himself. Sandy (1971), keen to find 'unity' in the *carmina maiora* in the theme of marriage, sees the Attis of this poem as a symbol of the broken pledge of married love, although he concedes that the details are 'not set forth in the poem but embedded in the myths and firmly lodged in Catullus' mind' (191). This cannot be the case: the poet has gone out of his way to transform the traditional tale of Attis as a legendary figure who dies and is resurrected into a very different man – a man of the city and its comforts who is whipped up into religious fanaticism and loses everything for it. There is no 'message' in this poem about marriage – at no point does Attis aspire to marry Cybele but rather to be a slave in communion with her, and after his castration he cannot marry anybody at all. Marriage is decisively rejected by him in order to pursue his religious mission as the servant of the goddess, much as it is in Euripides' *Hippolytus*, where Artemis his beloved goddess takes a similarly cool attitude towards his devotion (see especially 1440_1 (*pace* Barrett *ad loc*)).

Historical and biographical criticism of this sort of poetry is available but has severe limitations; Quinn argues, for instance, that the sudden appearance of Attis' snow-white hands and delicate fingers (8, 10) show that he was an effeminate youth already, and that 'the poem ... is a study of a young man who, along with others, had found (to their horror, or their shame) that they could not make the transition society demanded from the role of *puer delicatus* to that of husband, or Don Juan (*moechus*) ... Catullus ... offers us an ironic re-interpretation of the Attis legend in line both with his technique of bringing legend up to date ... and in a collection of poems about love and contemporary society' (Quinn (1972) 250). One problem with this line of argument is that it reduces the mythical and divine elements to the status of mere symbols: in real life *pueri delicati* did not find themselves severing their genitals and being chased by lions, and so Catullus' poem, if it is simply an exploration of a sociological phenomenon in the manner Quinn suggests, is absurdly exaggerated. Biographical criticism – equating Attis with the hapless Catullus and seeing Cybele as his implacable mistress Lesbia – is available (see e.g. Schmid (1974) 230-233) but usually and rightly dismissed as unnecessary, conjectural and inadequate as a tool with which to analyse any work of literature. The opportunity to do detective work in the society of Catullus' contemporaries and come up with the 'real' Attis is irresistibly tempting to some scholars, but the results will always be conjecture as history and of little use as criticism. After all, the interpretation and appreciation of this poetry is hardly likely to depend on the reader being able to pick up topical references which are not explained or even referred to explicitly. Poetry is not an encoded diary and should not be seen as such. Nor is it always 'moral' in tone: there are occasions when Catullus takes a moral stance, of course (poem 76 most obviously), but if no obvious moral point emerges from a reading of the poem, then that does not mean that either the reading or the text is worthless. There is no *a priori* reason to postulate a 'motive' for any poet to compose a poem; the common assumption that the poet is possessed of a 'feeling in search of a form' is often quite mistaken, and the truth is often that a brilliant poet is anxious to try out a form which he has not tried before – in this case the difficult Galliambics – and so wrote a poem whose subject matter is suitable to the genre. In the course of composition it may be that the writer discovers in himself feelings of which he may not have been aware prior to the act of composition, but the sequence is that of 'form in search of a feeling' rather than vice versa. Wiseman argues that the poem was composed – just as 61 was composed for a wedding – as a *Gelegenheitsgedicht*, a hymn to be sung at the annual *ludi Megalenses* in honour of the Good Goddess, a hymn combining prayer to the goddess with an uncompromisingly Roman attitude of disapproval towards the madness and the folly of Attis' behaviour . There can be no proof of this suggestion: and it may appear inherently unlikely that the organisers of a religious festival would commission a laureate poem which would deter devotion in this way, with 'the mystic god of the Galli portrayed as a Greek youth afflicted with a madness he cannot control' (Wiseman (1985) 206) and running away ingloriously from a lion.

This is not a straightforward poem, and any attempt to make it fit an occasion or a single unified tone is unlikely to succeed. It is, if anything, a poem of contrasts: the western Greek and the eastern Phrygian, the sophisticated city and the wild woods, the humble devotion of the mortal male and the proud arrogance of the divine female, the spoiled and popular youth with bands of followers becoming a wretched and lonely exile (notice how the companions disappear without comment, their purpose being solely to contrast popularity and loneliness), the beloved young man becoming a heartbroken lover of the unlovable Cybele, and so on; above all in its narrative drive this is a poem where rabid madness turns in the cold light of day to sick regret – a pattern familiar from the tragedies of e.g. Euripides' *Heracles*, and *Bacchae* and Sophocles' *Ajax*.

The poet gives us three narrative standpoints: Attis as seen by his companions, Attis as he then sees himself, finally Attis as seen by the goddess and the lion. The heroic self-mutilator becomes a tragic figure of sad regret, only to become a farcical figure running away from an animal who has been told not to harm him; the poet plays with the responses of the readers, forcing us to abandon our critical conclusions as soon as we have formed them and leaving our emotions moved but confused in this self-conscious exercise in irony.

Ironic clues are planted in many places: Attis' speech to his companions is 'full of the irony of ignorance and illusion' (Hutchinson 312) as he unconsciously reveals the excess (*nimio* 17) and folly (*erroribus* 18) of these 'exiles' (14 – he is doomed to become a permanent exile himself) who are the *vaga pecora* (13 – animal imagery looking forward to the lion later) seeking what is not rightly theirs (*aliena petentes* 14). His sentimental picture of the joys of worship in the woods (20-25) is shattered by the reality both of his situation (53-4, 68-72) and of his dread mistress (78-84), just as the dreamy picture of Phrygian revels is broken with the final word, the specifically Roman *tripudiis*. The only member of the *divae cohors* (25) whom he actually encounters is the savage lion who makes only too sure that he 'hastens' (*celerare*) where the goddess wants him.

His second speech employs similar rhetoric to different ends, the extended anaphoras* of *ubi* in 21-5 foreshadowing the anaphoras of *ego* in 68-71 as the unthinking hero becomes aware of his awful state, terms which he had idealised becoming terms of bitter regret (e.g. *Maenades* 23 – *Maenas* 69, *Phrygiam* 20 – *Phrygiae* 71), the heroic becoming the tragic. Even here, however, our emotions are kept in check by the 'exhaustive Ovidian ingenuity in the exploration of the paradoxical calamity' (Hutchinson 313) – the constant use of feminine endings to describe the emasculated male, the breathless string of self-descriptions (63), the tricolon crescendo* of

> *ego Maenas, ego mei pars, ego vir sterilis ero?* (69)

and especially the irony of *mei pars* (he has lost a part of himself – this is inverted into the conceit that what is left of him is only a part of himself); the high-flown language of compound adjectives (this aesthete cannot simply complain about the animals without describing them as *cerva silvicultrix ... aper ṅemorivagus* 72), the florid sensuous language describing his former florid sensuous lifestyle (64-7) and the mock-tragic wailing of

> *miser a miser, querendum est etiam atque etiam, anime* (61)

with that final 'o, my soul' a delicious ironical stance. It is also difficult to read lines 58-67 with much sympathy: the effete self-indulgent tone of the speech is self-parody of the foppish and spoiled youth who only has himself to blame for his plight and whose complaints after his self-inflicted injury are couched in plangent self-pity calculated to distance the emotions of the reader. Furthermore, there are plenty of negative aspects to his character: he has rejected Venus (17), he is like a heifer which has not been broken in and so is useless for farm work (33), or even worse a runaway slave leaving his master (51) – none of them calculated to win sympathy from a Roman audience.

Attis is not, then, an overwhelmingly attractive figure – but the divine heroine is no better. Cybele's speech is a parody of the 'angry god' figure; she opposes *furor* to Attis' flight for freedom (80) – but the *furor* which will drive him back is not the mad enthusiasm with which he mutilated himself, but simply blind panic in the face of a roaring lion. We thus imagine Attis from then on as being imprisoned in the woods by fear – bitter and resentful in the knowledge that he has thrown his life away. It would have been far kinder of the goddess to drive Attis mad and restore him to the frame of mind of lines 1-38, in which he was quite happy to serve her all his life; but then, kindness is not Cybele's strong point – she is herself a victim of the *furor* of anger as she shouts out with rhetorical repetition and alliteration*:

> *agedum, inquit, age ferox i fac ut hanc furor agitet*
> *fac uti furoris ictu ...*

and even the poor lion is made to suffer self-flagellation with his tail to serve the vindictive lusts of his mistress. Everybody suffers for her sake, and her vengeance is – as so often with avenging gods in classical mythology – unnecessary. Attis has mutilated himself irreversibly and will hardly be able to settle back into the urban life which he recollects wistfully. His 'excess of freedom' has been to regret his actions, and for this he will be locked up in fear and poverty for the rest of his life. The goddess shows herself to be a *magna ... domina* (91) indeed, to be feared rather than admired. The ending of the story thus overturns the beginning, where Cybele was seen through the rosy spectacles of the infatuated Attis, and substitutes for the fairy godmother a hideous witch. Her portrayal is also ironically Roman: Newman acutely observes: 'Cybele is a Roman (*imperia* 80) and her lion is a Roman soldier (*facit impetum* 89)' (Newman (1990) 217). The effect is not however political or even moral, but again ironic and distancing.

The poet's prayer at the end is a reaction to the story rather than a hymnic act of piety – this is not a hymn, *pace* Wiseman ((1985) 198-206) – but then, the final three lines are the supreme irony in the poem. A common form of closural* gesture in ancient poetry is to end with a personal touch bringing the poem back to the present and the truth (see e.g. Horace *Epode* 2) as a distancing device almost equivalent to the poet 'signing off'. So here, the notion of Catullus emasculating himself and being chased into the woods by a lion is patently ridiculous and sets the story we have heard into the perspective of reality, especially as the poet (speaking apparently *in propria persona*) uses the sort of language which Attis himself used in order to mimic and therefore mock the tone of the story. (So Hutchinson 312.)

In structure, the poem falls into two distinct halves: Attis' act of self-castration on day one (1-38), and his futile attempt to escape and repentance on day two (39-90), rounded off with a personal comment by the poet. The poem contains three speeches: Attis to his companions (12-26), Attis to himself (50-73) and finally Cybele to her lion (78-83). Each day begins with an 11-line narrative followed by a speech from Attis; on day one the reaction is to run towards the goddess, on day two the reaction is to flee from her. The overall structure then is as follows:

Day one
1-11   Attis' self-castration
12-26 Attis' speech to his companions
27-38 They all run to Mt Ida

Day two
39-49 Attis awakes and regrets his actions.
50-73 Attis' speech
74-84 Reaction and speech of Cybele
85-90 Attis driven back by the lion
91-3   poet's prayer to Cybele.

1-11 The poet launches straight *in medias res*: there is no background to the story and little explanation given for Attis' actions. The technique of stating the event and then allowing the milieu and the atmosphere to emerge from the reactions to it is a highly effective means of arresting the reader's attention and then keeping it.

1   **Attis**: the central character is named at once. Catullus tells us nothing about the background to this person, beyond that he is Greek and that he is inspired 'by excessive hatred of Venus' (17)

2   **the grove in Phrygia**: i.e. the forests of Mount Ida in the Troad. Notice here the jingle of *cupide pede*, and also the first of many uses of the word *citatus* and its cognates (cf. 8, 18, 26, 30, 42, 74).

3   **woodland-crowned**: *redimire* means 'to encircle as with a garland', 'to crown'; we thus imagine a clearing in the forest which is small enough for the surrounding trees to cast their shade, the metaphor* giving also a regal sense to the 'demesne of the goddess'.

4   A line devoted to Attis' state of mind. *stimulus* was a pointed stick used to goad animals into moving, here used to imply the involuntary nature of Attis' behaviour. Both *furor* and *rabies* have the sense of 'blind ferocity' appropriate here to an action of such violence and insanity. *vagus animi* is the more 'normal' Latin correction of the mss *vagus amnis*, although the plural *animis* may be correct.

5   **sharp flint**: The specificity of *acuto silice* led Wilamowitz to think that this was the prescribed implement for performing the operation: rather this is the product of historical imagination and an eye for the effect.

6.   **manhood**: For *viro* meaning 'manly part' or 'penis' see Adams, 70. The surprise is that one would expect Attis to be a *vir* without a *membrum*, rather than *membra* without a *viro*. The previous line is vague about exactly what he severed: castration normally assumes the removal of the testicles, whereas this line would imply that the penis also was removed: certainly the violence of the act in line 5 would sustain the interpretation that he removed both penis and testicles with the fateful flint.

7   **staining ... blood**: the grotesque detail goes on: he is still bleeding onto the ground.

8   **snowy**: With some implausibility, Attis at once has feminine hands (*niveis* is the colour of virgins such as Polyxena at 64.364) and despite his desperate medical condition, picks up Cybele's tambourine and begins to play it. The instant transformation into a woman is marked by the use from now on of feminine genders to describe Attis (beginning with *citata* here); Quinn ((1972) 250) argues that it is more likely that Attis must have always had an effeminate appearance, and that the poet is telling us something about him and his effeminacy in these epithets: see introduction to the poem. There is also an ironic effect in the constant feminine endings, something almost akin to Aristophanes' mockery of the beardless Cleisthenes as being a woman (e.g. *Thesmophoriazusai* 571-4). The gender functions as a constant reminder of the irrevocability of what Attis has done.

8-10   The beating of the tambourine is marked by repeated alliteration* of the letter *t*. *initia* here means 'the instrument of initiation' (Quinn).

9   *Cybebe*: The poet uses the Lydian form of the name *Cybebe* (with its long second syllable) here and elsewhere where the metre demands: *Cybele* has a short second syllable.

10   **making ... tremble:** an arcane mode of expression: the tambourine is called the *bursotonon kukloma* at Euripides' *Bacchae* 124, *bursa* meaning 'leather' or 'hide', presumably from a bull's back. Attis now has 'delicate fingers' to match his 'snow-white hands'.

12-26 Attis' speech: for comment see introduction to the poem.

12   **Gallae:** male followers of Cybele were called Galli: Catullus uses the feminine form Gallae to emphasise their castration. The origins of the name are obscure.

13   **Dindymus**: a mountain in Phrygia dedicated to the cult of Cybele (cf. line 91, and poem 35.14). The authority of Cybele is asserted several times in the poem: cf. 18, 91, 92. The status of the devotees as her 'wandering flocks' picks up the animal image in *stimulatus* (4) and looks forward to Attis' indignant account of the animals he will have to live with (53-4, 72) and also the lion the *pecoris hostem* (77).

14-17 Attis reminds his followers of how they have left their homes and abandoned their masculinity for love of Cybele.

14   **like exiles:** They are *velut* exiles in that they decided to leave their countries rather than being expelled.

15   **following ... guidance:**   *sectam ... secutae* is a good example of the *figura etymologica**, where the participle following the accusative shows the derivation of the words. Attis here stresses above all himself and his leadership: *meam ... duce me mihi.*

16   The line is a symmetrical one, the pair of (almost) synonymous adjective+noun phrases separated by the verb in the middle. *salum* is a direct transliteration of the Greek word *salos* denoting the rolling motion and restlessness of the sea, just as *pelagus* is also from the Greek *pelagos*.   The variation of vocabulary is strengthened by the matching pair of adjectives, *rapidum* suggesting *rapio* and therefore 'devouring', *truculenta* translated by Fordyce as the 'bullying' sea.

17   **unmanned:** *evirastis* picks up the use of *sine viro* at 6. The reason for the emasculation is here given as hatred of Venus (i.e. sex) rather than love for Cybele.

18   **gladden the heart:**   ironic, in the outcome. Attis is certainly not gladdened when he realises what he has done, and the goddess does not show gratitude as he appears to expect.

19   **slow:** *tarda* is technically redundant, put in here for rhetorical effect.

20   The repetition of *Phrygia(m) ad* + noun + goddess is striking.

21-5   **where ... where ... :** A long sequence of six anaphoras* introduced by *ubi*, painting an attractive picture of their destination: the first three focus on the music, the last three on the personnel.

22   **the Phrygian piper:**   the pipe had a curved lower end, and was a bass instrument (the player plays *grave*).

23   **Maenads** are properly the female worshippers of Dionysus, but the rites of the two gods are often associated. The tossing of heads is a peculiarly Maenad trait – cf. 64.255 – and the ivy symbolised in its evergreen quality 'the victory of vegetation over its enemy the winter' (Dodds on Euripides' *Bacchae* 81)

24   a line remarkable for its assonance* – three *a* vowels followed by three *u* vowels. The 'sharp yelling' of the devotees is again a feature of the Bacchic literature (e.g. Euripides' *Bacchae* 24)

25-6 **races:**   *volitare* is metaphorical*, as at 64. 251, but the speaker may be exaggerating also for persuasive effect. The alliterative* phrase *volitare vaga* picks up the sense of *citatis erroribus* in line 18, the speed of the movement brought out well by the three words *volitare ... citatis celerare*. If there were any doubt as to the Roman quality of the poem, the peculiarly Roman term *tripudiis* should allay it: the word denotes the wild dancing found in the rites of the Salii and the Arval Brethren.

27   **fake female:**   Attis is only a 'bastard woman' i.e. a false woman: for this use of the Greek word *nothos* cf. 34.15.

28-9 The followers respond to Attis' speech: the order is the reverse of that in the speech, as the *ululatus* here comes first, followed by the *typanum* and then the *cymbala* (contrast the order in lines 21-4).

28   Note the onomatopoeiac repeated *l* sounds of *linguis ... ululat*, and then the equally onomatopoeiac pair of answering *re-* verbs *remugit* (for the deep drum) and *recrepant* (for the clashing cymbals) complete with alliteration of *c*.

30   **swift ... hurrying:**   again, the speed is stressed with the emphatic *citus ... properante pede.*

31   **gasping and panting:**   The furious rushing of Attis is well brought out by the sequence of adjectives and descriptive phrases expressive of haste and fatigue: *anhelans* ('panting') is followed by *animam agens* ('gasping for breath')

32   **leading:**   *dux* is placed for emphasis at the end of the line; the groves are 'gloomy' as at line 3.

33   **like a heifer:**   the simile* is ironic: the heifer rushes to avoid the yoke, whereas Attis has voluntarily embraced it. In another sense, however, Attis has cast off 'the weight of his groin' (5) and thus is both unyoked but not 'untamed'. The simile thus teases the reader with elements which corroborate and also undermine its relevance.

34   A technically impressive five-word line ending with the compound adjective *properipedem.*

35   **tired little women:**   *lassulae* is a 'sympathetic diminutive' (Fordyce); throughout the poem Catullus treats these emasculated men as if they were real women and thus deserving of feminine attributes. *domum* will be regretted when Attis laments his loss of his home in line 58, flowery as it was (66).

36   **Ceres:**   the metonymy* of Ceres the goddess of crops meaning here simply 'bread' is discussed in Lucretius 2.655-660, immediately after his description of the rites of Cybele. The reason why the Gallae do not eat is presumably because

they are too tired to go looking for food, rather than any more anthropological reason.

37-8 The Gallae go to sleep, the pair of lines unfolding in a neat chiasmus* of: subject, ablative phrase, verb, verb, ablative phrase, subject. The *rabidus furor* is however left as a reminder of the insane earlier action in the mind of the reader. Thus ends the first half of the poem – the reader is left to wonder how Attis will feel about his irreversible action in the morning.

39-43 A single sentence describing the dawn in highly coloured language. The sun is 'of golden face' with 'eyes radiant', the triad of air, earth and sea are all given suitable epithets. For the awakening of reason in the clear light of dawn, Elder (1947, 399) well compares Sophocles' *Ajax* 21, 217, 258, 660, 672: the stories of mutilation under the influence of divinely-inspired madness are remarkably similar.

40   **cleansed:** *lustravit* means both 'surveyed' and also 'purified', implying (along with the 'white' air) that the new morning will cleanse Attis of his madness.

41   **sounding hooves:** *sonipedibus* is an effective expression for the horses of the sun and commoner than one might expect – see OLD s.v. b.

43   **Pasithea:** the name means 'goddess to all': she was one of the Graces and the wife of the god of Sleep Hypnos, given to him by Hera as a reward for putting her husband Zeus into a deep sleep in *Iliad* 14.

44-9 Attis realises what he has done and regrets it: his mental turmoil is stressed repeatedly (*liquida mente ... animo aestuante ... lacrimantibus oculis*).

44   **gentle ... ravings:** The chiastic* oxymoron* of *quiete molli rapida ... rabie* is effective.

45   **her doings:** Attis may have been under the influence of *furens rabies* (4), but the actions were still 'his own' (*sua*).

46   **lacked:** Attis sees what is <u>not</u> there any more.

47   **back to the shore:** returning to the sea symbolises Attis' wish to turn back the clock and reverse his operation.

48-9   **seeing the ... sea:** Rather like Ariadne, Attis gazes longingly out to sea weeping and addresses his father-land in the manner (e.g.) of Ajax about to die (Sophocles *Ajax* 859-61). The homesickness of the desperate is common in ancient literature.

50-73 Attis' second speech, different in tone from the brash first speech; the first speech was a rousing epic speech to his companions, while this one is a wistful soliloquy full of remorse and self-pity, a study in tragic 'learning the truth – too late'.

50   **country ... birth:** there is a nice parallelism in *patria ... creatrix, patria ... genetrix,* the adjectives being ruefully used here by a man now rendered incapable of procreation himself. Ellis remarks that there was a tradition in Rome that a man who castrated himself could not be a father and so could not continue the *patria*: 'to be a eunuch was therefore to play the parricide to one's own country' – a notion constantly behind Augustus' famous harangue of the celibate *equites* as 'murderers of their own posterity' (Dio 56.4-9).

51-2 **fugitive slaves:**   In the first part, Attis was happy to follow his mistress Cybele: now he regards himself as being like a slave who has run away from his master, only to become a slave to Cybele.

53   **snow ... icy:**   Attis gazes at the inhospitable landscape for which he has exchanged the comforts of home. stressing the coldness (*nivem ... gelida*) and the wild nature of the place and the beasts who live there (*ferarum*), a quality which he now shares in a sense (*furibunda*).

54   **concealed:**   *operta* is Müller's emendation for the jejune and unmetrical mss reading *omnia*.

55   **where:** Attis no longer knows even where his homeland is.

567   **while ... madness:**   Attis clearly lacks confidence that his madness (*rabie fera*) will not return.

59-60 **homeland ... gymnasia:** Attis runs through the catalogue of what he will be forced to eschew in his exile, both the general features (line 59) and the specific amenities of the city (line 60)

60   The *forum* is the market-place and general meeting-place in the city, the *palaestra* was the wrestling-school, the *stadium* the running-track and the *gymnasia* the training-school: the last three especially associated with young men and the life of the *jeunesse dorée*, as described further in lines 64-7.

61   **pathetic:**   The lamentation indulges in repetition (*miser ... miser, etiam ... etiam*) and self-apostrophising* (*anime*).

63   **woman ... boy:**   Attis goes over his four stages of life in reverse order, beginning with the latest. *ephebus* is a Greek work denoting a youth of 18-20 years of age.   Attis' autobiography is almost as impressive as that of the reincarnated Empedocles ('For I have been a boy and a girl, a bush and a bird and a leaping fish' Fr. 117).

64   **flower ... oil:**   The young man longs for his former comfort and fame with two elegant phrases: the metaphor* 'flower of the gymnasium' and the synecdoche* 'glory of the wrestler's oil'. There is a problem with the change of tense from *fui* (perfect) to *eram* (imperfect): Nisbet's proposal (Nisbet (1978) 86) that *fui* was originally *suus* ('I was the gymnasium's own flower') is extremely tempting – one ·manuscript reads *sui*, a possible case of assimilation to the genitive *gymnasi*, which was then 'corrected' to *fui*, f and s being often confused by scribes.

65-71 After a run of six *ego*'s, Attis now produces 3 *mihi*'s, before reverting to another six *ego*'s in lines 68-71.

65   **doors ... threshold:**   The doorways crowded and the threshold warm alludes presumably to the twin features of Roman life – the *clientes* who would throng the doorway to greet the occupant and escort him down to the forum, and also the serenading of the would-be lover who camps out on the doorway of the beloved. The latter was usually a pastime indulged in by males in love with females, on which see Lucretius 4.1177-9 ('often the weeping locked-out lover covers the threshold with flowers and garlands'), Copley (1956) *passim*.

66   **garlanded:** Attis' house used to be 'crowned' just as the demesne of the goddess was crowned in line 3, but in his case it was with the garlands of lovers left there during the night and discovered when he left the house at dawn.

67   **sunrise:** The time in the narrative is dawn – Attis contrasts this dawn with his usual dawns in the past.

68-73 In contrast to his former life-style, Attis now ponders his future: from being master he will be a servant, from being a man he will be a woman, from being admired he is now deformed, the warm doorway gives way to the icy woodlands, his admiring companions being replaced by the dumb beasts. No wonder he regrets his actions.

68   **handmaid ... :** From the general to the specific: 'servant of the gods' becomes sharpened to 'handmaid of Cybele'. *ferar* (' I shall be called') is of course deeply important to this proud young man.

69   **Maenad:** see 23n. *mei pars* is wonderfully expressive – a part of him has been removed, but he now feels that his remaining limbs are the 'part' – unpacked for effect into the brilliant oxymoron *vir sterilis.*

70   **cold, snow-clad:** The notion of cold is stressed with *algida ... nive*, the specific place Mount Ida leading to a more general expression *sub altis Phrygiae columinibus.*

72   **forest-haunting ... boar:** The two animals are chosen *exempli gratia*, the hind and the boar each given a compound adjective – as if the young aesthete cannot help thinking in lofty artistic terms even when contemplating the aesthetic desolation of life in the woods.

73   The shortest line in the poem (cf. Introduction # 'Metres'), the repeated *iam*'s 'coming like a series of blows, leading up to the terrible, final *paenitet.*' (Quinn)

74   **rosy lips:** Attis has womanly lips: cf. his snowy hands (8) and his delicate fingers (10).

76   **lions:** Cybele is usually shown in art and literature as being carried in a lion-drawn chariot: see especially Lucretius 2. 600-1 ('she, as our ancient and learned Greek poets sang, sits in a chariot and drives a pair of lions').

77   **flock's foe:** the *pecoris hostis* is the lion, traditional predator of cattle and sheep; the poet refers to the one on the left as being on the sinister or unlucky side. Cybele *stimulat* the beast, just as Attis himself was *stimulatus* (4), and his followers were compared to the *vaga pecora* of Cybele (13) at the beginning of the poem.

78-83 Cybele's speech, instructing the lion to frighten the rebellious devotee back to the woods, but not instructing the beast to hurt Attis.

80   **too freely:** Cybele's motive is injured pride – Attis now wishes to abandon her service.

81   **beat your back:** the lion is told to lash his back with his own tail and thus 'endure your own blows', borrowing an idea found first in Homer *Iliad* 20. 170-1 ('he lashes his ribs and his flanks on both sides with his tail as he rouses himself to fury for the fight').

82   **thunders ... roar:** The three 'sound' words are all needed for the cacophony: *mugienti* is the low-voiced snarling, *fremitu* is the roar itself, *retonent* is the re-echoing of the sound around the area.

83   a symmetrical line, the brawny neck inside the mane in poetry as in life.

85-6   The lion springs into life, spurring himself on (*sese adhortans* = *sese incitat*, the doublet stressing the idea). The beast (*ferus*) is also described as *rabidus* (linking him with the word *rabies*, Attis' word to describe his own madness in line 57). The three verbs in asyndeton* well bring out the impetuous movement of the lion: first a vague word (*vadit*, 'he rushes'), then the roar which he was instructed to produce, then the devastation caused to the undergrowth as he tramples it down.

88   **delicate:**   Attis is no wild beast and no match for one either. Note here the pacific setting of moisture and brightness (*albicantis* referring both to the white sand and also to the white foam in the waves, and leading nicely into the metaphor of the 'marble of the ocean' which is of course white), broken by the sudden impact of *facit impetum* at the end of the sentence but the beginning of the line.

89-90 **out of her mind:**   *demens* is ironic; Attis was lucid in seeking to escape the effects of her former madness, but now is scared out of her mind by the sudden apparition of the lion: similarly, *fera* could be taken as feminine singular agreeing with her – Attis is turned into one of the wild beasts in her terror and sudden loss of control. The rest of her life is well brought out in the juxtaposition of *semper omne*, with Attis becoming the *famula* which she dreaded being called at line 68.

91-3   The poet ends with his prayer to the goddess to spare him from this sort of madness, a poignant closure* bringing the text back abruptly to the present in the manner of the closure of 64 and 68. For the personal apostrophe* of the goddess compare 68. 77-8 and Callimachus *Hymn* 3. 136-7, 6. 116-7. Note here the repetition of *dea* (three times in a sort of tricolon crescendo*), the juxtaposition of *mea tuos*, the anaphora* of *alios age ... alios age ...* , the variation of vocabulary from *domina* to *era*, and then also *furor ... rabidos*. We are left with the words *furor ... rabidos*, referring us back to the beginning of the poem (*furenti rabie* 4).

6 4

This is the only complete surviving example in Latin of the miniature epic or *epyllion*, a form which dates from Alexandrian times – see especially Callimachus' *Hecale* and Moschus' *Europa* – but which found especial favour with the New Poets of the first century BC (others of the period are known to us by name: Cinna's *Zmyrna*, praised by Catullus and favourably contrasted with Volusius' *Annales* in poem 95; Calvus wrote an *Io*, Cornificius a *Glaucus*, Valerius Cato a *Dictynna*). The poem is not a simple linear 'short epic': the story of the marriage of Peleus and Thetis frames a 'story within a story', with more than half (216 of the 408 lines) of the poem given over to this 'digression' describing a tapestry adorning the marriage bed, the whole central tableau being an example of the device known as *ecphrasis** – the set-piece description of a work of art in narrative form – found in much ancient literature and discussed fully at 50-266n below.

The structure of the poem is as follows:

1-30   The meeting of Peleus and Thetis
31-49   The human guests arrive: description of the palace.
50-264   The tapestry *ecphrasis*
        50-1   bridge passage
        52-70   Ariadne on the beach
        71-5   bridge passage
        76-115   Theseus' earlier arrival in Crete: Ariadne falls in love
        116-31   bridge passage returns us to Ariadne on the beach
        132-201   Ariadne's speech
        202-214   bridge passage: Ariadne's curse prompts flashback to
                    Theseus' leaving of Athens
        215-37   Aegeus' farewell speech
        238-48   Ariadne's curse fulfilled
        249-50   return to the tapestry
        251-64   Bacchus and his entourage arrive
265-302   The human guests depart and the gods arrive.
303-383   The Fates sing the wedding song
384-408   Epilogue.

The meeting of Peleus and Thetis merges immediately into their wedding, the poet's handling of time and ordering of material allows an unusual degree of slippage and flexibility which both strengthens thematic links and also distances the text as an arbitrary literary creation rather than an 'iconic' or linear view of reality. In the ecphrasis in particular, the poet begins and ends with Ariadne as depicted in the tapestry: apparently doomed to die and lamenting her fate but in fact about to be saved by a divine saviour whom she cannot see. The background tales of Theseus and his father and the slaying of the Minotaur are brought in to explain how the central figure of Ariadne came to be where the artist has placed her and how her apparent impotence and vulnerability masks a powerful curse and imminent translation to divine company – the sort of union of god and human, in fact, which Peleus and Thetis exemplify and which the poet misses wistfully at the end of the poem. The viewer of the tapestry would of course see that Ariadne was about to be saved and so would know that her laments are wasted and needless: the reader of the poem is not let into the full details of the picture until her despair has been fully indulged. Thus the thematic coherence of the poem is easily seen: in both tales there is a human being married to a divine being, and the result of both unions is happiness at least for the moment: the magical meeting of the goddess and the man which opens the poem is cruelly shattered in the disillusioned epilogue where the poet laments that such unions do not occur any more. The sea is the peaceful idyllic element on which Peleus first sees Thetis and is also the cruel force (*truculentum* 179) imprisoning Ariadne on the beach until Bacchus flies in – the poet's treatment of the sea is not uniform and to some extent mirrors the mood of the tale (see Curran 175-9). The human sacrifice of Polyxena at the tomb of Peleus' son foretold by the Parcae towards the end recalls the sacrifice of Ariadne's 'brother' the Minotaur at the hands of Theseus and is in turn recalled by the massive sacrifice to Jupiter in 389. Theseus is *ferox* and able to slay monsters, while Achilles will exceed even Theseus in ferocity and carnage. The father of Theseus is a model of a caring parent, and Peleus and Thetis will also go on to have a highly successful son: in fact Peleus is most often seen (in Homer at least) as a sad old father whose son has abandoned him to fight in Troy, and Thetis is also often seen as a figure of mourning (Callimachus *Hymn to Apollo* 2.20-1 etc) for her son – an image which makes the relationship of Theseus and Aegeus analogous rather than contrasted with Peleus/Thetis and Achilles. Even tiny details become themes and find parallels in the inner and the outer narrative: the Nereids' breasts are seen by the mariners (18), Ariadne bares her breasts in despair on the shore (64-5), the mothers of Achilles' victims will beat their breasts (351) in despair at the death of their sons (for the complexity of this image see now Hunter (1991)). The trees are woven into a ship (10), the tale of Ariadne is told on a woven tapestry and features the life-saving power of Theseus' thread to come safely out of the labyrinth (113-5), and the Parcae spin the thread of the future (320-2 etc) which even includes the prophecy that Thetis will pass the *filum* test the morning after her wedding-night (376-80n). Even the language strengthens the unity of the different tales: compare line 19 and line 253 describing the love of Peleus and Bacchus respectively in very similar terms. What all these coherences establish is a feeling that it is a single world which this poem is describing, a world where both Peleus and Theseus are at home; the poet goes out of his way to confuse any sense of 'before and after' in the intertwining of the two tales, even foxing the reader's sense of chronology with the 'first ship' in the opening scene leading up to a tale which depends on a series of ships having been sailing between Athens and Crete for years (*solitam esse* 79). The past is all one, contrasted (ostensibly) at the end with the present, the whole poem creating a subtle *mise-en-abîme**.

Related to this thematic and narratological interweaving is the intertextual use of a range of earlier literature. Catullus alludes to phrases, themes, and characters in Greek and Roman literature and so deepens the texture and the significance of the poem. The opening of the poem, for instance, relies heavily on the echoes of Euripides' (echoed by Ennius') *Medea* and also Apollonius of Rhodes' *Argonautica*, texts which insist on the reader seeing the present poem as a narrative of the Voyage of the Argo with Peleus on board. This contrasts with the view of Apollonius (1.558) that Peleus married Thetis and fathered Achilles before the Argo sailed and the consequent idyllic courtship is astonishing both in chronology and content (Thetis was highly resistant to Peleus in earlier accounts (see below for details)). There are strong echoes of Lucretius in the poem, both of phrases (209), whole descriptions (e.g. the Bacchic noise at 251-64 recalls Lucretius 4. 545-8 and 2.618-20) and large themes (the human sacrifice of Polyxena owes a great deal to Lucretius' Iphigeneia (1. 84-100): the folly of Ariadne's love for Theseus is infused with Lucretius' scathing satire of romantic love at 4.1058-1287). Even the gloomy ending of the poem raises similar questions as the gloomy ending of the *de rerum natura*, and the final view of the gods out of contact with humans is Epicurean in effect if not in motivation (Epicurus' gods keep away to maintain their serenity, Catullus' gods do so out of abhorrence of man's behaviour). Echoes of Homer abound – the similes, the father-son sorrowing of Aegeus-Theseus recalling strongly that of Priam-Hector, the *aristeia* of Achilles – as well as of tragedy (Prometheus, Polyxena), the wedding hymn (the Parcae sing a sinister inversion of the traditional *epithalamium* – on which see introduction to poem 61), the Idyll of Peleus and Thetis falling instantly in love being a marine version of Greek pastoral poetry. Above all, the *ecphrasis* is a stylised but highly original version of a form of static description going back to Homer (see 50-266n). Detailed correspondences are picked up in the commentary: what is important here is the self-conscious manner in which Catullus has used the literature of the past to create a new poem, the echoes merging to form and also colour a new voice.

The predominant area of critical inquiry has been the poet's attitude towards his subject matter, in particular whether the poem is 'optimistic' or 'pessimistic' in its view of human nature and the heroic age. The classic statement of the 'pessimistic' viewpoint is still that of Bramble (1970), who sees disquiet in the poet's elaborate description of the idleness in the countryside, unease at the luxury in the opulent wealth in the palace and positive repugnance in the grisly prophecies of the Fates. The happy wedding of Peleus and Thetis is offset and undermined by the wretched state of the abandoned Ariadne, who thus gives the lie to the heroism and self-sacrifice declared as being the ethos of the past. The narrative itself is full of negative remarks and unhappy echoes – and to make the point inescapably clear the poet appends a gratuitous epilogue full of contemporary *Kulturpessimismus* showing the mood as one of deep disillusion. The *heroum virtutes* are ironically and bitterly 'corrected' by the poem's assertion that 'the Heroic Age was not so very different from contemporary times. It might have been happier in some ways than the present, yet still it contained the germs of future decline.' (Bramble (1970) 41). This powerful view is still with us in a large amount of the scholarly writing on the poem and deserves further critical examination. The assumption, for example, that the future brutality of the child renders the wedding unhappy is questionable, especially when the 'child' is without doubt the greatest warrior in the world of Greek myth. There is nothing to stop the happy couple in Catullus 64 from savouring the pleasure of their own happiness by contrasting it with the (future) unhappiness of others; as in the opening lines of Lucretius Book 2, it is a pleasure to see the sufferings of others when one is safe from danger oneself. This attitude might be seen as *Schadenfreude* but found little guilt in the breast of an Epicurean. Then there is the depiction of the luxury in the palace which would be viewed, Bramble argues, by the 'normal Roman', with 'disapproval' (Bramble (1970) 39); but this is contested by Jenkyns who sees the passage as one of sensuous

delight in the colours, textures (and of course poetic sounds) of the gorgeous palace
(Jenkyns, 90-91). Far from being a pejorative description, lines 43-9 are blazingly
happy: 'Laughter as a metaphor for bright colour or sparkling light is conventional
enough, but to make the house laugh at a scent, so that the visual picture is merged with
an element of sheer fantasy, and to make the scent so gorgeous that it is like a caressing
touch – this is indeed dazzling.' (Jenkyns 109). The familiar doom-laden reference to
Euripides' (and Ennius') *Medea* at the beginning of the poem is seen as sinister by
Bramble, but is well explained by Jenkyns as the poet's use of the 'colour' of an earlier
poet without automatically assuming his 'intention' as well.

The seeds of the pessimistic view had already been planted, in Kinsey (1965), who
notes the ironic elements in the poet's depiction of the heroic age but draws a different
conclusion from Bramble. 'Catullus does not take the grief of the mothers ... seriously
because neither he nor his audience take the stories of the heroic age seriously. His
attitude is ... that ... of the realist ironically retelling a story found in some romantic
novel which no one regards as anything except light entertainment.' ((Kinsey (1965)
930). This jocular debunking of the heroic age is one interpretation of the text, but not
one that has found much favour as it stands. Curran (1969) agrees that the poet's
depiction of the Heroic Age is ironic, but urges a more judicious judgement: 'Catullus'
attitude is a combination of a nostalgia for the glamour of the heroic world with an ironic
realisation that it is only an irrelevant dream ... Myth becomes a metaphor for the
present, an unpleasant present but, as the poem as a whole declares, it was never any
better.' (Curran (1969) 191-2).

Over against this is the argument of Putnam, who in an influential article (1961) urged
that Catullus was voicing his own anguish in his relationship with Lesbia in ths poem:
Putnam finds echoes of the poem in various of the 'autobiographical' shorter poems and
concludes that the poem is a 'personal statement', a sort of *roman à clef* which allows the
poet the disguise inside which he can indulge a moralising coda which he would have
found difficult *in propria persona*. The difficulty with this, as with all such documentary
interpretations, is simply that it demands the foreknowledge of the reader to understand
the poem. If our appreciation of this text is dependent on being intimate with the poet's
unhappy love-life, then one wonders why the poet did not make this more explicit and
accessible to the reader. The epilogue was the ideal opportunity to grind the personal
axes, but instead the poet here brings out instances of misbehaviour which elude the most
energetic detective-work in placing in contemporary Rome, let alone in Catullus' own
life. It is in this respect that Konstan's attempt to see the poem as an 'indictment of
Rome' falls down. It is not that the 'negative voices' in the text are not there – simply
that it reduces the text to a programme which would leave it a great deal less ambitious and
less successful than it is. Furthermore, the moralist using the poem as a stick with which
to beat contemporary society would have picked a more appropriate set of crimes to
shame contemporary Rome than the farrago of sexual and familial misdemeanours we find
here: surely the sort of critique which we find in Lucretius (who *does* attack luxury (2.20-
36) and political ambition (3.995-1002) and corruption (3. 59-73)) would have been
exactly the style and the material needed here – if that was the poet's intention.

There is undoubtedly a case for the 'pessimistic' view of the poem, then, but by itself
it will not suffice. This poetry is marked by coherences (already noted) and contrasts,
such as the use of tragedy in writing epyllion, or setting the happy wedding of Thetis

against the backdrop of the unhappy amour of Ariadne: above all, this is a poem of surprises where the reader is kept on his toes by the poet's refusal to supply the expected – the poem opens as if it is about the Argonauts but goes on to depict the wedding of Peleus and Thetis, the wedding-song is sung by the grotesque Parcae and is about the brutal future of their unborn son and not about their present happiness, the wedding-couch is decorated with a tapestry in dubious taste for the occasion, the coda of the poem is an unexpected account of why gods no longer consort with humans, full of sinister moral allusions, the indulgence of Ariadne's grief at enormous length deludes the audience out of expecting the depicted denouement in her salvation by Bacchus. Any interpretation of this text must take account of this constant shifting perspective, this self-conscious playing with the reader's expectations and sensitivities.

We must also be careful of judging the poem in anachronistic terms. The tale of Ariadne, for instance, is undoubtedly sad but has a happier ending which the viewer of the tapestry could see and the reader of the poem will soon be shown. The wrong done to her is real and her grief is genuine – but she gets ample revenge (albeit at the expense of the innocent Aegeus) and ends up married to a glorious god rather than to a fickle human. The pain is made bearable by the denouement. The result is something akin to the terrible 'Lying Tale' told by Odysseus to his father in the final book of Homer's *Odyssey*, where the old man is teased by his disguised son with a deceitful tale that his son is dead, only to find that his son is there all the time unrecognised telling the tale. This sort of teasing seems cruel to us, perhaps, but has the artistic effect of both dramatic irony (we and one character know something which another character does not) and also enhanced joy when the truth is told and the reunion is effected. The 'teasing' element in the tale of Ariadne is well-played out. Certainly, she is unhappy and laments her human lover's faithlessness – but we can smile at her misfortune knowing that she (like Peleus) has a divine lover waiting for her who will put everything to rights. This must to some extent give the lie to the 'pessimistic' critics who see her as a dark cloud on the wedding – although the poet does not forecast the future happiness of Bacchus and Ariadne as such a view could hardly be portrayed on the tapestry. The grief will become joy, the solitude and silence (186-7) is swiftly to be shattered when the Bacchic troupe roars into view: and all through the magic of Art.

If Ariadne is a sad woman about to be made happy, Thetis is the opposite: Homer describes Thetis as 'extremely reluctant' to marry Peleus (*Iliad* 18.434: Clausen (1982) 18) and had to be wrestled into it. Apollonius (4. 865-79) has her leave Peleus immediately after the birth of Achilles, who was brought up by centaur foster-parents but still 'longed for Thetis' milk' (Hunter (1991) 255 citing Apollonius 4. 813) and even suggesting that the name Achilles may be derived from the Greek *a-cheilos*, 'the one who did not bring his lips to his mother's breast'). In Homer's *Iliad* Achilles says of his father: 'he outshone all men for riches ... the gods gave him, a mortal man, a goddess for a wife: but even on him did the god pile suffering, for he had no generation of strong sons, but only one doomed child, and I give him no thought as he grows old ... ' (24. 534-40; cf. 19. 334-7)) Homer paints a very intimate picture of the relationship between Thetis and her son (e.g. *Iliad* 18.67-144), but the marriage of Peleus and Thetis was not harmonious in many ancient accounts of the tale except this one (Pindar for example praises Peleus' good fortune but recognises both the character of his wife (*Isthmian* 8.25-32), the struggle for her hand (*Nemean* 3.35f, 4.62ff) and the grief Peleus suffered in

losing his only son (*Pythian* 3.87ff)). Catullus does not prophesy the future of the happy
couple, contenting himself with the forecast of the deeds of their son Achilles, and the
resulting texture of his comments about the wedding match itself sound oddly
disingenuous (19-21, 334-6) in their naive simplicity. Even the chronology of the myth
is reversed: in most accounts, the wedding of Peleus and Thetis predates the voyage of the
Argo by a long time. Catullus' conflation of the voyage of the Argo and the marriage of
Peleus and Thetis allows him to play on the similarity between this couple and the tragic
pairing of Jason and Medea – a similarity played on by the echoes of Euripides' and
Ennius' *Medea* in the opening lines and by the resemblance between Catullus' Ariadne and
Apollonius' Medea. It does however allow the idyll of the wedding of Peleus and Thetis to
give way to the epic carnage of the Homeric hero Achilles and the tragic figure of
Polyxena, the narrative enlivened by outpourings of highly charged rhetoric, the text
then becoming a self-conscious exploration of generic boundaries which (again) shows
the magic transforming power of Art.

Jenkyns ((1982) 85-150) sees the artistic qualities in this text better than anyone and
shows well how the text resists reductive explanation. He urges comparison with the cult
of Dandyism and the aesthetics of *l'art pour l'art*, seeing the poem as an invitation into a
world of brilliance and colour and light. I would like to take this argument further.

Catullus is using the clash between the brilliant pleasure of the poetry and the (at
times) disagreeable details of the narrative to enhance the status of the text as a work of
art. The poet plants a 'pessimistic' view of love (as depicted in the plight of Ariadne), of
family life (as seen in Theseus and his father, in Ariadne and her 'brother' the Minotaur),
and of religion (in the poet's assertion that the gods have now given up all contact with
humanity because of our wickedness) and ends up with a gloomy conclusion. The only
'moral' inference from this which can be drawn is that none of these things is reliable as
an ethical ideal and that in fact the only ideals which could be entertained are aesthetic
ones, of poetry in particular. The 'epilogue' with which the poem ends is a familiar form
of personal closure* of a poetic text (see parallels in the commentary *ad loc*), bringing
the mythical past firmly back into the present, putting the poet's signature on the
narrative in a way which is self-referential and ironic. The sins which Catullus lists are
difficult to pin down to specific sinners (as shown by the wildly divergent views of
scholars on the respective culprits) and amount to a form of contrast between the heroic
past and the unheroic present which however fails to convince the reader with respect to
either the past or the present (fratricide, for instance, being the offence which Ariadne
assisted in to her cost but is named as a 'modern' vice). The very imperfection of the
subject-matter casts a satisfying glow back upon the perfection of the means of its
exposition and elevates the poet not as a moral Jeremiah casting abuse at his
contemporaries but as an aesthete who has found a way through the impure dross even of
the 'heroic' age (let alone his own age) to produce out of it all a pearl of perfection.

1-7 The opening sentence contains a typical piece of Alexandrian learning and allusion:
the pine trees 'born from Pelion's head' remind us of the goddess Athene was born from
Jupiter's head and this oblique image is to be deciphered by the reader as referring to the
ship *Argo* made from these trees. Equally striking is the element of surprise in the very
idea that pine trees can be born on the top of a mountain and later be swimming through

the waves; throughout the poem there is a sense of the 'monstrosity' of such perversion of nature, which allows the poet to enjoy teasing synecdoches* such as line 6 ('to run the salt ways on a swift poop'). The opening five lines contain six proper names, both to set the scene firmly for the reader and also to conjure up the world of legend in which this tale will unfold.

1   **Once ...** : the legendary, almost fairy-tale beginning locates the tale in the heroic past; and the repeated use of 'they say' or 'it is said' (1, 19, 76, 124, 212) also distances the narrator from his subject-matter in a lightly ironic manner typical of Callimachus (see fr.612 Pf ('I sing nothing which is not attested'), *Hymn* 5.56 ('not my words, but those of others'))

3   **Phasis** is the chief river in Colchis, flowing from the Caucasus mountains into the Black Sea. This line is the first of the 30 lines in this poem which have a spondaic fifth foot – a mannerism common to the poets of the generation, if Cicero is to believed (*Letters to Atticus* 7.2.1). The effect of such a rhythm is to slow down the pace of the line, especially when (as here) the fourth foot is also (unusually) spondaic, suggestive perhaps of the long journey to be made even when the ship was 'running'. The line is in fact forged from three lines of Apollonius Rhodius ('the streams of Phasis' (2. 1277-8) and 'belonging to Aeetes' (2. 1279)): the Greek names sandwich the rest of the line.

4-5   **chosen young men:** The Argonauts sailed from Greece to Colchis (eastern end of the Black Sea) in search of the Golden Fleece from King Aeetes: their leader was Jason, and his success in the enterprise was only secured with the help of Medea, the king's daughter, whom Jason took back to Greece and then abandoned in Corinth. The echo here of the treatment of Medea with that of Ariadne will be stressed as the poem unfolds, especially as Medea slew her brother.

        strength ... young: The second phrase is strictly unnecessary, being a decoration of the first: this kind of repetition is expansive and effective, part of the Homeric tradition of story-telling with its formulaic epithets, and sets Catullus in the epic tradition. There is something very appropriate about the poet describing the youths (literally) as the 'oak of Argive youth' – a metaphor indicating their choice quality but also summoning up the image of oak men sailing in pine trees.

6   **salt straits:** an epic synecdoche* for the sea, as *puppi* (literally 'poop deck') is synecdoche for 'ship'.

7   **sweeping ... fir-wood:** The sentence finishes with a flourish: the men are sweeping the sky blue plains with their fir-wood palms: almost a 'Golden Line' (adjective, adjective, verb, noun, noun, as at 59, 129, 163, 235, 351) but the second adjective and the verb are here inverted. The palms are metaphorical* for 'oars', *abiegnis* giving us the detail of the wood used for them which was not the same as that of the ship.

8   **the goddess:** Athene, the 'citadel' in question being the Acropolis of Athens. The Argonauts need divine help not only in building the ships but also in protecting their home-towns while they are away winning the fleece.

9   **she herself:** *ipsa* is somewhat surprising in the light of the usual tradition that Argus made the ship under Athene's guidance (Apollonius of Rhodes 1.18-19, 111-2). The quality of the ship is brought out by the fact that it can 'fly' even

when the breeze is only 'light', the metaphor *currus* (only here in extant Latin applied to a ship, althought the phrase 'chariot of the sea' is found in Greek) indicating that it is as swift as a chariot.

10   **web:** *texta* is a metaphor* drawn from weaving, in which the crossing of stitches is compared to the crossing of beams: the theme of weaving is important in the later depiction of the tapestry narrating Ariadne's plight. The metaphor also (again) stresses the enormity of the task – weaving with ... *pine trees* is something only a god could do.

11   **Amphitrite:** a Nereid, wife of Poseidon, and so stands by metonymy* for the sea. The reason for the circumlocution is not simply variation or erudition; it also sets up a theme of femininity being abused – in this case the sea by the ship, then the nymphs by the gaze of the sailors, finally of course the abuse of Ariadne by the 'perfidious sailor' Theseus. *prima* lands the poet in chronological difficulties, given the tradition that the Argo was the first ship ever to sail; for if the *Argo* was the first ship ever to sail, but Peleus has a tapestry of Theseus' voyage on his marriage-bed, then when did Theseus sail? Immediately after the *Argo* but before the wedding? But the Athenians had been 'in the habit of' (line 79) sending ships to Crete before Theseus went on his voyage, and the poet later uses the word *priscis* to describe the figures on the tapestry.

    imbuit is a surprising word to use here: its basic meaning is to 'drench' and it then has the sense of our 'baptise' 'initiate', usually and most obviously used of the first wetting of a new boat or new oars (e.g.4.17). It is paradoxical here to suggest that they 'wet' the sea (which is already wet) to introduce it to sailing.

12-13   **ploughed:** The perverse violence done to Amphitrite is well evoked by the strong verb *proscidit* ('ploughed', an action inappropriate for the sea) the general movement of the sea brought out by the mention of winds, the twisting of the waters with the oars and the consequent foaming waves. Note here how *aequor* means any plain surface, and so with *proscidit* we receive a metaphor of 'ploughing a field'. 'Man not only makes the trees of the mountain forest swim, but also ploughs the sea like a new field.' (Curran 176) *torta* is perhaps a metaphor for the action of curling-tongs (oars) to curl the waves of the sea, as Quinn suggests.

14-18 The sea-nymphs appear, never having seen ships before; one of them is Thetis, who falls in love with one of the sailors, Peleus. In Homer the funeral of Achilles (son of Thetis) is described to him: 'your mother, on hearing the news, came out of the sea, with immortal sea-girls all around her' (*Odyssey* 24. 47-8). Similarly, Thetis stirs up the Nereids and emerges from the sea to comfort her son weeping for Patroclus (*Iliad* 18.65ff)

14   The line cleverly leaves the key words until the end: 'out of the white swell of the sea they raised ... *faces*, watery Nereids ... ' The reader picks out the identity of the vision as slowly as the sailors did.

15   **prodigy:** *monstrum* conveys the notion of 'omen, portent' and is elsewhere used of the wooden horse at Troy (Vergil *Aeneid* 2. 245) and Cleopatra (Horace *Odes* 1.37.21). The ship is portentous in many ways – it presages the future of navigation, the marriage of Peleus and Thetis, the birth of Achilles and the deaths he will cause etc. What are effective here is the mutual wonder – no doubt the

nymphs are seen as *monstra* just as much as the ship is – and the slow gazing four-word line (one of very few in this poem – cf. 77, 115, 319 and none at all in the other poems), complete with fifth-foot spondee.

16-18 **On that day ... :**   The poet dwells on the vision of the nymphs. The insertion of *haud* (Bergk) is the most plausible correction of the mss reading: Goold's *haud ante alia* would suggest simply that this was the first time that sailors saw nymphs (but now it is commonplace), whereas Bergk's *atque haud alia* would mean 'never before or since', which ties in better with the epilogue's assertion that gods do not allow themselves to be seen any more (408).

17 **with their eyes:**   *oculis* is of course unnecessary but adds to the wonder and reinforces the idea of seeing already connoted in *viderunt* and also in the periphrasis *luce* ('light' meaning 'day'). Nor is it enough that mortal men saw nymphs, but they saw them naked – the poet expresses this as a general term first ('with bared body') before going for the specific point of focus in their breasts.

18 **breasts:**   *nutricum* is a surprising word to use for 'breasts': the word means 'wet-nurse' and may be an elaborate pun derived from Greek – the Greek words *titthos* (breast) and *titthe* (wet-nurse) both have the genitive plural *titthon*, an effect which the poet attempts to reproduce in Latin. The thematic relevance of breasts is important later in the poet's references to the milky breasts of Ariadne (65, ironic, as she has no possibility of rearing children) and again to the dried out breasts of the mothers whose sons Achilles will kill (351). Cairns (1984) notes that in Artemidorus 2.37-8 it is stated that a dream of Aphrodite emerging from the sea and naked to the waist was a particularly good omen for sea-farers. Closer to the present passage is Apollonius 4.940 where the Nereids reveal their bare legs (pointed out by Hunter (1991) 254).

19-21 **Then ... then ... then:**   The threefold repetition with polyptoton* of *tum Theti-* over these lines is emphatic and adds to the incantatory effect of the narrative. The two names are immediately juxtaposed in 19, just as the love of the two in the story is immediate.

20 **human:**   *humanos* picks up the mild outrage of *mortales* in line 17; though he was mortal, Thetis did not spurn him.

21 **father himself:**   The background to this is well-known: Jupiter (the 'father himself') wanted Thetis himself until Prometheus (or, in Pindar *Isthmian* 8, Themis) told him that the child of Thetis was destined to be greater than his father (Aeschylus *Prometheus Bound* 911ff).

22 **O heroes ... :**   The poet moves into apostrophe*, first of the race of heroes (22-4) and then of Peleus himself (25-30) This device was known in Greek as a *makarismos*, an exclamation expressing the degree of happiness enjoyed by the addressee: for a similar address to an individual see poem 51, to a group of people see Vergil *Georgics* 2. 458-74.   *saeclorum tempore* ('at that time of the generations') looks like a pleonasm* in the grand hymnic manner but actually reveals a debt to the 'Golden race' theory found in Hesiod *Works and Days* where the golden race gives way to the silver race, and so on: after the bronze race had wiped themselves out there came the race of heroes who were actually better than the bronze or silver races. Only the golden race surpassed them in quality of life;

and the poet plays with the pastoral idealism of typical 'golden age' themes later on.

23   **race of gods:**   *deum genus* may perhaps have been prompted (as Fordyce suggests) by Hesiod's phrase 'the divine race of heroic men' (*Works and Days* 159): the word 'hero' commonly came to indicate people who had one divine and one human parent (e.g. Hercules, Aeneas, Achilles) who thus rank midway between gods and men. The Veronese Scholiast on Vergil *Aeneid* 5.80 quotes this passage as *salvete deum gens o bona matrum progenies salvete iter ...* which demands the insertion of line 23b (missing from the manuscripts). The half-line cannot be recovered to finish 23b, and the most plausible filler is that of Peerlkamp who writes the line:

> *progenies, salvete iter<um salvete bonarum>.*

24   **often:** The sentiment is not implemented as they are not so addressed again, but the formula is common enough in hymns (see e.g. Homeric Hymn 3.546). Note here the inverted repetition of *vos ego ... meo vos*.

25   **wedding:** *taedis* ('wedding torches') here stands by synecdoche* for 'wedding'.

26   **mainstay:** *columen* is a metaphor for 'protector'. The privilege accorded to Peleus is emphasised by the epanalepsis* of *ipse/ipse* framed by the pair *Iuppiter ... divum genitor*. As we have seen (21n) Jupiter had very good reasons for 'giving up his love'.

28-30 **Was it ... ?:** The apostrophe ends with rhetorical questions with anaphora* of *tene*. Thetis was the child of Nereus and Doris (his sister), who were both children of Tethys and her brother Oceanus. In this passage the permission for the match seems to have been given by the grandparents rather than the parents, the poet showing his erudition in producing the names.

31-42 The Wedding guests arrive. The predominant tense of the verbs in this section is present, after the initial *advenere* (32). The theme of brightness is strongly established (*luces*) at the start and picked up again in 44-49.

31   **longed-for:** *optatae* picks up *optato* from 22 and remains a constant theme of the poem, where (e.g.) Peleus and Thetis have been longing for this day – and also Ariadne longs for Theseus, Aegeus longs for Theseus, the Fates sing of the future in terms which are alternately desirable and horrible. The tension between hope and reality is one of the poignant themes of this text.

32-3   **throngs:** The whole of Thessaly crowds into the palace just as the words overspill the line in enjambement*. Note here how the same statement is made twice: first in a 'straight' neutral tone and then with more telling description. *domus* becomes *regia*, *frequentat* becomes *oppletur*, *conventu* becomes *laetanti coetu*.

34   **gifts:** The humans' gifts are not described, whereas the gifts of the gods are revealed in detail (279ff).

35   **Cieros:** the mss read *siros* which would suggest Scyros, an island lying in the Aegean and geographically inappropriate here in a catalogue of Thessalian towns. The only connection of Scyros with our story is that it was there that Achilles' mother tried to hide her son to prevent him going to Troy: the sort of connection

which would prompt a learned scribe to 'correct' *siros* to Scyros, but not likely to be correct.

35-7 Cieros, Crannon, Larisa and Pharsalus were towns in Thessaly. Phthia is famous as the birthplace of Achilles and is in the south of Thessaly, while Tempe (the valley of the river Peneus between the mountains Ossa and Olympus) is actually in the north. For the proverbial beauty of Tempe see Theocritus 1.67, Horace *Odes* 1.7.4, Ovid *Metamorphoses* 1. 568-73: what is emphasised here is that for the wedding of Peleus and Thetis people will leave even Tempe behind. The poet produces variation in his list of names: note the chiastic* *Crannonisque domos ... moenia Larisaea* and the repetition of *Pharsalum ... Pharsalia,* the names being in key positions at the beginning of the line and immediately after the caesura. The verbs are also in two pairs: *deseritur ... linquunt* on the one hand, *coeunt ... frequentant* on the other.

38-42 The neglect of agriculture as the farmers leave their land to go to the wedding. Catullus has taken the familiar 'golden age' theme of men not working the land (Tibullus 2.1.5-7, Vergil *Eclogues* 4.40-1 etc) but ends his picture of rural idleness with detail much less glamorous as the ploughs rust away. The whole vignette is of course hyperbolic: the length of time it takes to attend a wedding is hardly enough to see all this ruin in the fields, and Catullus' purpose is therefore either playfully ironic (sending up a literary theme) or else darkly moralistic (as urged by Bramble). The style of the lines is moreover highly organised: note the extreme assonances* and alliterations* of (e.g.) *mollescunt colla ... humilis curvis purgatur* etc.

38   **grow soft:** *mollescunt* i.e. because the bullocks are no longer pulling the plough and so their hardened necks grow soft again.

39   **low-growing:** Vines were often made to grow supported on trees (as in 62. 49-55), but sometimes as here were allowed to grow low towards the ground, when the weeds around them would need clearing.

40   As Fordyce notes, the four spondees which begin this line well express the lumbering effort of the bulls.

41   **pruners' hook:** the pruners have to thin out the shade of trees to allow the sunlight to reach the grapes, especially if the vines are growing up the trees.

42   Like line 7, almost a 'golden line'.

43-49 **The master's house:** Quinn well compares the sequence to that of foreshortening the distance in a work of art: first we see the crowded palace, then 'the crowds which stream towards it, then the deserted countryside; lastly we follow the crowds in the palace through the scenes of splendour to the centre-piece, the marriage-bed.' The description of the palace is one of lavish and extravagant wealth – again, it is unlcear whether the poet intends us to feel envy, disgust or simply admiration for this affluence. There is no doubt about the contempt which Catullus' contemporary Epicureans would have felt – see the sneering mockery of precisely this sort of wealth at Lucretius 2. 20-36.

43   **master's:** *ipse,* as often, means here 'the master'. *recessit* is also an artistic term, denoting the receding of the palace away from the eye of the beholder, and the word *regia* itself 'recedes' (by enjambement*) into the next line.

44-6 **brilliant ... gleaming:** the poet stresses the idea of brightness and light with the sequence: *fulgenti splendent auro ... argento candet ebur ... collucent ... splendida.* The shining brightness in the palace contrasts with the scaly rust in the fields; some of the imagery is tautologous* – the *regia* has *regali gaza,* for instance.

46 **rejoices:** *gaudet* is a nice use of the pathetic fallacy*, as the house shares the joy of its guests; compare the joy and laughter of Lake Sirmio in 31.12-14.

47-9 **wedding-couch:** The marriage-bed is the climax of this description: the *lectus genialis* was placed in the atrium during and after a Roman wedding: the word *pulvinar* connotes the couch reserved for the images of gods, and is of course appropriate here for the wedding of a goddess.

48-9 **Indian ... purple ... crimson:** The colour contrast is pleasing: the bed adorned with Indian tooth (i.e. white) is covered with a purple bed-spread. The dye *purpura* (derived from the *conchylus* i.e. the shellfish *murex brandaris*) denotes both the colour and also the wealth of its owner, being a universal symbol of affluence and status in the ancient world – senators for example wore togas with a purple stripe upon them.

50-266 ECPHRASIS.

We now move to the *ecphrasis*, the story within the story, the depiction on the tapestry of Ariadne abandoned by Theseus on the island of Naxos. As will immediately be obvious, the poet does not tell the tale in strictly chronological sequence. The tale of Ariadne in 'fact' went as follows:

1. Theseus leaves Athens
2. Theseus meets Ariadne and slays the minotaur
3. Theseus takes Ariadne away and abandons her
4. Ariadne awakes, abandoned.
5. Ariadne curses Theseus
6. Theseus forgets to change the sails and causes his father's death.
7. Bacchus rescues Ariadne

The order in the poem is: 4, 2, 3, 5, 1, 6,7.

The links between the outer and the inner story are many and various – a male mortal (Peleus) marries a goddess, a female mortal (Ariadne) ends up being married to a god (Bacchus): happy love of the outer story is contrasted with (temporarily) unhappy love, wedding oaths are kept by Peleus but broken by Theseus, and so on. The beginning (50-1) and the end (265-6) of the section is clearly marked by similar wording, a form of rhetorical closure imitated also in the beginning and ending of the two speeches within the ecphrasis (Ariadne's lament 130-1, 202 and Aegeus' speech 213-4, 238-40).

In ancient criticism the term *ecphrasis* meant any 'poetic or rhetorical description, including descriptions of landscape (*topothesia*), buildings, battles and storms.' (Laird (1993) 18). In modern criticism the term tends to be used especially of the set-piece description of a visual work of art, such as the depiction of the Shield of Achilles (Homer *Iliad* 18. 478-613), the mantle of Jason (Apollonius Rhodius 1.730-767), the shield of Aeneas (Vergil *Aeneid* 8. 608-731). In crudely simply terms, this story 'freezes' the narrative of Peleus and Thetis on their wedding day in order to 'unfreeze' a decoration observed by the human guests at that wedding: when the *ecphrasis* is over the wedding 'unfreezes' and continues (267ff) directly from 49, as if nothing has happened.

The fascinating aspect of this particular *ecphrasis* is just how 'disobedient' it is, in Laird's terminology: i.e. it does not content itself with describing what a real picture before the poet's eyes could reasonably show but goes beyond the picture to a narrative prompted by it. It is not simply that the poet gives us flashbacks of explanatory narrative material (*nam perhibent* ... (76) etc): nor that the poet conveys sound-effects, thought-processes, and feelings; not even that the two-dimensional silent characters in this picture utter long speeches which no painter could ever have conveyed and which no other ancient *ecphrasis* ever attempted. The poet turns the spatial distance between Ariadne and Bacchus into a narrative/temporal distance between her waking up alone and abandoned to the point where she is about to be rescued. This deliberate confounding of one artistic illusion by subverting it into another is one of the most strikingly original features of the whole poem. To underline this process the poet interrupts the time-sequence with flashbacks and then delays the arrival of Bacchus – which on the tapestry is of course there 'all along' – leaving the reader to deduce that on the picture the heroine had her back to the saving god. To make the artistic contrast of temporal/audible narrative and static mute visualisation all the more pregnant, the poet deliberately juxtaposes references to the sounds of the 'narrative' with a reminder of the (obviously silent) 'picture' (the Bacchic troupe is a band playing and shouting (255-64) followed immediately by the reminder that this noisy scene is in fact a silent picture (265), discussed by Laird (1993) 21) and leaves teasing reminders of the pictorial quality of the tale paradoxically in the words which the (silent) characters speak ('all is silent' complains Ariadne 186) alongside descriptions of the noises to be heard (e.g. the shore is *fluentisono* (52)).

The poet, it might be urged, is using the tradition of the *ecphrasis* simply as a literary convention to tack two stories together. Rather as later on Ovid uses more or less successful connections to link tales in his *Metamorphoses*, so here Catullus wishes to tell the tale of Ariadne inside the tale of Peleus and uses this literary device to effect it. Nobody is fooled by this trick and Catullus mocks himself several times for doing so, both implicitly (the 'sound effects' listed above) and explicitly (the apology for digressing at 116-7 followed by a digression). The poet's use of the *ecphrasis* shows that he is a *doctus poeta* indeed, well versed in the Alexandrian artifices of poets such as Callimachus and aiming to tickle the palate of his cultivated, equally *doctus* readership with this oblique and self-referential bow to the artistry of the past.

There is, however, more to it than that. Catullus <u>is</u> using the artistry of the past in a learned and skilful manner, of course, and his purpose <u>is</u> primarily aesthetic rather than ethical or protreptic*: but the blurring of the distinction between genres and then the confounding of narrative and pictorial, of static and dynamic, of tale and picture is intended to do more than simply entertain readers thirsty for novelty. The whole poem is cast into doubt as itself a limited expression of verbal signs, whose significance is forever in flux and yet whose magic can convey the past and even bring the dead to life. The *ecphrasis* shows us the dead image animated: the poem as a whole similarly aims to animate the irrecoverably past world of legend and mythology, of gods walking with men and heroes slaying their enemies like a man ploughing a field, the idyll of love, the epic of warfare and the tragedy of bloodshed. The irony of course is that the pictorial silent characters do all the talking, while the 'real' characters (Thetis, Jupiter, Peleus etc) are in fact silent until we get to the Parcae who paint a vision of the future in words, their prophecy taking over the narrative voice (marked by the refrain) from the poet. Often the reader has the impression that the whole text is a series of 'tableaux' (as Quinn urges), set-piece descriptions of (e.g.) love at first sight, a wedding feast, a procession of gods. The mastery of narrative perspective is such that the reader might well wonder whether the distinction between *ecphrasis* and *non-ecphrasis* is itself false, and that far from being merely a way of cobbling together two tales this device holds the key to the whole poem as an exercise in poetic artistry inviting admiration and pleasure by the sheer mastery of form, content and narrative skill.

51   **heroisms ... great:** The language here is ironic. The only man who qualifies for the title 'hero' in this tale is Theseus, and his behaviour is anything but heroic. Quinn has a problem with the poet's ironic stance towards the past, but the apostrophe* at 22-30 is all part of the 'heroic' mood which the next episode will shatter, while the epilogue 384-408 is itself hardly to be taken at face value as a recommendation of the past over the present.

52-57 **gazing forward ... :** The eye fixes first upon the island, then on Theseus sailing away, and only then on Ariadne, who is not named until line 54; she then monopolises attention for the rest of the sentence.

52   **Dia:** is the island where, according to Homer (*Odyssey* 11.321) Ariadne was killed on her way from Crete to Athens, a different version of the legend from the one we are reading here. In classical times it was called Naxos. The compound adjective *fluentisono* is one of several in the poem (cf. *clarisonus* 320, *raucisonus* 263; such compounds are common in Lucretius). There is of course no way in which a pictorial representation of a scene can convey sounds – part of the convention of the *ecphrasis* is that it fleshes out the limitations of the pictorial form with details of non-visual aspects of the scene. *prospectans* on the other hand is quite clearly an indication of the direction in which Ariadne is facing – out to sea looking at Theseus' departing ship.

53   The alliteration* of *Th ... c ... c ... c ... c ... t* is striking.

54-5   **uncontrolled madness:** *indomitos ... furores* is almost a tautology, as it is in the nature of *furor* (madness, love, passion) to be *indomitus* (unrestrained). What gives the word *furor* added edge here is the following line; 'nor does she believe that she is seeing what she sees' picks up the strong theme found in Lucretius that romantic love is a form of hallucination in which the lover does not see the truth about his beloved (4. 1037-1287, esp. 1153-76). Catullus, in a playful allusion to this idea, has Ariadne full of *furor* and hence blinded with passion but because of her passion she does not yet believe her eyes although as a matter of fact they are telling her the truth: she cannot yet believe what is true, but has all along believed the lies that Theseus has spun her. This theme of truth and deception is further amplified in *fallaci* (56).

57   **lonely:** *sola* is an example of transferred epithet (hypallage*) – it is not the sand which is lonely but the girl who is standing upon it. The poet manages to juxtapose the three strong adjectives *desertam ... sola miseram* in the first half of the line, thus giving the greatest possible emphasis to the girl's plight.

58 The young man's rapid flight is well evoked by the sequence of dactyls and the uneven rhythm of the ending of the line, where *pellit vada remis* produces clash of ictus and accent at a point in the verse where ictus and accent normally coincide.

Being *immemor* is later to prove Theseus' undoing (200-250).

59 **leaving ... storm:** A neat combination of natural description and metaphor* in a 'golden line': mention of a windy storm is natural at the seashore, but here we also have a literary cliché of faithless words being cast on the winds – cf. 142, 70.4.

60 **seaweed:** a vivid detail; note also the affectionate diminutive *ocellis*.

61-2 **statue ... tosses:** A paradoxical phrase: a static work of art (a picture) shows a woman frozen like a statue – but it is a statue of a Bacchant, who is the least static of all women, and her surface immobility hides deep emotional turmoil underneath – and then we see her clothes falling off in sequence. The mention of the Bacchant is of course ironic in view of her later salvation by Bacchus himself, and the lament *eheu* may be either a reminder of, or in ironic contrast to, the cry of Bacchic joy *evoe* (255 Laird (1993) 21). Note here the epanalepsis* of *prospicit* (cf. 26n) and the appropriate use of *fluctuat* to describe the flood of feelings she has – a word well suited to the swelling and tossing of the sea.

63-7 **not keeping ... veiled:** Ariadne's loss of her clothes is partly ironically futile sexual signalling to a departing lover, partly unconscious sexual signalling to a new lover whom she cannot see (Bacchus), partly an expression of her grief that she does not care about looking 'decent', exactly as is done by Andromache lamenting at Homer *Iliad* 22. 468-70. The clothes are described as 'delicate' and 'light' – their removal being thus easier and the eroticism enhanced.

63 **blonde:** *flavo* most heroes and heroines have blonde/fair hair; see 66.62, 68.130 and notes.

The *mitra* was a bonnet, fastened with ribbons under the chin, associated with the East.

63-5 **veiled:** A general statement (her torso no longer clothed) followed by a specific focus (her milky breasts not bound) exactly as at 17-18. The breasts are 'milky' in an ironic statement of futility as they will have no chance of suckling Theseus' children; the *strophium* (also known as the *mamillare*) was the band tied around the body with a twist between the breasts. Nisbet (386), however, points out that *velatum* is probably wrong, as the group of lines 63-5 is perfectly balanced: each of the three lines has six words which perfectly correspond to a word in the other two lines (*non – non – non: retinens – contecta- vincta; mitram – amictu- strophio; subtilem – levi – tereti; vertice – pectus- papillas*) The exception is *flavo – velatum – lactentis*, where the two outer words denote colour while the middle term does not. Nisbet proposes therefore *variatum* to suggest the breasts lined and coloured with veins: this would point forward to *variabunt* in 351 (used there of the aged breasts of the Parcae) and would also neatly correspond to *flavo* and *lactentis* with a minimum of emendation.

66-7 **slipped right off:** The casting of her clothes – which would be a significant act for a Roman woman – was mocked by the waves which lapped them at her feet (*alludebant* has the element *ludus* in it).

68 **headband** ... : The poet picks up *mitra* from 63 and *amictus* from 64, adding the descriptive epithet *fluitantis* – most plausibly applied to the largest item of clothing named.

69-70 **all ... all ... all:** Note the tricolon* *toto* ... *toto* ... *tota* and the alliteration* of *pendebat perdita.* To add yet more emphasis the poet apostrophises Theseus.

71-5 Having shown the scene, the poet now begins to explain the background to it. The exclamation has no main verb, as the verbs are all in relative or temporal clauses.

71 **drove her mad:** *externavit* derives from *sterno* with the meaning 'drive out of the mind'.

72 **Erycina:** The 'lady of Eryx' is Venus who had a famous temple on Mt Eryx in Western Sicily, from where the cult spread to Rome: in Catullus' own day there was a temple of Venus Erycina in Rome itself. The metaphor* in *spinosas* ('thorny') is maintained by *serens* as we picture the goddess sowing thorns in the soil of Ariadne's heart.

73 **savage:** *ferox* is no insult at this stage – anybody who hopes to defeat the Minotaur needed to be so – but this man acts in the same way to his beloved as he did to his enemy.

74 **Piraeus:** the harbour of Athens. The rhythm of the ending of the line is again rough: a spondee and a strong caesura in the fifth-foot.

75 **Cretan:** Gortyn is in Crete, and the epithet comes to mean simply 'Cretan'. The proverbial injustice of King Minos was part of the Greek tradition (e.g. [Plato] *Minos* 318d-e) – and yet he ends up as the lawgiver in the Underworld. His wife Pasiphae fell in love and mated with a bull, conceiving the monstrous Minotaur which it was Theseus' purpose to kill. The epithet *iniusti* is perhaps more fitting in view of the human tax he demanded from Athens for the death of Androgeon, as explained next. *templa* is palaeographically more plausible as the correct reading behind the mss *tempta*: the word *templum* can simply mean an 'enclosure or building – hence palace' (Quinn), but it also strikes a nice oxymoron* with *iniusti.* Parthenius' emendation *tecta* loses this point.

76-79 **for ... :** this explains why Theseus was concerned with the Minotaur. *perhibent* again appeals to the tradition as witness (cf. 2n). Minos' son Androgeon was killed in Athens by rivals whom he had defeated at the Panathenaic Games; one version has it that he was killed by Theseus' own father Aegeus. Minos therefore besieged the city of Athens which held out quite successfully until it was beset by plague, when it submitted to terms. These terms were that the Athenians had to send seven young men and seven young women to the Minotaur in his labyrinth every year.

78-9 **chosen young men:** This recalls the phrase in line 4 describing the Argonauts. One wonders how these youths were 'chosen' – Vergil tells us the choice was by sortition (*Aeneid* 6.22). This and the following two lines all have fifth-foot spondees.

Cecrops: the legendary first king of Athens. Athens had got into the habit (*solitam esse*) of giving these people as 'dinner to the Minotaur' – the last few words conveying the stark truth in a brief compass.

80   **these evils:** Theseus' action is seen as heroic act of self-sacrifice seeking
either death or glory. Of course, if his father Aegeus had been the one to kill
Androgeon in the first place, then it would be only fitting that his son should go
out to exact revenge. The battlements are *angusta* – a telling reminder that little
Athens can not afford to lose its best youths.

82/3 **undead deaths:** *funera nec funera* is a paradox ('dead but not dead') especially in
the manner of Greek literature (e.g. Euripides *Alcestis* 521, *Iphigeneia in Tauris*
512, *Phoenissae* 272, mocked by Aristophanes (*Acharnians* 396)).

84   **light ... gentle:** The fragility of Theseus' quest is well evoked by the
syllepsis* of light craft and the gentle breezes which he was 'pressing on'.

85   **great-hearted:** Minos, having just been called the 'unjust king' is now given
the epithet *magnanimum* – the Latin equivalent of Homer's *megaletor* (*Iliad*
13.302, used sardonically of the Trojans at 21.55) which combines the meanings
'great-hearted' and also 'haughty' as found here in the two separate words
magnanimum ... superbas. At *Odyssey* 19.176 the epithet is applied to the
Cretans by Odysseus (in a lying tale to his wife Penelope).

86   **saw ... eye:** As often in ancient literature, the eyes are the doorway of sexual
desire: cf. Euripides *Hippolytus* 525-6 and especially Propertius 1.1.1 ('Cynthia
first captivated lovesick me with her little eyes').

87ff **soft ... pure ... :** The royal maiden enjoys a life of luxury and safety in sharp
contrast to the wild risk she takes for her lover. The poet almost implies that her
naiveté was a by-product of her sheltered life up to that time, her virginity (*castus*)
unprepared for the courting of Theseus, the long drawn-out childhood well evoked
in the leisurely relative clause over four lines (*quam ... colores*) and being sharply
terminated by her love at first sight.

87-8 **bed ... nurse:** Ariadne had a sweet-smelling bedroom symbolic of her
innocence, as had the (much less innocent) Helen in Homer *Odyssey* 4.121. The
bed does not literally 'feed' her of course, but the phrase conveys both her
virginity and her growing to maturity. Understandably, the poet does not name
Ariadne's infamous mother Pasiphae (see 75n) as that would ruin the atmosphere
of innocence so artfully built up here.

89   **Eurotas:** the river that runs by Sparta: Catullus specifies this particular river
presumably for some reason, but the only association the river has is with Helen
of Troy (cf. Ovid *Amores* 1.10.1), hardly a rôle-model for marital fidelity.

90   **colours:** *colores* is here synecdochic* for 'flowers'.

91-3 **blazing ... flame ... :** Her eyes are 'burning' with love, leading to her whole
body receiving the fire and then bursting into flames right down to the marrow of
her bones. The tricolon* form of the image of love as fire is thus sustained as far
as it can physically go in a hyperbolic* manner, assisted by the alliteration* and
enjambment* of *cuncto concepit corpore flammam funditus*. Note here the ironic
use of *concepit*; the only conception she received from Theseus was the fire of
love: cf. 198-9n. Similarly, Peleus (19) and Bacchus (253) also catch fire with
love.

94-5 **divine boy ... :** Apostrophe* of Cupid, complaining as does Apollonius of
Rhodes 4.445 ('wicked boy, source of great pain, great hatred for men ... ').
misere as often has the sense of 'love-sick' (Lucretius 4.1076 etc). Paradoxically

Love himself has a cruel heart in instilling these mad feelings (*furores* - on which see 54n) in others. The mixing of joys and sorrows is a common theme of divine providence; Venus does so at 68.18, and the twin jars of human fortune which Zeus dispenses to men allot their destined mixture of good and bad luck (Homer *Iliad* 24. 527-8)

96   **Golgi** and **Idalium** are both in Cyprus and famous as cult centres of Aphrodite/Venus.

97-8   **streams ... aflame:** A mixed metaphor* – Ariadne is 'aflame' but also being 'tossed on waves' of care.
        Theseus is 'fair-haired' as Ariadne herself (63)

99   **fears:** Ariadne's fears are for Theseus as he faces the Minotaur. Note the assonance of *corde timores*.

100   **paler than ... gold:** 'Ariadne, an olive-skinnned Mediterranean beauty, would naturally turn pale yellow (the colour of pure gold), rather than white, with fear.' (Quinn). There is also perhaps another oblique reference to the affluence of her upbringing.

102   **death or ... praise:** sounds like the rhetoric of warfare: 'either death or glory' is the typical heroic programme, and the enemy is here easily cast as a *saevum ... monstrum*.

103-4   **small gifts:** Ariadne made promises of offerings to the gods in return for Theseus' safety: these 'little gifts' (*munuscula* is an affectionate diminutive) were evidently not unpleasing to the gods – the juxtaposition of *ingrata ... frustra* stresses that. For details of the practice of making such *vota* see Ogilvie 37-9: such vows were often written down and attached to the statue of the god being invoked, whereas here Ariadne simply makes them secretly to herself 'with silent lip' (as her love for the stranger was of course disloyal to her father and her 'brother').

105-9   **just as ... :** An impressive simile* in the full epic manner, modelled on Apollonius Rhodius 4.1682-8 (and cf. Homer *Iliad* 13.389-93). The Taurus mountain range in Cilicia is chosen perhaps to suggest the word *taurus* (bull): the tree being laid out by the wind has anthropomorphic features – arms for branches (*bracchia*) and sweating bark (*sudanti*) – to confirm the parallel with the Minotaur. We see the tree struggling for two lines before being shown what is destroying it, and the decisive verb *eruit* comes in the most emphatic position at the end of the phrase but the beginning of the line. The labour to uproot it is well conveyed in the fifth-foot spondee *exturbata*, while the twisting movement of the wind is stressed with the juxtaposition of *turbo contorquens*. The final scene of devastation is appropriate for a fallen tree but of course hyperbolic* in the context of a single combat between man and monster; but it adds to the drama and the magnitude of the scene.

110-11   **laid out:** Theseus' victory is despatched quickly after this impressive simile. The monster is laid out just as the tree *prona cadit*, the monster shakes its horns just as the tree shook its branches, with the extra piquancy that the powerful agent of destruction in the simile is now useless to assist – the *turbo* has become merely *vanis ... ventis* on whom the bull relies *nequiquam*.

113   **thread:** Ariadne helped him find his way out of the labyrinth by giving him a
       ball of thread which he simply rewound to retrace his path.

114-5 The Latin well evokes the labyrinthine journey, the few long words (9 words in
       two lines) suggesting the long journey, line 115 – with the one weak third-foot
       caesura – also connoting the unbroken set of paths for Theseus to wander. The
       language is also expressive: *tecti ... error* is a striking phrase – the whole
       construction is one giant 'wandering', but simple observation will not help
       (*inobservabilis*).

116-23 **Why ... more?:** A familiar rhetorical trope (*quid plura?*), justifying the tale
       and also skipping over areas of the tale which he does not wish to tell at length,
       and returning to Ariadne on Naxos.

117-8 **daughter ... father:**   Ariadne's family bitterly regret her leaving – as does
       Ariadne herself now. Her father conspicuously fails to embrace her as do her sister
       and mother, whose grief is the greatest and the most fully explored – both the
       sister Phaedra and the mother Pasiphae being no strangers to dangerous love, of
       course; on Pasiphae see 75n, while Phaedra later on married Theseus and then fell
       disastrously in love with his son Hippolytus and took her life when he rejected her
       – as told in Euripides *Hippolytus* and Racine's *Phèdre*.

119   **grieved:**   The mss simply read *leta* at the end of this line: most editors print
       Lachmann's *laetabatur,* reasoning that this expresses the mixture of emotions
       proper in a mother happy to see her daughter in love but sad to see her leave home.
       If correct, this is the one reference to happiness in the whole sentence, and
       Conington's *lamentata est* ('she grieved') is more likely to be correct.

120   **sweet:**   *dulcis* is a common word in these poems, especially of happy love (cf.
       e.g. 66.6, 67.1, 68.106). Again, there is an ambiguity about the genitive *Thesei*:
       if objective it is accurate (she did love him), if subjective, it is merely wishful
       thinking. (cf. 19n).

121-3 **departed ... sleep:** The enormity of Theseus' crime is well expressed: he did
       not even tell her her fate but waited until she was 'tied up in sleep' and stole away.
       immemori means more than that he forgot to take her with him, but has the sense
       of 'deliberately neglectful' and is a *Leitmotif* of this whole section of the poem
       (see 58, 231, 248). *coniunx* is deliberately left to the end as the crowning insult.

124-31 The narrative returns to Ariadne on the beach, picking up the tale from 75.
Ariadne's first instinct is to climb the steep cliffs to keep Theseus' ship in view (126-7),
then when it has vanished over the horizon, to run into the water after it (128), but no
longer so self-forgetful as she was at 63-9, as she now lifts her dress clear of the water.

124   **they say:** *perhibent* is another reference to the legendary tradition – irony as
       this is part of the tale-telling itself. Notice the hyperbole* of *ardenti ... furentem*
       and then *imo e pectore.*

125   **piercing:**   *clarisonas* (cf. 320) is ironic as her words, however, eloquent and
       clear, cannot be heard by their addressee.

126   **mountains ... gaze:** she climbs up to a vantage point to keep Theseus' ship
       in view for as long as possible, but the object of her vision is almost all sea rather
       than ship, as is shown in 127 *pelagi vastos aestus.*

128   **trembling:** *tremuli* is elsewhere used of people: 61.51 *tremulus parens*, 17.13
       tremula patris in ulna, 68.142 *corpus tremulum* of old age, as of the Parcae at 307.
       The reader might expect it here to apply to Ariadne shaking with anger/fear: it in
       fact goes with *salis* used in metonymy* for the sea which moves in a regular up-
       and-down manner.

129   **bared:** the poet shows a flash of bare flesh again, but unlike the earlier occasion
       she is now conscious of the water and lifts her skirt up to avoid getting it wet –
       contrast 66-8 (Quinn). *nudatae* sounds enticing and recollects the loss of clothing
       of 63-7, but will only reveal the ... *surae* (the calf of the leg).

130   **sad:** *maestam*: cf. *tristem* (126). *extremis* is rather premature as she is not
       actually going to die (cf. 76. 18). Quinn explains: 'i.e. her last words as a mortal;
       when her lament is over she is rescued by Dionysus (see 251-3); there is an echo
       in Propertius 3.7.55'. It is thus an example of dramatic irony, the reader knowing
       more than the character and the 'narrator' at this point.

131   **icy little:** *frigidulos* is a pathetic diminutive (cf. 103, 3.18): the sobbing of
       singultus combined with the detail of her wet face is perhaps chilly because of the
       effects of wind and water together.

132-201 Ariadne's lament: the 'longest section of the poem' (Quinn), and of course
having no possible source in the tapestry being described. There is a similarity between
this speech and the soliloquy of the abandoned Palaestra in Plautus' *Rudens* 185ff, a
similarity at least of rhetoric: as in the dramatic context there is also irony here. For a
character to proclaim that she is all alone when she is in front of an audience there is what
Laird calls 'meta-theatrical irony' (Laird (1993) 28): similarly, for a figure in a picture
which is being avidly gazed at by the youth of Thessaly (267) to lament being alone, and
to be described as uttering a plangent lament to that effect, is irony raised to a higher
power. The context and some of the detail of her lament is familiar to us already from the
previous narrative, but the rhetoric allows the poet to do several things: firstly, to repeat
and reinforce the abandonment of Ariadne; secondly, to expand our vision of the narrative
with events in the past (e.g. Theseus' promise of marriage (139-41) and Ariadne's leaving
home (180-3)) and the future (e.g. her being eaten by wild beasts (152-3)) as well as
alternative scenarios of what could have been (160-3); thirdly to draw attention to the
contrast between the visual/spatial and the narrative/temporal in this *ecphrasis*. Earlier
the poet has animated the picture into a sequence of movement (126-30) as he will later
animate the picture into a sequence of sounds (251-64): here he freezes the picture into a
static position but animates the emotions and brings out the energy and passion locked
in a static imprisoned form.

132-4 **traitor ... :**   the epanalepsis* of *perfide*, combined with the stress on divine
       powers (*aris ... neglecto numine divum*) allies Ariadne and the gods who uphold
       oaths against the 'traitor'. Ariadne has been 'abducted' from her ancestral altars
       and Theseus has neglected the power of the gods – all pointing towards her rescue
       at the hands of a god.

134   **is this ... is this:** repetition of *sicine* from 132

135   **carry home:**   *portas* he carries a freight ... of broken promises. *devota* here
       means 'under curse'.

The point here is that his ship ought to carry Ariadne, but all it bears is the weight of broken promises and curses resulting from her abandonment. Note the high emotional use of *a!*.

136 **turning ... mind:** 'Turning the mind of ...' usually refers to men praying to gods, but is here used of Ariadne beseeching Theseus in vain. Note the enjambement* of 136-7. The catalogue of complaints builds up from *perfide ... immemor ... crudelis ... inmite*, this last having recently been used of Cupid (94). The sardonic tone is here evident: 'you had no *clementia* available at the time so as perhaps to be prepared to consider (*vellet*) taking pity on me ... ' She speaks with sarcasm, as if what she was asking was a favour when in fact it was his duty.

139-41 **These were not ... :** contrasts the past, Theseus' promises and flattering tone (*blanda voce*) with the grim reality of the present. The promises were freely given (*dedisti*), not wrung from him reluctantly.

140 **love-sick:** *miserae* referring to Ariadne. Then she was *miser* in the sense of love-sick (as in Lucretius 4. 1076 etc); now she is *miser* in every sense of the word. *iubebas* is a strong word – you forced me to hope, almost against my will. 'Then you gave me happiness, ordering me to hope, now you have stolen my happiness and ordered my death.'

140-1 **love-sick ... joyful:** The *miserae* is contrasted with *laeta ... optatos*. The collocation of *conubia ... hymenaeos* is imitated in Vergil *Aen* 4.316. Note the chiasmus here and the lack of a strong caesura; there is no coincidence of ictus and accent in foot 5. 'The line can be read as a combination of a glyconic and a pherecratean, the metre used for wedding songs (cf. poem 61), to which this is a pathetic allusion' (Goold)

142 **winds ... nothing:** cf. 59, Vergil *Aeneid* 9.313. This line is a perfect summary of Ariadne's futile despair, leading into a generalised jeremiad against man's selfish cupidity.

143 **From now on ... :** Partly in contrast to an assumed 'in the old days' (for which see 384-407): no longer will there be any trusting men. This leads to the assumption that Thetis ought not to trust Peleus, as they are clearly posterior to the events on the coverlet – despite the idyllic words used of their love earlier. No men can be trusted, she says.

Note also the jingle of *nunc iam nulla viro*, the repetition of *nulla* and *viro/i; iuranti* picks up the oath theme of *periuria* (135). The words form the neat scheme of man swearing, woman believing, with the sentence ending up with the sad word *fideles*; *speret* picks up 140 *sperare iubebas*.

145-7 **lustful ... making:** Men, says Ariadne, will say anything to get what they want, and then will ignore their words once their desire has been satisfied. NB the vagueness of *aliquid* is redeemed by *cupiens* and it is their *animus* (the Greek *thymos*), the appetitive side of the mind, which is anticipating (*prae-*) the acquisition (*apisci*), a word often used of acquiring property.

146 **nothing ... no ... :** Note here the rhetorical repetition of *nil ... nihil,* and the chiasmus* of verb+infinitive followed by infinitive+verb.

147 **once ... slaked:** Catullus seems to be using the language of Lucretius 4, but is interestingly different. Lucretius argues that sex is futile because 'as soon as it is all over there is a brief respite and then it is back to square one' (Lucretius 4.

1115ff); Ariadne feels that the sexual bond between them has been a mere pretence
to secure the ulterior motive of slaying the beast. *cupidae* picks up *cupiens* from
145.

148   **fear:** *metuere* is suspect as a gnomic perfect alongside the present tense *curant*.
Czwalina's *meminere* (1867), adopted by Goold and Quinn, removes the problems,
but is not compelling.

149-50 **I saved you:** Ariadne expected Theseus to love her for what she had done for
him, but her reward is desertion without even the honour of burial. The phrase 'in
the middle of the eddy of death' is striking, reminding us of the *turbo* which was
compared to Theseus in the simile* at 105-9; *medius* is an intensive word here.
Note also the enjambement*.

150   **brother:** her brother is the Minotaur, the half-brother offspring of her mother
Pasiphae and the bull. *crevi* is legal language. It may seem odd of Ariadne to
affect any great affection for the Minotaur – she brings him in here firstly as a
desperate emotional argument (I gave up my brother for you as well as my home
and my future ...) and secondly as it focusses on the theme of human (or half-
human) sacrifice as elsewhere in the poem (especially 362-70): thirdly, it points
a contrast and comparison between Minotaur and Theseus. Who is the monster
now?

151   **cheat:** *fallaci* a word last used of the sleep which 'deceived' her in 56.

152-3   **given ... to wild beasts:** A familiar terror in the ancient world is that of the
unburied dead lacking peace in the underworld: both the fear of the soul wandering
eternally and the horror of the corpse being eaten by birds and animals; cf. Homer
Iliad 1.4-5, Sophocles *Antigone*, Lucretius 3. 888-93.

152-3   **torn apart ... dead:** notice the chiastic* *dilaceranda feris – alitibusque
praeda*, the enjambement* and the impressive five-syllable word with which 152
ends.

154   **lonely:** cf. 60.1-3.

155   **sea ... :** is not mere rhetoric, but is appropriate to her position on the sea
shore. *conceptum ... exspuit* might suggest abortion or miscarriage: it implies
rejection of the child (cf. Lucr. 2.1041). The literary source for this passage is
Patroclus' rebuke of Achilles in Homer *Iliad* 16.33-5: 'Pitiless man, your father
was not Peleus, nor was Thetis your mother, but the grey sea gave you birth, and
the steep cliffs, for your heart will not bend.'

156   **Syrtes ... Scylla ... Charybdis:** An impressive tricolon crescendo*. The
Syrtes are the shallows off the African coast; Scylla was loved by Poseidon and
turned by her rival Amphitrite (see 11n.) into a sea-monster who devoured sailors
who sailed near her cave; Charybdis is the whirlpool off the coast of Sicily, a peril
faced successfully by Jason and the Argonauts. The sense of *vasta* is "the
emptiness or desolation which repels or appals the beholder" (Fordyce)

157   **returns ... sweet life:** all the positive words are strung together: *dulci
praemia vita*.

158   **if your heart ... :** i.e. your heart had never been in our marriage, because of
your father's orders. 'Aegeus was ... one of the old school (*prisci*, cf. Hor *Odes*
3.21.11 *prisci Catonis*) who had strong ideas (*saeva praecepta)* about their sons
and foreign women' (Quinn). Ariadne is perhaps saying that Theseus was less

honest than his father, who never concealed or disguised his feelings about a
'foreign wife'. The irony here is that this tapestry is covered with *priscis* ...
figuris (50) but among them is someone harking back even further to men who are
even more *prisci*.

161   **slave ... love:** Ariadne would have preferred the life of a slave to no contact at
all with Theseus – she would even enjoy it (*iucundo*) – unless, that is, *iucundo*
means 'pleasant for you' and she is thus saying that Theseus would enjoy it. Note
the concentration of *famularer serva labore*, all words of service.

162   **soothing   ... waters:**   a lovely line for an unappealing act. *permulceo* is 'I
soothe, pacify, alleviate'. He has beautiful feet (*candida*). It is not obvious why
the poet calls the water *liquidis:* it may be stressing the liquid element as Ariadne
is on the sea-shore. Note also that this picture is not actually part of the coverlet
but is simply in Ariadne's mind as she speaks, and yet the 'colour' words are still
there and the scene is painted as if it were being described from sight. *vestigia* for
feet by metonymy* – this is the first use of this (Fordyce).

163   **garment of crimson:**   A nice ironic touch, the coverlet prompting a tale
where a coverlet is imagined – and it is purple also as at 47-9.

164-70 **But why ... ?:** Ariadne pulls herself together and reminds herself that she is
alone and unheard. This may be a naturalistic device, or else a gentle mockery of
the tragic address to sun, moon, earth etc (as in e.g. Sophocles' *Ajax* 856-865)

164   **in vain:**   Another reference to the theme of futility; note the juxtaposition of
ignaris nequiquam and cf. 111.

165   **out of my mind:** for *externo* cf. 71. There may be a Lucretian echo in *nullis
sensibus auctae* – cf. Lucretius 3. 630, mocking the artists (among others) who
have depicted the soul as endowed with physical senses.

166   **cannot hear ... :**   The line contains further echoes of Lucretius: (3.931-2
(Nature speaking) and 4.577 (echoes)). Catullus' purpose in this imitation is
debatable; possibly to mock Lucretian rationalism, or again simply the
incongruity of this highly disturbed woman's using the language of Epicurean
*ataraxia** (serenity) to try to calm herself down. The reminder of the echo is
especially apt in the *loca deserta* setting of this speech: and poignantly Lucretius
describes (4. 575-6) being 'with companions' but she has none (168). There is
also a nice irony in Ariadne 'complaining that she cannot be heard or addressed
because she is in a picture'. (Laird 29)

167-8   **By now ... :**   Ariadne imagines how by now he is in the middle of the sea
whereas she has gone nowhere and is alone. Notice the sandwiching of the (non-
existent) man in the middle of *vacua ... in alga* and the gritty detail of seaweed
rather than the poetic sandy shore.
mortalis looks forward to the god Bacchus who is going to arrive any minute: it
is again dramatic irony in her mouth.

169-70 **spiteful ... exsultant:**   This is a personification of fate: but the reader
thinks that *nimis insultans* etc must refer to Theseus, until the feminine ending on
saeva. There is surely a wry joke in the play on *auris* as breezes/ears: I have no
aures (ears) but only *aurae* (breezes) to hear me! *nimis* is unusual – more even than
is normal for fate?

171 **Almighty Jupiter:**   Ariadne, deprived of human audience, directs her
apostrophe to Jupiter. The form of the wish is well-known from Eur *Medea* 1ff,
Ennius *Medea* 253-4.

172 Notice how the juxtaposition of the place-names forms a 'golden line*'. *tempore
primo* is clearly (and chiastically*) opposed to *extremo tempore* in 169.

Even in her distress, Ariadne can still speak with a learned allusive style of
Cnossian (for Cretan), Cecropian (for Athenian). Even more striking is the string
of understatements: if only just the *poops* of *Cecrops* had not even *touched* the
shore of *Cnossos* ... This suggests that her fate was sealed by this tiny act, the
bomb detonated by a spark.

173 **dreadful ... bull:**   almost a golden line*, with the unpleasant words together
at the front and the adjectives and nouns in chiastic* formation.

174 For *perfidus* cf. 132-3; Theseus is now just a sailor, and a treacherous one at that.

175 **wicked ... guest:**   The *perfidus ... navita* is now (variation) a *malus hospes*,
the cruelty of his plans hidden inside the phrase *dulci ... forma*. The word *hospes*
is sardonic – to think we invited him in and looked after him ... and note the
enjambement* of 175-6

177-87 Ariadne is trapped, as are many characters in epic and tragedy – most closely
comparable being perhaps Philoctetes (abandoned on the island of Lemnos by the
treacherous Greeks, a fate similar to Ariadne's) and Daedalus and Icarus who seek to escape
from King Minos (Ariadne's father) by flying.

178 **Ida:** Mount Ida is in her native Crete.

178/9 **rough:** *truculentum* ('angry' or 'stormy') is a nice touch of pathetic fallacy*: as
if the sea were cross in thwarting her homecoming.

180-1 **my brother's blood:** The sentiments are rhetorically pleasing, but less than
fully reasonable. One wonders how much affection her father bore for the monster
born of his wife's bestiality, whom he locked in the labyrinth. The theme of
brotherly slaughter is picked up again at 399 in Catullus' moralising epilogue,
where the poet laments that 'modern society' is barbaric enough to commit such
acts – which the heroic age also committed. The image of being spattered with
blood is gruesome and effective.

182 **faithful ... husband:** Ariadne's words are sardonic again – her 'faithful
husband' is now fleeing from her. *memet* is perhaps self-pitying – 'everyone else
has a husband (and father, and family) but not me ... '

183 **bending his pliant oars:** The rower bends over the oars, straining to go
faster: if the word *lentos* means 'sluggish' then we have the sense of Theseus'
impatience, whereas if the word means rather 'pliant, flexible' it suggests then
that the rower is applying such force to the oars that they are bending. Ariadne
imagines that Theseus is rowing his own ship.

184-7 Ariadne's despair finds its expression in two series of anaphoras*: *nullo ...
nulla., ... nulla* and then *omnia ... omnia ... omnia*, the latter being an obvious
tricolon crescendo*.

184 The mss reading *litus* is awkward: it demands to be taken in apposition with *sola
insula* and is only perhaps to be explained as the inelegant expression of a

distraught woman. More likely is Palmer's *colitur* – palaeographically easy to corrupt to the shorter *litus* and supplying the missing verb.

186   The final syllable of *nulla* is scanned long by position before the double consonant which begins *spes*.

186-7 **all is silent:** Ariadne's words are ironic in view of what we know is coming to her; far from being 'silent' (*muta*) Bacchus and his entourage make a terrific din (254-264), nor is the island *deserta* once the troupe of bacchants will have arrived, and Ariadne will wed a god and thus be an immortal when Theseus is merely a dead hero.

188-91 **demand ... punishment:** Ariadne announces her intention to appeal to the gods and secure vengeance for her ill-treatment. Her need for revenge is no less because she will as it happens be saved by Bacchus – his rescue is motivated by sheer desire, not by any wish to see justice done, and anyway Theseus has still done wrong even if the tale ends happily.

188-9 **droop ... withdraw:** *letum* ends the previous sentence: Ariadne expresses fatigue (*languescent ... fesso*) but rouses herself now to state that she will not die until she has secured vengeance. Death is expressed in two images: the eyes drooping and the senses withdrawing from the body, the second of which is evocative of Lucretius' view of the *anima* as linking the senses together in what we would call the nervous system, whereby sleep is a temporary, and death a permanent, disconnection of the channels of sensation.

190   **punishment:** A *multa* was strictly speaking a fine – ironic understatement here in a highly rhetorical passage to use so pedestrian a word.

191   **faith of the heavenly ones:** Ariadne clearly trusts in the justice of the gods – if only because she has nobody left to turn to.

192   **Kindly Ones:**   the Erinyes who punished murder – especially murder of kinsfolk as in Aeschylus' *Oresteia*. They also punish perjury (Homer *Iliad* 19. 259-60, Hesiod *Works and Days* 803-4). For the image of them having snakes entwined in their hair see e.g. Aeschylus *Choephoroi* 1049 and also Sophocles *Ajax* 835-40. *multantes* picks up *multa* from 190, and the three words *multantes vindice poena* add up to a devastating amount of vengeance.

194   **anger:** The poet uses a lively image of them hissing out their anger (*exspirantis etc*) and spitting their venom with the alliteration* of the letter p.

195-7 The level of rhetoric is high: repetition of *huc huc,* emotion of *vae misera* and the impressive four-adjective catalogue *inops ardens amenti caeca* sandwiched by the basic phrase *cogor ... furore:* note also the tricolon crescendo* of 1. *inops* 2. *ardens* 3. *amenti caeca furore.*

198-9 **sincerely:**   Ariadne implies that insincere feelings deserve to be ignored, but hers are too genuine to be insignificant. The source of her feelings is *extremis ... medullis* (196) and here *pectore ab imo*, just as at 93 and 125. Note again the bitter irony that the cares 'are born' (*nascuntur*) continuing the theme of the sterility of Ariadne's 'marriage'.

202-14 Bridge passage linking this speech with that of Aegeus.

203   A neat symmetrical line: noun A – adjective B – verb – adjective A – noun B.

204   **ruler ... nod:** Ariadne's faith in the gods is justified in the event: Jupiter here
        nods assent, and later on Bacchus rescues her. The source of Jupiter's earth-
        shaking nod is Homer *Iliad* 1.528-30 ('The son of Cronos (Zeus) spoke, and
        nodded his dark brow in agreement, and the ambrosial locks waved from the
        immortal head of the king; and he made great Olympus shake'): here the use of the
        word *numen* suggests its origin in the word *nuo* – the collocation amounting to a
        figura etymologica*. *caelestum rector* is an epic epithet to describe Jupiter.

205-6   **earth ... sea ... firmament:**   The three spheres of earth, sea and sky
        (represented by the three divine sons of Rhea: Pluto/Hades, Neptune/Poseidon and
        Jupiter/Zeus respectively) all shake at the nod, the phrase being ideal for the
        tricolon crescendo* which climaxes with Jupiter's own sphere of the heavens.
        horrida is predicative in expressing the effect of the nod.

207-8   **planted:** Theseus was 'sown with unseeing darkness as to his mind'.

209   **instructions:**   The word *mandata* is repeated at 214 and 232 'as a kind of
        Leitmotif (Quinn). The phrase recalls Lucretius 2.582 *memori mandatum mente*
        tenere ('to hold the instruction in an unforgetting mind').

210   **welcome ... sad:**   The juxtaposition of *dulcia ... maesto* is deliberate, the
        white sails would indeed have been 'sweet' to the 'sad' parent: the tale is here
        sketched in rough outline, to be elaborated in greater detail below.

211   **Athens:** Erectheus was the great-grandfather of Aegeus, and so Erecthean means
        'Athenian'.

212   **they say:** *ferunt olim* is an appeal to the legend as at 2, 76, 124 etc.

215-37 Aegeus' farewell, couched in two long sentences composed in difficult syntax and
awkward structure, suggestive perhaps of 'an old man's rambling way of speaking'
(Quinn).

215-6   **son ... son:**   The father repeats the word in emphatic anaphora*. The son is
        choosing to go off to Crete (81-2), and so the only compulsion the old man is
        under is that of the will of his son and his fate (218), forced to *dimittere* his son
        who then *dimisit* his father's instructions (208)

217   **just recently:** Theseus' father Aegeus did not meet his son until the latter was
        grown up and had made the journey to Athens to meet him; Theseus grew up with
        his mother Aethra in Troezen. *reddite* is the perfect word to denote the giving
        back of a child to its rightful father.

218   **boiling:** *fervida* is 'boiling' or 'blazing', often used of anger and passion, as in
        describing Aeneas as *fervidus ira* ('boiling with rage') at the end of the Vergil's
        Aeneid.

219   **you ... me:**   again, emphatic juxtaposition of *mihi te*, with *cui* therefore
        ambiguous until the phrase unfolds in full. The sense of *languida* is that of eyes
        'drooping' in sleep or death – reminding us of Ariadne's words at 188, whereas the
        sense of *saturata* is clearly 'feasted full'; the old man uses the language of the
        banqueter who will sleep easily after feasting – ironically here as he is anything
        but happy and the dreadful feast in question is one of human flesh to a Minotaur.

221   **rejoicing ... glad:**   The old man makes the almost tautologous remark
        gaudens laetanti pectore to stress to his son that he views the enterprise with no

pleasure, a feeling evinced by the colour of the dark sails which he will instruct his son to fly on the mast.

222 **ensigns of good fortune:** these would perhaps be tempting fate and so the old man counsels the opposite.

223 **laments:** 'A note of distancing irony' (Quinn); cf. 164-70. The lamentation is of course premature, even if it is justified in the event.

224 **defiling ... dust:** defiling the head with earth and dust is a gesture of grief, as performed by Achilles over the dead Patroclus (Homer *Iliad* 18. 23-25), Priam over his dead son Hector (Homer *Iliad* 24. 163-5) and later Evander over his dead son Pallas (Vergil *Aeneid* 10.844).

227 **Iberian purple:** 'Spanish rust' is the colour, not of fresh rust, but rather 'the deep blue colour of heavily weathered iron' (Quinn). The term reminds us of the rusting farm implements neglected while the rural folk attend the wedding in line 42. Hector

228 **Itonus:** a town in Thessaly with a famous sanctuary of Athena.

230 **spatter ... blood:** the phrasing recalls 181 where Ariadne describes Theseus as ' a young man spattered with my brother's blood', a theme picked up again at 399.

231 **unforgetting:** *memor* and its opposite *immemor* are the terms by which Theseus is constantly tried and found wanting: cf. 58, 248.

232 **blot out:** *oblittero* means the defacing of an inscription by the passage of time and the effects of the elements; Aegeus wishes his words to be 'engraved' and not to be 'worn away' with time.

234-5 **cloth of death:** the sails are *funestam* both because they (falsely) betoken the death of Theseus and also because they (truly) bring about the death of Aegeus. For the word cf. 201, 246. There is a neat contrast and parallelism in these lines, as *funestam* is placed at the beginning of one line, *candida* at the beginning of the other, and likewise the two antonymic verbs are placed midway in their respective lines. *undique* adds emphasis – 'all the sails' (Quinn) The ropes are 'twisted' because they are made from plaited threads and rushes.

236 **joys ... glad:** *laeta gaudia* are juxtaposed for emphasis. *aetas prospera* is perhaps an odd phrase to use, suggestive of the several 'ages' of man: it would be easier to emend it to Dousa's *fors*, but this would lose the theme of age and time which Aegeus stresses throughout his speech.

239-40 **as clouds ... :** An epic simile*, Theseus being the lofty mountain who forgets his instructions just as the clouds fly away from the mountain-top when blown by the wind. The 'source' of the simile is perhaps Homer *Iliad* 5. 522-6. Not all the features of the simile are equally important, of course; the mountain-top is 'snowy white' and 'lofty' simply to add atmosphere and panoramic scale, rather than for any symbolic reason.

241 **from the top ... :** The father gazes out (naturally enough) from a high vantage-point to see Theseus sailing towards him, just as in similar fashion Ariadne sought a high vantage-point from which to gaze at Theseus sailing away from her (126-7). Here Aegeus' desperation is well brought-out as he 'sought' a 'glimpse' from the 'very top' of the citadel.

COMMENTARY: LXIV 159

242 A line of great artistry, almost a golden line* in its word-order and employing a pleasing degree of assonance*: *anxia in assiduos absumens lumina fletus*. The pathos of the poetic conceit that the old man is 'wearing out' his anxious eyes simply by looking too much and too hard is also striking.

243 **billowing:** The reading of V is *inflati*, a word which makes perfect sense ('billowing' in the wind) but which, it was felt by many editors, fails to explain the event in the way which Sabellicus' *infecti* ('stained') does. Catullus, it might be argued, has already explained the situation thoroughly, and the billowing of the sail would bring it to the old man's attention more quickly. The mss reading is a nice piece of understated realism.

246-50 Catullus ends this part of the *ecphrasis* with verbal echoes recalling the beginning of the episode: central themes of the episode are run through quickly once again, unravelling the story much as Theseus unravelled the thread in the labyrinth. *funesta ... paterna* refers to the latest incident described (i.e. the death of his father Aegeus); *morte ferox* reminds us of the killing of the Minotaur (73-4, 105-111) – suggested also by the term *Minoidi* to describe Ariadne; finally we see the picture with which the scene began (52ff) of Ariadne sad on the seashore. The correlative *qualem ... talem* reminds us of Ariadne's curse *quali ... tali* (200-201), and the sentence ends with an appropriately maritime metaphor* for the many-layered rolling waves of care inside her, recalling the early description of her in line 54. Individual words add to this 'ring-composition' effect: *immemori* in 248 looks back to *immemor* in 58, *prospectans* in 249 picks up *prospectans* in 52, *cedentem* (249 – 53) *maesta* (249) picking up *maestis* in 60.

251-264 While Ariadne is gazing out to sea, behind her the god Dionysus/Bacchus is coming towards her with his retinue, about to save her; a form of dramatic irony whereby we know more than the character in the story.

251 **Iacchus:** a form of the name of the Greek god Dionysus, often termed Bacchus or Liber in Latin. This mysterious god was himself the child of Zeus/Jupiter and a mortal woman Semele, brought up by the nymphs of Mount Nysa after his father's self-revelation had incinerated his mother still carrying him. The worship of this god was carried out especially by women (Maenads, Thyiads, Bacchants) who would take to the mountains and there practise forms of ecstatic religious rites involving the killling and eating of wild animals. The males who also attended the god were grotesque – both the young Satyrs (goat-like creatures in a permanent state of sexual arousal) and the old Sileni (usually drunk). Dionysus was also the god of the theatre and his worship is best examined in Euripides' tragedy *The Bacchae*, a play which may be the source for some of Catullus' phrases here.

flowery ... flying: *florens volitabat* is a striking pair of metaphors: flowering and flying at one and the same time.

252 **Satyrs ... Sileni:** see 251n. The *thiasus* is a Greek word for the company of Dionysiac worshippers, used also of the frenzied band of Cybele's worshippers at 63.28. Nysa was traditionally seen as the source of Dionysus and his cult; opinions varied as to its geographical location – Thrace, Arabia, Ethiopia and India all being contenders.

253   **for you ... :**   Catullus again addresses a character directly in apostrophe*; cf. 22-30 and 69.

254-5   **raging ... distracted:**   The phrase *lymphata mente furebant* emphasises the madness and frenzy of the Maenads, as does the repeated *euhoe* interrupting the sentence. 'tossing their heads' refers to the familiar spectacle (in Art) of the Bacchants 'in ecstasy flinging back the head in the dewy air' (Euripides' *Bacchae* 864-5)

256   **bacchic wands:**   The *thyrsus* was a stick or staff tipped with vine-leaves or ivy: its touch was enough to induce frenzy.

257   **torn apart:**   Another familiar aspect of Dionysiac ritual, the *sparagmos* or tearing asunder of an animal: the most notorious *sparagmos* was that in which the mother and aunts of King Pentheus tore him limb from limb thinking that he was a lion, as Dionysus' punishment for Pentheus' spurning of his rites in Thebes – the tale told in Euripides' *Bacchae*. The deliberate postponement of the noun *iuvenco* here may lead the reader to wonder exactly who or what is being dismembered. The poet dwells on the savaging of these rites in a manner which might lead us to wonder just how happy Ariadne's union with the god is destined to be.

258   **snakes:** Bacchants were able to take venomous snakes into their hands without suffering harm, even being able (as here) to 'bind their speckled hide-garments with snakes which licked their cheeks' (Euripides' *Bacchae* 697-8).

259   **ritual objects:**   *orgia* denotes both the rites themselves and here the secret exotic (*obscura*) cult-objects contained in the wicker-baskets (*cistis*). The same word *orgia* is repeated in epanalepsis* in 260, where its meaning is more general 'rites' rather than the specific 'cult-objects'. *audire* is a difficult word in either case; if it means simply 'hear', then we imagine the uninitiated striving in vain to catch the cries of worshippers and *orgia* means 'rites', whereas if *orgia* means 'cult-objects' again the verb would have to mean 'hear about' (OLD s.v.9).

261-4   **drums ... cymbals ... horns ... pipe:**   The sound of the Dionysiac worship is described in some detail – although of course sounds cannot be portrayed in two-dimensional art such as the tapestry which Catullus purports to be describing. The whole passage is rich in sound-effects: the alliteration* of (e.g.) _plangebant ... proceris tympana palmis/_ ... _tereti tenuis tinnitus_, the assonance* of _raucisonos ... cornua bombos_.

261-2   **drums:**   The *tympanum* was more like a modern tambourine than a drum, consisting as it did of hide stretched over one side of a wooden hoop, with tiny pairs of cymbals attached to the side of the hoop; the two actions in these lines are both performed with the same instrument, depending on whether it is to be beaten or shaken.

263-4   **horns ... pipe:** From percussion to wind: the horn produces the low booming *bombus* while the *tibia* (a reed instrument) emits a more blaring high-pitched sound well evoked by the adjective *horribili*, the verb *stridebat* (a screeching sound) and the *i* assonance of the two together. The whole passage appears to be a conflation of two passages in Lucretius: 'a thunder of drums (*tympana*) attends her, tight-stretched and pounded by palms, and a clash of hollow cymbals; hoarse-throated (*raucisono*) horns (*cornua*) bray their deep warning, and the hollow pipe

thrills (*tibia*) every heart with Phrygian strains' (2.618-20) and then also: 'when
the trumpet lows with a deep bass boom, and the boxwood pipe, the virtuoso
foreign instrument, re-echoes its hoarse roar ... ' (4.545-6: for the reading *buxus
cita* see my commentary *ad loc*).

265-303 The *ecphrasis* has ended and we are put back into the original context of the
marriage of Peleus and Thetis. There now follows a procession of divine guests coming
to the wedding-feast: a procession marked by discord (Prometheus still bearing the scars
of his quarrel with Jupiter) and pointed absences (Apollo and Diana). These three divine
beings are named when the other major gods are not, giving the impression that the poet
is lingering on the discordant element: but the contrast is surely drawn therefore between
quarrelsome and spiteful gods on the one hand and a supremely harmonious couple on the
other.

267-77 The human guests depart from the palace, politely leaving before the gods arrive
in a spirit (presumably) of deference; this sits oddly with the poet's insistence that in the
heroic age the gods mingled freely with men.

267-8 satisfied: The youth of Thessaly was 'filled up' with looking, a metaphor* to
    express the sensuous enjoyment of the wedding and the palace whose mere sight
    was enough to satsify the appetite: this is in sharp contrast to Lucretius' barbed
    jibe at lovers who 'cannot sate themselves with looking' and 'neither can they
    remove any part from the delicate limbs by rubbing them with their hands ... '
    (4.1102-3).

269-75 just as ... : A beautiful simile* comparing the departing guests to the waves
ruffled into increasing movement by the West wind towards the rising sun. The simile is
based on Homer *Iliad* 4. 422-5: 'just as when on the much-sounding shore the swelling
wave of the sea rises up more swiftly under the moving power of Zephyr: out on the sea it
forms a crest first of all, and then breaks on the land roaring greatly ... '
269-70 breath ... forwards: The word *flatu* is placed early, then the sea is seen in
    its calmness in the morning, the new line starting off with the expressive
    horrificans which produces sudden motion (*proclivas incitat undas*) which looks
    like that of a stream flowing downhill (*proclivus* is thus used at Lucretius 6. 728)
    although the sea is flat.
271 forwards ... to the ... sun: Quinn notes that 'the waves move ... out of
    darkness into light, like the crowd'. The phrasing of this line is 'high' poetic
    style in the extreme, with the striking metaphor* *vagi sub limina solis*.
272-3 slowly at first: The waves take time to accumulate motion and so move
    slowly at first; the crowd, by contrast, are lingering because they are reluctant to
    leave, but the phrase *clementi flamine pulsae* suggests that the driving force of the
    gods is benevolent, just as the mood of the crowd is happy and laughing
    (*cachinni*).
275 crimson ... reflect: The crimson light of the rising sun is reflected in the
    water, the distance between the waves and the light being expressed in the
    separation of *purpurea ... luce*. Note here also the poetic conceit of waves
    'swimming' or 'floating' on the sea.

276   **the royal household ... forecourt:**   The opulence of the house is stressed
once again as three words are used to denote it.   The emphasis on the word
vestibuli causes concern: why should the poet pick out the portal?   One
possibility is that the word is put in to match the metaphorical *limina solis* of
271, as suggested by Fraenkel's note on Aeschylus *Agamemnon* 1180ff: Nisbet
notes this ((Nisbet (1995) 388) but then conjectures that the correct reading might
be *vestiflui* 'with flowing robes', which would be wonderful in the context of the
simile if it could be supported with more textual evidence: it would 'point back to
the flowing water of the simile' and bring the texture of the simile into the
narrative proper.
277   **all departed:**   The breaking up of the crowd is well brought out by the short
words and the broken rhythm of the line, the fifth-foot spondee suggestive of the
slow movement.

278-302 The gods arrive and bring gifts.
279   **Chiron** was the wise centaur 'from the cave on Mt Pelion' (Homer *Iliad* 16.144)
who later became the tutor of the young Achilles.   Here he brings 'gifts of the
woodland' which are then explained as coming from all over Thessaly and not
solely from woodland.
280-2 **flowers:**   The poet delays the noun *flores* leaving the reader in suspense as to
what he is talking about.   'Instead of a list of places where the flowers came from,
the reader is offered a series of images of Thessaly, its fields and mountains, the
river Peneus, and left free to explore these; the strictly denotative word *flores*
necessarily inhibits this process, so it is delayed as long as possible.' (Quinn).
281/2 **the river:**   the Peneus, the main river in Thessaly
282   **Favonius** is the West Wind or Zephyr.   The line is similar in wording and feeling
to Lucretius 1.11 'in all its force the fertilising breeze of the West wind is
unlocked', both of them perhaps remembering Callimachus Hymn 2.80-1 ('your
altars wear flowers in spring – all the flowers which the Hours bring out in their
different colours when Zephyrus breathes dew.') In all three cases the West wind is
described as a wind producing fertility.   The mss reading *perit* is clearly wrong,
and Housman's lovely *aperit* (the breeze 'opening up' the flowers) is far preferable
to *parit* adopted by most editors.
283   **mingled:**   Quinn asks interestingly whether the poet wrote *in distinctis* ('in
separate') rather than *indistinctis* ('in unsorted'); unfortunately word-division is
not part of the paradosis of a Latin text and so the editor must decide which reading
makes the more sense.   Most feel that Chiron had gathered such a plethora of
flowers that the effect of this plenty would be lessened if they were few enough to
be sorted into separate bunches, and so the 'unsorted posies' suggest that there
were simply too many different sorts to be regulated in that way.
284   **house laughed:**   The metaphor* of the house 'laughing' (cf. 46) is here
strengthened by the extra touch *permulsa* ('caressed' 'soothed') appropriate in the
context of a gift of flowers.   *domus* of course often means 'household' as well as
simply the building in which they live.

285 **Peneus:**   here the river is personified as a river-god.   Tempe is the valley between the mountains Olympus and Ossa through which the river Penios flows: it became a byword for beauty of landscape.

287 **daughters of Thessaly:**   A famous crux.   The mss read *minosim linquens doris* which makes no sense.   What may have happened is that the scribe found a proper name he did not recognise and 'corrected' it to a word looking like the proper name *Minois* (60, 247) but put into something like the Greek dative plural case.   If this line of thought is correct, then Heinsius' *Haemonisin* (a Greek word meaning 'for the daughters of Thessaly') would fit well: *Haemonides* is a feminine toponymic* from Haemonia, a poetic name for Thessaly.

    doris still causes difficulties: the adjective sounds as though it should mean 'Dorian', but the word *dorus* (for *dorius* or *doricus*) is unparalleled, and anyway there is nothing Dorian about the girls or their dancing.   Of all the suggestions, the least implausible is Lachmann's *crebris* which strengthens the following two words both in its alliteration and in its sense.

288 **He ... high ... roots:**   *ille* is deictic or pictorial, as Fordyce convincingly explains: 'there he was with trees in his hands'.   The juxtaposition of *radicitus altas* is deliberate to emphasise the great size of these gifts – they were tall anyway, but he had them roots and all.

289-91 Five different sorts of tree: beech, laurel, plane, poplar and cypress trees all gathered together into a giant dendroid bouquet.

289 **tall ... straight:**   *recto proceras* are another effective juxtaposition to emphasise that the trees are tall and straight.

291 **Phaethon** had foolishly taken the chariot of his father the Sun-god but found himself unable to drive it; running dangerously close to setting the earth on fire, he was blasted with the thunderbolt of Jupiter; his sisters who had yoked the horses for him and so conspired in his misdeed and death, were changed into poplar-trees – trees which weep tears of amber.

292 **woven together:**   *contexta* tells us that Peneus wove the trees into a 'screen of foliage' (Fordyce): *late* confirms that there were a great number of trees which covered the property.

294-7 The arrival of Prometheus: Prometheus was a Titan, famous for giving fire to mortals, an act for which he was chained to a rock in the Caucasus while an eagle ate out his liver by day, only for it to grow back during the night.   He was released from his captivity and punishment by Jupiter in return for the secret which he knew, namely that the child of Thetis was destined to be greater than its father, a secret which changed Jupiter's feelings for Thetis as shown at line 21 above.

294 **intelligent:**   *sollerti corde* well describes the inventive and clever Prometheus (whose name in Greek means 'forethought') who created man out of clay and invented most of the arts.

295-7 **traces of ... :**   what begins as a description of Prometheus' appearance gives the poet the opportunity to narrate (briefly but effectively) the tale of his punishment at the hands of Jupiter, the god who is right behind him in the line of deities entering the house.   The poet stresses the strife between Jupiter and

Prometheus to display the disharmony which can exist even among the gods: see also 299n.

297   Note the p alliteration* and the fifth-foot caesura and spondee, well expressing the agony of the punishment.

298   **father ... wife ... sons:** A family group of Jupiter, Juno and their children, described in familial terms as 'father with his wife and children'. This line is hypermetric – that is, there is a surplus short syllable on the end which is to elide with the vowel which begins the next line; this is the only such line in Catullus' longer poems – it is found later in (e.g.) Vergil *Aeneid* 4. 558, 629.

299/300 **Phoebus ... sister:**   Phoebus Apollo and his sister Diana/Artemis are not present at the wedding, partly because they are supporters of Troy (which Achilles is destined to overthrow) and partly because Apollo is destined to kill Achilles. This is a departure from earlier poets who had Apollo at the wedding (Homer *Iliad* 24.63, Pindar *Nemean* 5.41) and releases the god from the charge of treachery levelled against him by Thetis (Aeschylus fr. 450, Plato *Republic* 383b) that he sang of blessings to come at her wedding and then went on to kill her son – a future which as god of prophecy he would certainly have known when he sang his song.   Catullus thus shows Apollo either as a god of integrity – or as a god with an already burning hatred of Achilles.   There is no parallel for the absence of Diana/Artemis; presumably the poet invented this version to suggest the lack of total harmony among the gods.

300   **twin:**   *unigenam* usually means 'only child' but cannot sustain this sense in a sentence which has only just mentioned her brother.   Probably Catullus intends it to mean 'born along with' or 'Twin', which Artemis was of Apollo; the epithet is often applied to Hecate, the only child of Perseus and Asterie, and associated with Idrias in Caria, a famous cult-centre of hers founded by Idrus.   Hecate was often associated with Artemis, and so paradoxically this 'only child' has a brother.

303-22 The Fates introduced.

303   **bent their limbs:**   the gods do not recline in Roman style on couches, but rather sit at ivory ('snow-white') chairs, their limbs 'bent' (*flexerunt*) rather than extended horizontally.

304   The rhythm of the line is uneven, with caesuras only in the third and fifth feet, suggestive perhaps of the table groaning under the weight of the meal, the uncommon singular word *dape* showing that this mighty array of food is only one single meal. (cf. *dapem* at 79.)

305   **The Fates:** The Parcae are named as three separate women in Hesiod *Theogony* 905. The name Parcae derives, it seems from *parere* (to give birth) and denotes an ancient goddess of childbirth.   The juxtaposition *veridicos Parcae* emphasises their honesty; *veridicus* is used of Epicurus by Lucretius (6.6).
        shaking ... uncertain: There is a neat irony throughout this description of the Fates as infirm old women who however hold tremendous power in the knowledge they have of the future.   At their first appearance here they are weak and shaking, as old people are often portrayed in Catullus (see *tremulum* below and cf. e.g. 68. 154, 61. 51).

307-9 **white ... crimson ... rose:** The colour-contrasts are repeated and striking: *candida purpurea* of their white robes with a crimson border followed by the similar *roseae niveo* to mark the shock of red ribbons on white hair.

310 **plucked ... task:** As befits goddesses with the future in their hands, they never stop spinning the thread of destiny.

311-319 The poet indulges in a highly Alexandrian description of the spinning of the Parcae, the details precise and learned, the vocabulary accurate and technical. The poet focusses on pairs – the left hand and the right hand first, and then the fingers and the thumb, then finally the teeth and the lips. These women are engaged in 'the most familiar of female household tasks in antiquity' (Quinn), while they sing of the grisly future of the greatest hero of them all.

311-4 **left ... thread:** The left hand holds the distaff or spindle covered in soft unspun wool, while the right hand draws strands of wool down from it and shapes them into a thread: every so often the right hand turns its palm downwards and twirls the weighted spindle balanced on the thumb. As in much didactic poetry, the sheer poetic skill with which the poet has managed to turn the above prosaic description into hexameter verse is superb, rounding off with a balanced line (314) to display a balanced spindle (A-B-C-B-A).

315 **tooth:** To assist the work of the hands, the old ladies use their teeth to 'smooth off' the thread: provocatively, Catullus only credits them with a singular tooth, both to express their extreme old age and also to keep the balance here of: one hand, then the other hand, then one tooth. The rhythm of the monosyllabic ending is almost unparalleled in Catullus (68.19 is the only other example) and well brings out the sharp tugging and the snap of the thread.

316 **dry little lips:** the phrase animates the picture of the Parcae into a *tableau vivant*, the (apparently) pathetic figures brought to life before they are heard to speak.

318 **soft:** *mollia* picks up *molli* in 311: the essence of the wool itself has not changed.

319 a four-word hexameter in two pairs of alliterative words.

320-22 **Carding ... :** introduces the song of the Parcae. *pellentes* is an odd word to place here – it would mean 'beating out' the fleeces to stop them tangling. Fruterius' *vellentes* makes far better sense and would be (as Fordyce comments acutely) a *figura etymologica* pointing out the linguistic connection between *vellera* and *vello*.

320/1 **poured out:** *fuderunt* gives the sense of plenty, of unstinting and unsolicited outpouring of song. *talia* ('of this kind') does not prevent the poet from quoting what appear to be the *ipsissima verba* of the Parcae.

322 **song ... mendacity:** the poet describes the words as being a *carmen* and then immediately states that – unlike many another *carmen* perhaps – this one will not be treacherous or untrue. The Parcae will sing, but not the 'wretched stories of poets' (Euripides *Heracles* 1346); the Muses know 'how to speak many false things as if they were true' (Hesiod *Theogony* 27) but these songsmiths will tell no such falsehoods. The irony, of course, is that the exploits of Achilles are the very stuff and essence of poetic legend, and so we are presented with legendary

women in a heroic age announcing future legendary exploits – but then we are told that this will be no mere legend.

323-81 The Marriage Hymn. Unlike the hymns in poems 61 and 62, this hymn begins and ends with conventional passages of felicitation (323-36, 372-81) but then concentrates more on the exploits and character of the child of the union rather than discussing the union itself. Had the song been sung by the Muses (as in the version of the legend found in e.g. Euripides *Iphigeneia at Aulis* 1040ff), then there would have been less scope for the poet to turn his eyes towards the next generation as he does. The hymn – like poems 61 and 62 – makes use of the refrain at slightly irregular intervals, but the refrain here is peculiar to the activity on which the women are engaged rather than the more common exclamation to the god of Weddings. The device of using a refrain is a feature especially of Alexandrian poetry (see e.g. Theocritus 1 and 2) imitated by Roman poets.

323-4   **You:** The hymn begins with an address to Peleus in three phrases: first general praise, then more personal address. *eximium magnis* is emphatic juxtaposition, the two nouns *decus* (natural and/or inherited quality) and *virtutibus* (chosen acts of valour) held apart by the two adjectives. Peleus adds to his already rich fund of glory with freely chosen bravery.

324   **fortress of Thessaly ... :**   cf. 26:   Emathia is roughly equivalent to Thessaly; strictly speaking the name refers to Macedonia. Ops is the Roman equivalent of the Greek goddess Rhea, mother of Jupiter, Neptune and Pluto. The phrase 'dearest to the son of Ops' is modelled on the Homeric *diiphilos,* although Homer does not actually use it of Peleus.

325-6   **on this happy day** the sisters will give the couple a gift of the truth. *luce* is no mere poetic synonym for 'day' but adds to the imagery of light and brightness found in the whole description of the wedding and the palace, and is appropriate here as the sisters bring what is hidden (the future) out into the light.

326-7   **drawing ... run:** On its first appearance, the refrain has an explanatory gloss in the preceding line which is not repeated later on. The *subtegmina* are the 'transverse threads woven in between the warp threads in a loom, the weft' (OLD s.v.) which rather anticipates the use to which this spun thread will be put and implies the traditional picture of the Fates cutting the thread of a man's life and thus determining its length.   Quinn acutely observes that 'spinning implies weaving ... and it is not hard to imagine an elaboration of the traditional image, in which human existence becomes a pattern of warp and weft upon the loom.' The Fates, it is asserted, follow the weaving of the yarn; the spinning of the threads is of course a metaphor for the spinning of men's fates.   Note here the repetition of *currite* in the first and fifth foot, and cf. the repetitions in the refrains in *o Hymenaee Hymen, o Hymen Hymenaee* (61.4-5 etc) and again *Hymen o Hymenaee, Hymen ades o Hymenaee* (62.5 etc).

328-32   Sentiments similar to those of poem 62: the Evening Star Hesperus will unite the newly-wed couple.

328   **The Evening Star:**   personification of Hesperus is increased here with the poetic conceit of the star 'carrying' what husbands desire: note also that the name of the subject of the verbs is delayed until the following line.

329   **will come:**   repetition of *adveniet* to give a pleasant accumulatory ring to the list of who is going to come: the star, and with the star the wife ... Hesperus is a *faustus* star in that he brings the joy of the union, less so in the tragedy which its offspring will wreak.

330   **soul-twisting:**   *flexanimo* is an effective compound adjective equivalent to *animum flectens*; the imagery of diverting the mind with floods of love is redolent of the seduction of Zeus in Homer *Iliad* 14. 153-351 (cf. especially Aphrodite's 'zone, on which are ... beguilements ... and passion of sex, and the whispered lovers' talk which steals the mind away even from the thoughtful (214-17)) or then again the seduction of Mars by Venus in Lucretius 1. 33-40.

331   **languid little sleeps:**   the diminutive is effective.

332   Catullus deliberately chose not to write a Golden Line* *levia robusto substernens bracchia collo*, perhaps feeling that the intimacy of the lovers did not require such grandeur. There is a still a contrast between the 'smooth' arms of Thetis and the muscular neck of Peleus, the whole phrase looking forward to the coupling which will take place.

334-6   **No home ... :**   A felicitation or *makarismos* akin to that at 22-30. The sense that this is the 'best ever' union is emphasised by the double anaphora* of *nulla ... tales: nullus ... tali* and then also *qualis ... qualis*. The imagery of shelter is there in *contexit*, the function of the house being perfectly executed, as was the house of the poet's friend when loaned to him for his meetings with his lover in 68.68. *foedere* is a typically Catullan word to refer to the 'bond' of mutual love (cf. 373, 87.3, 109.6)

338-71   **Achilles**   and his deeds are prophesied, bringing out the full force of Prometheus' secret that the child of Thetis would grow up to be greater than its father.

339   **front ... not ... back:**   Achilles' bravery is assured by the fact that his enemies never see him running away, but only attacking.

340-1   **running:**   A nice unpacking of Homer's common epithet 'swift-footed Achilles': and also a reference to his legendary hunting abilities whereby 'he killed stags without dogs, for he excelled in swiftness of foot' (Pindar *Nemean* 3. 51-2). Note here the double alliteration* of *vago victor certamine cursus* and then the same alliteration varied in *praevertet celeris vestigia cervae*.

343-6   **hero:**   *heros* is concessive in force: – nobody – not even a hero – would dare ...

344   **The Phrygian plains:**   the fields around Troy; Teucrian means 'Trojan', as Teucer was the first king of Troy. Note the poet's variation of vocabulary here. Here also is the first hint of brutality as the fields are 'seeping' with blood.

345   **drawn-out:**   *longinquus* means 'long-drawn out' rather than 'far-flung' and refers here to the 10-year siege (*obsidens*) of the city-walls (*moenia*).

346   **third heir of ... Pelops:**   According to Homer (*Iliad* 2.105ff) Pelops left his sceptre to Atreus, who in turn left it to Thyestes, who in turn left it to Agamemnon, who thus is named here the 'third heir of Pelops'. Myrtilus was Oenomaus' charioteer, bribed by Pelops with a promise of half his kingdom if he

would help him win the race and secure the marriage with Hippodameia but murdered after the event. The whole line is a typical piece of allusive, learned poetry which tests the reader's knowledge of the legends and the literature: Catullus is also carefully not stating that Achilles routed Troy – he was dead before the end of the Trojan War – but in his allusion to treacherous Pelops he is hinting at the use of trickery and treachery in the final defeat, implying that after the death of Achilles, dishonest tactics had to be resorted to.

348-51 **mothers ... hands:**   A startling sentence: the brilliant successes of Achilles will be reported by grieving and ugly old women whose sons he has killed; the tone of heroic pride and glor' quickly turning to pathos and then the grotesque. For the sadness of parents lamenting their sons killed in battle, cf. Croesus in Herodotus 1. 87 ('in war fathers bury their sons, instead of sons burying their fathers') and also Hecabe and Priam over the dead Hector in Homer *Iliad* 22.405-36, especially Priam's appeal (420-2) to Achilles' father Peleus ('He too has a father like me, Peleus, who sired and reared him as a suffering to the Trojans ...'). For Achilles' ruthlessness towards the young, see e.g. Homer *Iliad* 20. 460-489.

350-1   The two common expressions of female grief are the letting down of the hair and the beating of the breast. The first of them is made more poignant by the telling detail *cano* – their hair is white with age: the second is made grotesque by the adjective *putrida* – unlike the breasts of the sea-nymphs at 18 or the *lactentis papillas* of Ariadne at 65, these breasts are decayed and incapable of nursing any new sons to replace the dead. *variabunt* is then visual: they will 'colour' their breasts with bruises.

353-5 **harvester:**   Commentators point to Homer *Iliad* 11. 67-71 as the source for this image of Achilles harvesting the bodies of the enemy in the blazing heat: 'as reapers against each other drive their swathes in a field of wheat or barley belonging to a rich man, and the handfuls are falling thick and fast ... ' *Iliad* 20. 495-503 also uses an agricultural simile to compare with the slaughter of Achilles: 'as when a man yokes ... oxen to crush white barley on a strong-laid threshing-floor, and quickly the barley is stripped beneath the feet of the bellowing oxen, so the horses trampled bodies and shields before great-hearted Achilles, and the axle under his chariot was splashed with blood ... ' Catullus has echoed the language of *Iliad* 11 but the mood is that of *Iliad* 20 – note especially the verb *prosternet*.

354   **blazing sun:**   The poet mentions the blazing sun to give more point to the colour of *flaventia* and also to evoke the stifling heat as the hero mows his meadow of corpses.

355   **sons of Troy:**   The epic name *Troiugenum* begins the golden line* with a suitably elevated sound: epic is of course the genre in which the exploits of Achilles always were celebrated.

357   **Scamander** is the main river in the area of Troy, a river at which Achilles totally defeated the Trojans in Homer *Iliad* 21.

358   **which ... Hellespont:**   A needless geographical placing? 'An ornamental, distancing line' (Quinn)? There is a (distant) thematic linking in that the Hellespont is named after Helle, who perished after falling off the golden-fleeced

ram which was carrying Helle and Phrixus (children of Athamas) away from their evil stepmother Ino: Phrixus arrived with the ram in Colchis, and was received kindly by King Aeetes – the ram was sacrificed and its golden fleece hung up, to be captured by the Argonauts in due course. The sailing of the Argo was hinted at in the opening lines of this poem, and so it is perhaps fitting that the same event should be alluded to towards the end, in the context of the water swallowing up the bodies of the dead. There is also a nice contrast of the rapid current of 358 being choked and stopped in 359–60.

359-60   **stream ... blood:**   A grim piece of realism: the channel of the river is narrowed (*angustans*) by the dam of bodies choking it: these bodies are piled high (*acervis*) and the warm blood raises the temperature in the river water (*tepefaciet*).

362-4   **sacrifice:**   The sacrifice of Polyxena is here referred to in general terms: a more specific account of this ghastly event follows in 368-70, the Parcae (and the poet) emphasising the horror by the repetition.   Polyxena was the youngest daughter of Priam and Hecuba, sacrificed at the tomb of Achilles to appease his ghost, an act of human sacrifice to mirror that at the beginning of the war when Agamemnon slaughtered his daughter Iphigeneia to make the wind blow the fleet from Aulis where they had become becalmed: Catullus' version of this sacrifice owes something both to Euripides' account in the *Hecuba* (521-82) and also to Lucretius' account of the death of Iphigeneia at 1. 84-101.   For a full account of Euripides' version of the tale in *Hecuba* and its symbolism, see now Mossman (1995) 142-163.   Even more interesting is the fact that Polyxena was slain to be a 'bride' for the dead Achilles, thus neatly fitting the context of a wedding song with grim irony.

362   **even ... dead:**   The greatness of the hero (and the futility of the sacrifice?) are well brought out by the phrase *morti quoque* – even when he is dead he will still receive booty (*praeda*).

363   **rounded ... lofty:**   The whole line focusses on the tomb of Achilles, built up (*coacervatum*) and rounded (*teres*) and grand as befits a great hero.

364   **snowy ... struck dead:**   The pathos is obvious as Polyxena is referred to as the 'knocked-out maiden' and her limbs are 'snowy-white'.

366   **tired:**   The Greeks are understandably tired after ten years of war: it is only 'fortune' which gives them the chance to defeat Troy, presumably in the trick of the wooden horse.

367   **untie the Neptunian bonds:**   refers to Homer's phrase 'undo the holy coronal of Troy' (*Iliad* 16.100) meaning the walls of the city which had first been built by Dardanus and then later rebuilt by Neptune for Laomedon, father of Priam.   Note here the concentration of names *Dardaniae Neptunia*.

368   A form of Golden Line*, with the nouns and adjectives arranged chiastically*. The tomb of Achilles will be made wet with the blood of Polyxena.

369-70   **two-edged ... buckle:**   the tone becomes suddenly realistic: note the detail of *ancipiti* and the telling obsɜrvation *summisso poplite*, her reaction to the blow given in three separate verbs: first she 'gives way under' it (*succumbens*), then she throws her torso forward (*proiciet*) and her knees buckle, leaving her at the end of the sentence a mere body (*corpus*), anonymous and dead.   The rhythm of *truncum summisso* is slow and heavy with assonance of *-uncum summ-*.   The knees buckling reminds us of Lucretius' Iphigeneia who 'sank to the ground giving way at the knees' (1.92).

372   **And so:**   *quare* is breathtaking: does the slaughter of Polyxena justify and recommend the marriage of the parents of Achilles?   The Parcae appear to slip into traditional Marriage-hymn style without considering the link with what immediately precedes it, or else the irony is poignant and deliberate.

373-4 **Let the husband ... let the bride:** The balanced pair of lines linger on the giving of the bride to the groom: in the first line he is to receive her, in the second she is to be givent to him in his desire. For *foedere* as a bond of love and/or marriage, see 335, 87.3, 109.6.

376-80 **wind her neck ... :** i.e. the neck-band of yesterday will no longer fit the bride: 'Among the ancients an old wives' tale held that the consummation of a marriage was confirmed by the bride's expanded neck-size' (Goold, citing Nemesianus 2.10) The word *filo* here recalls the *filum* given by Ariadne to save Theseus (113) and also the thread spun by the Parcae (317).   The text here is difficult: most editors agree to omit the refrain put into line 378 and first excised by Bergk, although it is not impossible for the poet to break up the stanza into two groups of two lines each, the one referring to the nurse giving the girl the neck-band test, the other referring more generally to the would-be grandmother.

379-80 **fearful ... sad:**   The mother is given two adjectives here, *anxia* at the possibility of marital discord and then *maesta* if it occurs.

384-408 EPILOGUE: for discussion of this section see the Appendix at the end of the commentary.

384/5 **pure ... heroes:** Gods came in person, because the homes of men were chaste (*castas*), and their owners were (enjambement*) heroes (*heroum*).

385/6 **gathering:** *coetu* has the sense of social and sexual union here – literally so as Peleus has married a goddess. The theme of 'showing' is important here also, reminding us of the showing of the Sea-nymphs' bare bodies at lines 16-18.

386   **heaven-dwellers:** The poet employs the grand epic term *caelicolae* (cf. *pater divum* in the next line) to promote the grandeur and the greatness of men of old. *solebant* is also emphasised: they were actually in the habit of coming down – this was not an isolated occurrence – cf. *saepe ... revisens* in the next line.

387   **gleaming:** The temple is perhaps described as 'shining' both in the gleaming of the gold and silver which was laid down there and also in the imagery of brightness and light which permeates the poem, especially where the grand abode is being described: cf. 43-9.

389   **saw:** Jupiter both saw and was seen; note the alliteration* of *c* and *t* here. The sacrifice is a suitably grand hecatomb (for which see Homer *Odyssey* 7.202); the language reminds us of the sacrifice of Polyxena in 369-70.

390   *Liber* is Dionysus or Bacchus, who has already appeared in this poem rescuing Ariadne. Note here the evocative use of names (*Liber Parnasi ... Thyadas ... Delphi*). Parnassus is the mountain overlooking Delphi and reckoned to be a dwelling of Dionysus and his female followers.

391   *euantis* is an onomatopoeic* word (= *euazein* in Greek) for the ritual cry of the Bacchants. The female worshippers of Dionysus are called Thyiads here and are a

familiar feature of his worship, as in lines 254-64. The poet here reminds us of the figure of Dionysus rescuing Ariadne, as indeed he reminds us of Ariadne compared to a statue of a bacchant at line 61. Bacchants usually have their hair down in a spirit of abandonment ... rather like Ariadne who was literally abandoned and let her hair down in line 63, and like the grief-stricken frenzy of the old women whose white hair was dishevelled at line 350.

392   **Delphi** is here the people of Delphi, who were *laeti* to receive the god on altars smoking with sacrificial offerings.

394   **death-delivering:**   *letifero* is another epic compound, and Mavors is the archaic form of the name Mars as in Lucretius 1.32, 1.475, 5.1296. The gods here are referred to in a highly allusive and scholarly manner, in the tradition of epic poetry.

395   **racing:** *rapidi* is not just quick but also 'snatching' (deriving from *rapio*). The mistress of the Triton is Athena, Homer's *Tritogeneia* (cf. Lucretius 6.750), who was born on the river Triton. The mss then read *ramunsia* which was emended to *Amarunsia* by Baehrens ('Amarunsian maiden') and would presumably refer to Artemis (deriving from Amarynthus in Euboea), a goddess who does indeed come down to fight in Homer (*Iliad* 20. 39) along with Ares and Athena. Others argue however that the simpler emendation *Ramnusia* is correct, referring to Nemesis as at 66.71 and 68.77 (from her shrine at Rhamnus in Attica). 'Catullus is very likely thinking of Hesiod's Nemesis, who will desert mankind at the end of the iron age (*Works and Days* 197-200).' (Quinn) There is no certainty here, but the context does favour Artemis – indeed the original reading *Amarunsia* might have been 'corrected' to *Ramnusia* and then corrupted to *ramunsia*. The present context is one of Homeric-type fighting where the goddess actually appears and encourages the troops, not a personified force leaving them at the end of the iron age.

397-406   The jeremiad against contemporary immorality brings out four specific examples of wickedness involving relationships between: brothers, children, parents and gods. The metaphor in *imbuta* is liquid, reinforced and specified in the following line as brothers' blood.

398   **lustful:** There is no moral objection to being *cupidus* in itself: it is simply that these people allowed their desires to overcome their sense of justice, with the strong metaphor of Justice being routed and made to flee.   Note also the juxtaposition (over two lines) of *fugarunt, perfudere*: the one leading inexorably to the next.

397/9   **soaked ... wet:** The liquid imagery in *imbuta* is now made specific as it is blood being poured on to hands – and brothers' hands at that. For the repetition of *fraterno ... fratres* compare Lucretius 3. 72 ('they cruelly rejoice over the sad death of a brother'), Vergil *Georgics* 2.510.   The worst example of brotherly killing is probably the murder of Remus by Romulus – from the 'heroic age'. Note here how the verbs are all placed emphatically at the start of the three lines.

400-1   **the son** stops mourning his parents (which is bad enough), then the father actually wishes his son dead (worse still). The force of the first statement is that sons ceased to mourn for parents *at all*, rather than that they began to mourn and then stopped.

401-4 The corruption of marriage and the corrupting power of sex – both appropriate in this poem – are explored in grotesque and perverted forms.

402   **new young wife:** Many editors follow the mss reading *innuptae novercae* with the paradox of 'unmarried stepmother'; the sense then is that the man murders his son so that his son will not be in the way when he marries a woman young enough to be his daughter. For the crime Quinn compares Sallust *Catiline* 15 of Catiline's incestuous marriage with Orestilla, 'because she hesitated whether to marry him, fearing his grown-up son, it is believed that he murdered his son and thus rendered his house empty for his wicked wedding'. *novercae* is thus anticipatory of the relationship that the bride would have had with the son if he had not been killed. Much better sense, however, is found in Maehly's *uti nuptae* with Baehrens' *novellae* for *novercae*, so that it is (possibly) the son's wife whom the father is marrying after he has killed her husband – although the text does not specify that it is the son's wife. There is no obvious topical reference here of a man who killed the son and married the daughter-in-law – but then the wicked man might have killed the son simply to avoid the rivalry over his young new wife which his son might present, and the whole scenario is strongly redolent of 67.23-4 and the plot of Plautus' *Casina*. For the imagery of plucking the flower of love cf. Lucretius 4.1105-6.

403-4 **laying ... unwitting:** the clearest parallel to this story (noted by Dee (1982) 109 n.20) is that found in Parthenius *Erotic sufferings* 17: it concerns the mother of Periander, tyrant of Corinth, who conceived such a desire for her son, that she tricked him into becoming her lover in the following way: she told him that a certain beautiful lady wished to be his lover but that she refused to be identified and so insisted on the lights being put out when she visited him. When Periander discovered the truth he began to develop the insanity for which he became famed (suggested by *furore* 405); this is certainly closer than either Pasiphae tricking the bull (who was not her son), Gellius and his mother (in Poem 74), or Oedipus and Jocasta, who both acted in complete ignorance, at least in the Sophoclean version of the story. It is still difficult to explain why Catullus should round off his 'contemporary' catalogue with a tale from old Corinth, however – unless the whole sequence is taken from a Greek source and this original *cause célèbre* was transmitted along with the rest.

405   **speakable and unspeakable:**   *fanda nefanda;* the asyndeton* reveals the muddled state of morals in a muddled form of words, made explicit in *permixta*. *furor* ('madness') is used in Latin both of intense emotions of love, anger etc and also of hallucination whereby we are 'out of our minds'.

406   **turned:**   is almost a repeat of 398, but whereas there it was mortals driving justice out of their minds, here it is the justice-making mind of the gods being repelled by our behaviour.

407-8 **That is why ... :**   *quare* brings us back to the topic, as at 372. *lumine claro* suggests both 'the light of day' and also 'clear vision' (cf. Lucretius 4.824 'the bright lights of the eyes were created so that we might see our way').

COMMENTARY: LXIV   173

APPENDIX: 384-408 EPILOGUE: the contrast is drawn between the heroic past and the unheroic present; the days when gods mixed with men are now gone. The wistful longing for the old days of familiarity between gods and men is at least as old as Homer *Odyssey* 7. 201-206, where King Alcinous says of Odysseus ' ... for in the past they have always appeared plain to see as gods when we sacrifice sumptuous hecatombs, and they feast sitting with us where we sit. Even when a lonely traveller meets them, they make no concealment, for we are close to them, like the Cyclopes and the wild tribes of the Giants.' Of even greater interest here is the manner in which the poet switches from an (apparently) impersonal narrative account of the past to a more involved personal assessment of the present. The epilogue divides into two sections: 13 lines of glorious description of the past followed by 12 lines explaining and decrying the present. The tone of the first half is rich in evocative proper names (*Liber Parnasi ... Thyadas ... Delphi* etc), in epic usages (*caelicolae ... Mavors*) and epithets (*rapidi Tritonis era, letifero belli certamine*) and the poetic voice is unashamedly hyperbolic* in its approval (the homes of these *heroum* were chaste (*castas*), the sacrifice was of a hundred oxen, the worshippers 'ran' out of the 'entire' city 'racing' each other to receive the god). The tone of the second half is equally hyperbolic, the wickedness of the present being every bit as extreme as the piety of the past: the earth is now 'soaked' with 'evil crime', the hands 'wet' with brothers' blood (the 'wetness' image of *imbuta* being both reinforced and made specific), parents and children wish each other dead (the reciprocity brought out by the chiastic *gnatus ... parentes ... genitor ... nati*, the pathos intensified by the adjective *primaevi* – the first child being the occasion of great rejoicing in 'normal' marriages as shown in the sentimental picture of 'little Manlius' in 61. 209-218), or even commit incest, lust (in all its forms) pushing aside all moral principles.

The two sections of the epilogue have a wry and ironic symmetry about them: just as the 'father of gods' was pleased with the death of a large number of animals (387-9), so also the modern father seeks the death of his son: the god Bacchus is called by his title *Liber* to point up the contrast with the wicked father who kills his son in order to be *liber* (402). The last image of the first part is that of the god Mars and the goddesses Athena (Minerva) and Artemis (Diana) rousing the troops to do battle in the 'death-bringing struggle of war': the second section begins with the earth soaked in 'unspeakable crime'. The glorious war of the one and the unspeakable crime of the other, the hecatomb of Jupiter and the murder of a son all produce death as their end-product; but they are not judged in the same way. This is perhaps behind the rather odd phrase 'everything both speakable and unspeakable mingled together in wicked madness' (405): actions which in other contexts might be quite respectable are corrupted into wickedness by the 'madness' of the age. The gods are the guarantors or justice: when men put justice out of their minds the gods ceased to consort with them (398) and human wickedness turned 'the just-making mind of the gods' away from us, the household gods being 'adulterated' by the incestuous mother. The poet leaves the gods literally in obscurity, removed from contact with 'the clear light of day' and thinking it beneath them to visit 'such unions' – unions like that of Peleus and Thetis which can no longer happen – unless the gods consent to marry us.

The ending of this poem has aroused acute interest. On the surface it shows self-evidently the poet lamenting that the sort of events he has described do not occur any more and is one of several pessimistic endings in Roman poetry, arousing similar questions to those surrounding the ending of the *Aeneid* and the *de rerum natura*. Like those of those two poems, the ending has its roots in earlier texts in addition to personal comment: first of all Hesiod concludes his catalogue of the degenerating races of humankind with the following condemnatory account of his own times:

'Now is a race of iron, toil and grief all day and death by night ... the father will not agree with his children, nor they with him, nor guest with host, nor friend with friend, nor will brothers be dear to each other as they once were. They will be quick to dishonour their ageing parents, they will censure them, carping with words of bitterness in their hardness of heart and ignorance of the fear of the gods ... and then Shame and Nemesis, wrapping their fair skin in white garments, will leave the broad-pathed earth and abandon mankind to go to Olympos to join the gathering of the immortal gods. Painful grief will be left to mortal men, with no defence against evil.' (*Works and Days* 176-201)

The parallels with our text are obvious: the breakdown of relationships and the departure of the gods leaving us to suffer. It is inconceivable that Catullus could have composed the ending of this poem without reminiscence of Hesiod, and equally inconceivable that his readers would not recognise it also. Hesiod does not of course have all the gods departing, as does Catullus: the point Hesiod is stressing is that if Shame and Nemesis (personified forces which inhibit us from doing wrong) have left the earth, then there really will be no protection from a jungle mentality and we will be prey to evil of our own making, the verbs being decisively in the future tense. Catullus adapts this idea interestingly: the gods are the preservers of justice and right, but their departure is the result of our wrongdoing and not its cause as in Hesiod, and what is in the Greek poem an elegant anthropomorphic metaphor for human loss of respect for society's laws becomes in Catullus an aetiological myth explaining the observable fact that gods do not share our human lives although legend states that they once did. We rejected Right, and the gods have rejected our company as a result.

Closer still to Catullus' view of things is Aratus, who in his *Phaenomena* explained the departure of Justice from the earth to become the constellation Virgo on the grounds of our wickedness. Human history began with a Golden Age – something like the world evoked in the opening 49 lines of this poem – and for a while all was well:

'Justice ... of old lived on earth and met men face to face, and did not despise (cf. *dignantur* 407) the races of men and women, but mingling with them sat down (cf. 303), although she was immortal ... not yet did men have any knowledge of grievous fighting or insulting disagreement or the noise of battle (cf. 394-6), but they lived a simple life. The cruel sea was far from them, not yet did ships (cf. 1-13) bring their livelihood from miles away, but oxen, the plough (cf. 38-42) and Justice herself, giver of just things ... plentifully supplied all their needs' (Aratus 100-113)

(The golden race gives way to the silver race: Justice still lives on the earth but less willingly so and she tends to stay high up on the hill away from the cities: from there she would address the assembled crowd and threaten them:)

'What a race your golden fathers produced – worse than themselves. You will produce even worse yourselves. Wars and savage bloodshed (such as that of Achilles in 338-360) will be the lot of men and painful suffering shall come upon them' (123-6).

The subsequent race of bronze were the first men 'to forge the brigand's sword, the first to eat the meat of the plough-ox' and so Justice flew up to the heavens where she is visible as a constellation.

COMMENTARY: LXIV 175

Once again, it is almost certain that Catullus had these lines in mind when he composed this text. The literary reminiscence of Hesiod through Aratus places Catullus in a tradition of didacticism which he exploits, using the colour of the earlier poets in an archly allusive manner. On the one hand it is totally appropriate that the poem which has been narrating legendary deeds should finish off with this flourish of an aetiological myth to draw a terminal line under the tale with the explanation of why such tales can never be repeated, using one myth to close the others; on the other, it is surely over-simplistic to see the 'moral' criticism of society in lines 397-408 as straight-faced and sincere when its 'sources' are so clearly literary rather than sociological. The individual crimes referred to are suggestive of the world of tragedy (fratricide and incest occuring in the pages of Sophocles more often than on the *Via Appia*) or perhaps the psychological contorted Love-romances of Catullus' contemporary Parthenius, rather than to the well-documented sources on the Roman vices of corruption and ambition.

The result of this 'borrowing' from earlier Greek poets is paradoxical and two-fold. On the one hand it allows the poet to append his own signature to the poem by bringing the tale of 'once upon a time' (*quondam* 1) right up to his own age (*nobis* 406): this form of closure reflects the poet's shifting of perspective from the past to the present, from the lofty to the degraded, from god's-eye to worm's-eye, and is echoed in poems such as Horace *Epode* 2, the ending of the *ecphrasis** on the Shield of Aeneas in Vergil *Aeneid* 8. 729-31 and Propertius 1.3. Somewhat similar is poem 68, except that Catullus here waits until the end before showing us what appears to be a personal standpoint, while there the mythical and the personal are intertwined throughout. On the other hand, this closure is supremely 'literary' and is therefore unlike those of Vergil and Horace: the poet here masquerades as a moralist, but the fact that his words are so close to earlier sources has the effect of putting them into inverted commas and casting ironic doubts on their 'sincerity'. Catullus does not lack moral convictions – poem 76 is full of moral feeling, for instance – but the allusive language in this epilogue does leave us with a disturbingly unclear picture of the poet's 'own' view. It shows a poet signing off his poem with an irony which both enhances its artificiality and distances our emotional involvement: it signals to the reader that the whole of the foregoing is artefact and not document.

Finally, the epilogue contains hints and echoes of earlier parts of the poem: the slaying of bulls for Jupiter and the spilling of brother's blood both remind us of the slaying of the Minotaur, (Ariadne's 'brother' 150, 181), the sacrifice for the gods recalling the sacrifice of Polyxena, the entrance of Bacchus with his entourage is a clear reminiscence of 251-64, the warfare of Mars recalls the battles of Achilles in 338-360 or the 'death or glory' of Theseus in 101-2, the expulsion of justice by lust recalls Ariadne's bitter account of male lust in 145-8, the death of parents reminds us of Theseus 'killing' of Aegeus by his forgetfulness, while the man who kills family to secure his lover is a gender-reversed reminder of Ariadne who did exactly that. The poet's final instance of human wickedness (the mother deceiving her son into incest 403-4) is quite unlike anything in the poem and emerges hyperbolically out of the sexual desire of the previous line. The effect of the epilogue is, then, a recapitulation of key themes and events in the poem, a teasing adaptation of earlier material into an apparently new and contemporary piece of comment. Once again, we are pleased by the artistry of this but our sureness of the poet's intention is unsettled by it. It is the last of many paradoxes and ambiguities with which this poem leaves us.

6 5

This poem is the first of the collection to be written in elegiac couplets, the metre in which all the rest of the collection is composed (See Introduction § 'Metres'). It is a verse epistle to a certain Hortalus, usually (but by no means certainly) identified with the Quintus Hortensius Hortalus (114-50 BC) who was Cicero's great rival in forensic oratory and who was also known as a composer of erotic poetry himself (cited by Ovid *Tristia* 2.441). The purpose of this poem is to introduce and accompany the following poem (66) as a poetic gift of a translation from Callimachus (16), rather as 68.1-40 introduces (with a similar disclaimer) the rest of poem 68. The poet expresses his sorrow at the death of his brother and apologises that his grief has hindered his poetic creativity – though the poem before us shows no sign of flagging inspiration.

The poem is a single sentence of 24 lines, its main verb being in lines 15-16: the poem reads like a spontaneous outpouring of grief for his brother filtered through the poetic artistry of the medium. The structure of the poem is elegantly symmetrical:

1-12		**3x4 lines**
1-4	poet's inability to write	(4 lines)
5-8	brother's death stated	(4 lines)
9-12	apostrophe to brother	(4 lines)
13-24		**3x2 lines + 1x6 lines**
13-14	Procne simile	(2 lines)
15-16	poet to Hortalus	(2 lines)
17-18	image of carelessness	(2 lines)
19-24	simile of girl and apple	(6 lines)

Notice the way in which the two halves each break down into smaller parts: the first half into three even thirds, the second half into two halves, one of three short couplet units, the second the longest single unit in the poem: this makes the final lyrical simile (19-24) seem all the longer and more impressive. The address to Hortalus is interrupted by the outburst of the poet's feelings for and then to his brother, the poetry thus embodying the emotion which it attests as a reason for not writing poetry.

The grief for the poet's brother is here expressed for the first time and is articulated in mythical and poetic terms; this passage, like poem 101 – and in contrast to the somewhat self-centred grief in poem 68 (19-26, 91-100) – is focussed on the plight of the brother rather than that of the poet. The unwelcome Lethean waters and the weight of the Trojan soil are brought out by the spondaic slowness of *nuper Lethaeo* and also *Rhoeteo quem subter*, by the pathetic alliterative* diminutive phrase *pallidulum ... pedem* enclosing the line and also by the strong verb *obterit*. The depth of emotion produces unusual enjambement* from the pentameter to the following couplet in 10-11 assisted by the repetition of *numquam* (assuming that the lacuna began with this word) and then epanalepsis* of *semper*: words like 'never' and 'always' being highly fitting for this grief.

The mood lightens as the poem continues: the grief is compared to that of the mythical figure Procne allowing the poet to revert to his theme of his duty to compose the poem and to conclude with the touching vignette of the girl whose love-token is discovered. The poem thus begins and ends with the figure of the 'maiden' (*virginibus* (2), *virginis* (20)), the poet's *cura* answered by the *miserae ... tristi* girl. The poet's grief for his brother is no less, but the tone manages to lift itself from the exploration of sorrow to the perspective of the dedication of the following poem, so that 66 is 'prepared' by the ending of 65, as Wilamovitz suggested (cf. 19-24n.).

1-4 An elaborate concessive clause to explain the poet's difficulty in writing, awaiting the explanation in lines 5-8. The poet's grief over his brother causes sexual and poetic frigidity also at 68.5-8, 15-20.

1   **care:** *cura* is frequently used of the passion of love (cf. 64.62): this passage reminds us that the primary sense is of emotional upset (cf. 66.23+n.). The linking together of *assiduo confectum cura dolore* is very strong, ending with a very physical word denoting pain.

2   **The Learned Maidens** are of course the Muses. The word *doctus* is one of great importance in the literature of this period, denoting the 'learned', erudition which was both well-read in the works of earlier (especially Greek) writers and was able to turn out poetry which alluded (often obliquely) to that common fund of poetry. The Muses are *doctae* in that they control the whole realm of poetry and so hold the material whose use will make the new poet himself *doctus* (they are similarly described later by Tibullus 3.4.45, Ovid *Tristia* 2.13, *Met*.5.255: further references in Syndikus 195 n.13).

3   **sweet offspring:** The imagery in *Musarum fetus* is close to Cicero's phrase *fetus animi* for the different branches of philosophy (*Tusculan Disputations* 5.68, cited by Syndikus 195 n.14) and is suggestive here of childbirth – the poet is unable to push out the baby of poetry – a somewhat paradoxical notion in the case of virgin Muses. The 'offspring of the Muses' is expected to be *dulcis* – a prime purpose of poetry being always pleasure, even in the case of verse with other motives besides (e.g. Lucretius 1. 922-950): Horace later epitomises the ideal of poetry as being to mix what is pleasurable with what is useful (*Ars Poetica* 343 (on which see Rudd (1989) 206, 231-2)).

4   **tossing:** For the imagery of being in distress at sea cf. 68.3, 13, 64.62. The phrase *mens animi* sounds like a tautology: strictly speaking the *mens* is solely the seat of reason, the *animus* the seat of thought including emotion as well as reason, and so the 'mind of the heart' ought to mean 'reason unclouded by emotion' – but the two together as a single concept denoting both 'mind' and 'heart' are to be found in Lucretius (e.g. 3. 94-5, where see Kenney ad loc.: 4.758). Catullus here is arguing that his poetic intelligence cannot function because of the swell of emotions in his heart: his *mens animi* is overwhelmed by the rest of his *animus*, his reason is totally clouded by emotion.

5   **Lethe:** the river Lethe in the Underworld was traditionally regarded as the river of forgetfulness, whose waters were drunk by souls about to be reincarnated which thus made them forget their previous lives: e.g. Plato *Republic* 621a, Vergil *Aen* 6. 703ff. The poet alludes to this particular river here presumably to set up a pathetic contrast between his brother who is now in the world of oblivion and the poet himself who will continue to love him (11), although the emotion is now one-sided and futile (as clearly expressed in poem 101). A *gurges* is 'an engulfing

178   CATULLUS

body of water which swallows or sweeps away' (Fordyce) and is the ideal word here
to express the violent removal of the poet's brother, even though the following
line is comparatively gentle.

6.   **poor little pale:** The diminutive *pallidulum* is affectionate: cf. 66.16, 3.18,
17. 15. The line is 'golden'*, with the adjectives and their nouns at opposite ends
of the line framing the verb. The understatement of *manans alluit ... pedem* – all it
takes is a gentle oozing from this water onto the foot to show death immediately –
is expressive of the fragility of human life and contrasts with the more violent
image of *ereptum ... obterit* in the following couplet.

7.   **Rhoetium** is on the Troad: the poet here begins with the general location and
then immediately gives the more precise position of the dead man, with the two
names juxtaposed, just as *litore tellus* shows us the same process in reverse as the
specific leads into the general.

8.   **presses ... down:** *obterit* is used of the dead 'buried and crushed under a weight
of earth' in Lucretius 3.893. *eripio* is used at 68.106 of the snatching away of the
beloved brother: it is also used in 76.20 of the poet's wish to have the 'disease' of
love 'removed'. The word here must go with *nostris ... ex oculis*, 'stolen from our
sight'.

9.   The fact that a line is missing in the MS is perhaps due to the scribe's seeing lines
9 and 10 beginning with the same words and jumping straight to line 10 (after
writing the initial *numquam*, perhaps). A late manuscript (D) has the following
words in place: *alloquar, audiero numquam tua facta loquentem* but, as Syndikus
asserts (194 n.9) this is simply a cobbling together by a scribe, and better sense
is made by Palmer's conjecture in 1896:
numquam ego te potero posthac audire loquentem
('Shall I never again be able to hear you speaking?').

10-14 Apostrophe* to the dead brother, as at 68.20-24, 92-100, broken off with an
emphatic *sed tamen* in line 15. The effect of this apostrophe is of course to demonstrate
the grief which the previous four lines have stated: as if the emotions were so strong that
they burst out even in the middle of a poem addressed to somebody else.

10   **I ... you:** The poet juxtaposes *ego te* in lament that their bond has now been
broken: more bitter still as the brother who now lacks life was dearer to the poet
than life itself. Lines 10-11 are bound by the enjambement*, by the repetition of
amabilior ... amabo, and by the contrast of *numquam ... semper.*

12   **always ... songs:** The poet does not in fact 'always' sing of his grief in the
future – although poems 68 and 101 certainly do so. The statement here is partly
to follow the remark about his poetic incapacity – he cannot write original poems
for grief, but he *can* certainly write elegies over his brother.

13-14 **the Daulian bird** was the nightingale: according to legend (Apollodorus iii.
14.8), Procne and Philomela were daughters of Pandion. Procne was married to
Tereus, king of Daulis, by whom she had a son Itylus or Itys: Tereus raped
Philomela and tore out her tongue to prevent her telling anybody, but she
managed to weave the news into a robe, at which Procne in her fury killed Itylus
and served him up as food for his father. Tereus discovered the truth and pursued
the sisters but the gods transformed all three of them into birds: – Philomela was

turned into a swallow, Procne into a nightingale, Tereus into a hoopoe. She is a fairly common figure in Roman and Greek poetry, her son often being called Itys: cf. Aeschylus *Agamemnon* 1144, Sophocles *Electra* 148f, Horace *Odes* 4.12.15. For the full story see Ovid *Met.* 6. 442ff. The simile* is originally from Homer *Odyssey* 19. 518-23. The comparison is excellent here: Catullus is lamenting his dead brother just as Procne laments her son – but of course Catullus did not murder his brother, and the ramifications turn the reader aside from the surface meaning of the passage. It was Procne's love for her sibling which made her commit the murder which she is now forced to lament, whereas in Catullus' case the dead man is the very sibling whom he loves. Procne lamenting thus combines the themes of a) lament for a beloved dead man b) love of sibling and of course c) the poetic theme of the nightingale (cf. Callimachus' famous image of Heraclitus' poems as his 'nightingales' (*Epigrams* ii, *A.P.* 7. 80)).

13   **thick shades of the branches:**   *densis ramorum umbris* is a direct allusion to Homer's version of the nightingale, the daughter of Pandareos 'sitting in the dense foliage of the trees' mourning Itylus her son (*Odyssey* 19.520). The poet here spends a great deal of the simile describing the setting, little describing the song.

14   The line is framed by the two names: Procne is called *Daulias* after Daulis in Phocis where her husband Tereus lived. *fata* suggests that the death of Itys was somehow 'destined' to happen – whereas in fact his death was deliberately encompassed by his mother as revenge. This is perhaps Catullus tilting the simile towards the brother (who died of 'destiny'; that is, natural causes) rather than the ostensible subject.

15   **And yet ... :**   *tamen ... tantis* is a nice touch of rhetoric: even though the sadness is so great, nevertheless ...   The logic of the poem would suggest that Hortalus had requested (*tua dicta* 17) precisely what poem 66 gives him, and that the poet – grief-stricken though he is – has still (*tamen*) managed to fulfil the request.

16   **Battiades** is Callimachus: the name meaning "son of Battus". Battus was also the name of the legendary founder of Callimachus' native city of Cyrene, and Callimachus calls himself Battiades in *Epigram* 35 Pf. Ancient languages are free with their use of patronymics (cf. e.g. *Amphitryoniades* in 68.112, *Anchisiades* ("son of Anchises") for Aeneas in Vergil's *Aeneid*) both for variation and also for effect. The effect here is of a learned, allusive reference such as Hellenistic poets (such as Callimachus) loved to use: only the learned reader would recognise Callimachus behind the patronymic. *expressa* here means 'translated'.

17   **entrusted ... to the ... winds:**   for the well-known image of promises being entrusted to the winds cf. 30.9, 64.59, Homer *Odyssey* 8. 408, Apollonius Rhodius 1.1334-5, Vergil *Aeneid* 9. 312-3. Catullus here emphasises the point with the effective juxtaposition of *vagis nequiquam*.

18   **poured:**   Catullus perhaps changes the metaphor* with *effluxisse:* from being blown in the wind to being washed away – a combination perhaps of the "wind and running water" on which the promises of women should be written (70.4), as well as looking forward to the rolling out of the apple in the following simile.

19-24 A brilliant simile*, whose relation to the context has been much discussed. Quinn asserts that the apple 'stands for the version itself which C. had been working at when his brother's death caused him to put it aside. To the arrival of the mother and the girl's jumping up corresponds the letter from Hortalus to which poem 65 is Catullus' reply: it said perhaps, "What has happened to that translation of Callimachus?" The letter elicits the translation, which C. will watch tumble forth upon the world, as embarrassed as the girl at its untimely appearance.' This interpretation assumes that the translation was requested by Hortalus, (as is suggested by *sed tamen* in 15), and that the delay has been caused by the adverse effects of his grief. Quinn's unpacking of the simile is perhaps, however, over-precise: the point of contact between the girl and the poet is the sense of forgetfulness and shame, and any more detailed contextual correspondence between the two is unnecessary. Rather, the reason for the simile is stylistic – the poet expresses his embarrassment in 'mock-heroic splendour' (Williams (1980) 48) and thus passes off his feelings in an arch poetic vein which avoids overloading the emotional tone as a 'straight' expression of apology would have done. The simile also undercuts the primary expression of poetic sterility announced in lines 1-4, with a wry irony, whereby this poetically impotent poet can compose a passage as rich and beautiful as this one.

So far, so good: but there still remains the question of whether the love element in the simile has any special significance: the love of a child (Itylus line 14) or a brother (5-12) has been expressed: so why does the poet cloud the issue with this simile of sexual love? Wilamovitz' idea that the love motif looks forward to the love-story which is poem 66 is probably the best theory adduced so far (Wilamowitz (1913) 269, cited by Syndikus (198)).

19   **apple:** For the apple as a gift of love see Aristophanes *Clouds* 997, Theocritus 5.88-9 (with Gow's encyclopaedic note ad loc). The apple was a secret gift from the girl's fiancé (OLD s.v. 'sponsus' shows its primary meaning to be present or future husband), but her virginal status is reinforced in *casto virginis* (20). This apple was clearly not simply thrown as an invitation to sex (as in the parallels quoted from Aristophanes and Theocritus) but treasured as a souvenir of affection: the girl has nothing to be ashamed of, but she is still embarrassed at the revelation of her private (hence *furtivo*) feelings to her mother. What is crucial here is that the simile links together the twin themes of the poem – the poet's sadness (*malis ... maesta ... maeroribus.///.miserae ... tristi*) along with his shame at not sending the promised poetry before now, even though he has nothing to be ashamed of.

21   **soft:** *molli* strengthens the idea of 'feminine'.

22   **shaken ... leaps:** The two verbs (*prosilit excutitur*) are put expressively together at the end of the line, the one movement causing the other as an instantaneous reaction.

23   The whole line looks solely at the movement of the apple, prolonging the girl's agony for the whole line, a line which is spondaic and slow – all but the fourth foot being spondees.

24   **guilty ... sad:** *tristi conscius* go nicely together: she is sad in her guilt being discovered. Note here the effective assonance* *ore rubor*, and the hypallage* whereby the blush is called *conscius*. The spreading of the blush recalls the spreading of the wave at line 6, the sadness of the girl mirroring the poet's

sadness at his brother's death, and also bringing back the 'maiden' theme from the 'Learned Maidens' in line 2: thus the final simile manages to combine the twin elements of grief and shame into a fine vignette whose secondary form and skilful language distills the primary emotion into poetry.

6 6

The background to this poem is thoroughly Alexandrian in every sense. Queen Berenice of Egypt was married to her second cousin King Ptolemy Euergetes when he succeeded to the throne in 247 BC. Shortly thereafter he set out to make war in Syria and his anxious new wife vowed to sacrifice a lock of hair for his safe return. He returned triumphant and the lock was duly sheared and put in the Pantheon at Alexandria. Not long after it mysteriously disappeared, whereupon the court astronomer Conon claimed to find it translated into the heavens as a new constellation. Callimachus used the story to compose a poem in the mouth of the lock itself, explaining and bemoaning its fate: and it is this Greek poem (surviving in part) which Catullus here translates into Latin: for a similar translation of a Greek original see his version of Sappho in poem 51, and for the relation of this poem to the remains of the original Greek poem, see the Appendix, Clausen (1970), Horvath (1962), Putnam (1960) and Wormell (1966).

The poem – like its original, which found its way into the fourth book of Callimachus' *Aetia* – is an aetiological explanation of the constellation *coma Berenices*. The didactic purpose is buried, however, in both poems, behind the personification of the lock itself and the consequent burlesque of human feelings which it expresses. The sentiments are well expressed and perfectly reasonable, but the setting and the inherent eccentricity of the tale lend a distanced air to the poem and give it an unreal quality. The result is a delightfully witty and elegant pastiche of dramatisation (the whole poem is spoken by the lock *in propria persona*), of learning lightly worn (astronomical details casually dropped as they would be by one who was herself a star (65-8), the historical *exemplum* of Xerxes (43-7), the finer points of metallurgy at 49-50), of moral advice (not found in Callimachus, but rendered less than whole-hearted perhaps by the advice intermingled with the lock's insistence on being given scent), of punning (the playing on Zephyrus and Zephyrium at 52-7) and mythical allusions (52-3, 70 etc.), of epic grandeur (36) and of sexual frankness (81) and of both together (12-14). The lock speaks both as a commentator on human affairs who has grown up with Berenice and knows her better than anyone (19-26 etc.) and also as a person in her own right with her own emotions to share (63 etc.): and as the poem nears its end we see that the happiness of Berenice is secured at the price of the happiness of the lock (75-6), and the idyll of the royal couple – both of them capable of brave deeds (27, 36) – gives way to the lament of the discarded lock who might look regal and splendid (line 8 sees her puffed up to her full importance) but is actually a sad and lonely female who would bring the universe down to return to her former anonymity (93-4). All she can expect now is offerings of perfume such as she would have enjoyed daily had she stayed attached to the royal head. There is pathos here – and yet the tone manages to stay predominantly light (see e.g. 63-4), only now and then slipping into elegiac mode (e.g. 75-6) – and there is above all elegance and charm in the poet's exploration of the fanciful story which makes the moral didacticism of the rejection of adultery (84-6) appear as an instrument of ironic distance rather than as a clumsy 'message' to the reader. So proud and haughty a royal lock would have such lofty ideals of sexual propriety – *noblesse oblige*, after all – a pride which is is brought out by her request for generous offerings of decent scent. Irony is never far away in this sort of poetry, and the rhetoric of the lock is always slipping into self-parody and hyperbole*: while it is tempting to see the poem as in some sense an expression of 'real feelings' on the part of the poet, the inherent absurdity of the situation surely renders the exaggerated emotion burlesque rather than tragedy – exactly the sort of burlesque which Alexander Pope achieved in his *Rape of the Lock*.

Clausen (1970) sees the poem as 'an oblique elaboration of the mood expressed more directly in 65', and there are clear points of contact between the dedicatory poem and the gift itself, as one might expect. The lock grieves over the loss of its mistress, just as Catullus grieves for his dead brother, (with a sea-shore involved in both cases), and furthermore the lock explores the temporary grief of Berenice missing her 'brother', contrasted with the permanent grief of Catullus whose brother is lost for ever; the chaste girl at the end of 65 is embarrassed by an apple rolling out of her clothes and would hardly need the stern advice of the lock at 66. 84-88, the same mood of faithful modesty emerging from both poems. Edwards (1991) sees 66 as an antitype to poem 64, and (again) the parallels are there to see. This lock is placed near Ariadne in the heavens (60-61), the sacrifice of bulls is used to express piety (64.389, 66.34), the lock even speaks (66.42) as if she were a 'human sacrifice' (as was Polyxena (64. 362-70)), and grief for a brother is expressed by Ariadne for the Minotaur (64.150, 181) and by Berenice for Ptolemy (66.22) – although neither of them were exactly brothers. The lock speaks as a powerless female in the hands of male strength (66.42-7), and Ariadne is powerless in her abandoned state (64.177-87); the marriage of Berenice and Ptolemy may be idyllic (as was that of Peleus and Thetis), but the speaking lock is almost as unhappy in her desolation as Ariadne: and the grief of Berenice is a healthy expression of love and soon to be ended, while the poor lock, like Ariadne, can see no way out. The only way out for Ariadne is provided by divine intervention, and the lock's final wish implies an equally miraculous translation of distant stars. Ironically, the lock wishes to leave the heavens and return to earth, while Ariadne in 64 wishes to be removed from the seashore where she is, and her crown (in 66.60-61) has been elevated to the heavens as a mark of the love of Bacchus. Both poems end with the moral and contemporary closure which leaves the distant world of the poem behind and places the poet and his readers in the centre of things – there is nothing in the (admittedly fragmentary) Callimachus poem to correspond to 66. 77-88 (see Putnam (1960) 223-8).

Finally, the poem looks back to poems 61 and 62: in particular, the question of false tears shed by the bride has already been raised cynically by the young men at 62.36-7, just as the proposed baring of breasts at 66.81 recalls 61.101. The idyllic marriage of Berenice and Ptolemy mirrors that of the happy couples in 61 and 62, just as it looks forward to that of Laudamia and Protesilaus in 68: it contrasts with the unhappy sexual relations of 67 and of Ariadne in 64. One might even suggest that the shearing of the lock is an oblique reminder of the mutilation of Attis in 63. The thematic links in this collection are indeed strong: and we do not do Catullus justice if we suppose that poem 66 is merely an exercise in linguistic and metrical skill.

The structure of the poem is as follows:

1-14   Self-introduction by the lock
15-32   grief at weddings: two-fold contrast between 'normal' brides and Berenice and between B's earlier bravery and her grief at her husband's departure.

33-38   the lock paid as offering for Ptolemy's success
39-76   the sufferings of the severed lock.
77-94   exhortation to preserve the lock's honour with scent – and moral advice.

1-38 and 39-76 form two exact halves, to which 77-94 have been added as a coda. The metre of the poem is elegiac couplets: see Introduction # 'Metre'.

1-7 The man who: Conon is named after a series of descriptive phrases lasting six lines: for this pattern cf. the opening of Vergil *Georgics*. Conon of Samos was a friend of Archimedes and a distinguished astronomer and mathematician: his works on both subjects earned him renown but are now lost (OCD s.v. 'Conon' (2)).

The symmetry of these opening lines is striking: two lines of *qui* + verb, then two single lines of *ut* + verb followed by a double line of *ut* + phrase; lines 4-6 thus form a tricolon crescendo* (1. *ut* + part of a line; 2. *ut* + a whole line, 3. *ut* + two lines forming a complete elegiac couplet.)

1   **all ... great:**   Note the emphatic opening joining *omnia ... magni* and the 'golden line'* ABCAB pattern of adjectives, verb and nouns. *mundus* is often used of the sky/firmament, as at Lucretius 4.137:   it can also suggest the whole universe ('the earth is placed in the middle of the *mundus*' writes Cicero in *Tusculan Disputations* 1.40.

2   **stars:**   After the catch-all phrase 'lights of the great firmament' (stars, planets, sun, moon) Catullus now singles out the stars.

3   **sun:** The sun is characterised effectively: *flammeus* has the heat and brightness, *rapidi* the speed (paradoxical, as the sun appears to be slow but the heavenly bodies actually move quickly: cf. Mimnermus' reference to the 'swift sun' (frag. 11a West)) and also the sense of voracity (from *rapio* – used of the heat of the sun also by Vergil *Georgics* 1.92: see Mynors on *Georgics* 4.425) and *nitor* the dazzling quality. This is all effectively dampened by the spondaic ending to the line *obscuretur*, just as the sun is darkened at dusk.

4   **fixed times:** Conon the mathematician would have calculated these times.

5   **Trivia:** properly a cult-title of the goddess Hecate: together with Diana she is associated with the Greek moon goddess Selene (as explained by Fordyce on Catullus 34.13). This goddess fell in love with the shepherd Endymion and enjoyed romantic encounters with him on Mount Latmos in Caria. The aitiological myth explained the seasonal disappearance of the moon as being the times when she was on the mountain with Endymion.

Catullus' decision to describe the moon's movements in these romantic terms here is perhaps surprising. He could have simply alluded to the waxing and waning of the moon, as it is the prediction and calculation of the heavenly movements which is the point of the praise of Conon. The poem is in fact a bridal poem and love is its theme; hence any reference to such themes in mythology will be gratefully snatched up by the poet. The love of the goddess is irregular and stolen (*furtim*) (cf. 7.8) but none the less *dulcis* for that: and this love causes the moon to depart from its prescribed pattern of movement, love being an anti-

social, disruptive force as ever. Ironically, the moon's departures from the rules
are themselves regular and can be predicted by one so clever as Conon.

7   **floor:**   *limine* is the reading of Heinsius and makes more sense than the MSS
reading *numine*: the epic phrase the 'sparkling floor of heaven' is pleasing, as is
the idea of a lock of hair dropped on the floor ... of the sky.

8   **me:**   The speaker at last identifies herself with all the grandeur appropriate to her
queenly status. The long adjectival *Beroniceo* and the grand *caesariem* produce a
line in essentially three words. For this slow, stately style of introduction cf.
64.1 (complete with nominal adjective) and cf. also Lucretius 3. 907, Vergil
Aeneid 6. 792.

9   **all:**   The MSS read *multis*, but it is difficult to see the point of mentioning
'many': Haupt's conjecture *cunctis* ('all') is clearly preferable on grounds of sense.
Furthermore, Callimachus' original has Berenice offer the lock to 'to all the gods'.

11   *auctus*:   There is a problem with the MSS *auctus*; a hiatus before its initial vowel
and the need to lengthen its final *-us* before *hymenaeo*. The form of the word
auctus is paralleled at 64.25, but the metrical oddity is still here. The initial
hiatus is more common in Greek, and Vergil uses it in 'Greek' contexts (e.g. *Aen*
1.617 *Dardanio Anchisae*, 3.74 *Neptuno Aegaeo*) as does Lucretius in contexts
which are not specifically Greek (e.g. 3.374 *animae elementa*, but the *-ae* genitive
ending is rarely elided (for details see Kenney ad loc). The Greek word *hymenaeo*
often has this sort of lengthening before it: cf. 62.4, 64.20, Vergil *Aen.* 10.720,
7.398, as do other Greek words (see Fordyce ad 64.20).

12   *vastatum*:   is the so-called supine of purpose, common after verbs of motion.
Assyrian: for Assyrian, read Syrian. Ptolemy Euergetes went off to Syria to
defend his sister, expelled by her late husband's first wife Laodice. By the time he
arrived in Syria she was dead.

13-14   **grappling:**   There is a nice irony here: Ptolemy goes off to fight bearing the
scars of a *rixa* already, a struggle over *exuviae* (spoils). The difference is of course
that this fight took place by night (*nocturnae*) and it produced pleasant (*dulcia*)
marks and the spoils were his new wife's virginity. For poetic conceit of love as
fighting see (e.g.) Lucretius 4.1049-51, Ovid *Amores* 1.9 and for the Greek
background to this see Kenney (1970) 380-385. Note again Catullus' preference
for putting adjectives early on in the line and supplying the nouns to which they
refer later.

15/16   **of ... randy men:**   The sequence of thought here is: most brides cry fake tears
at their wedding, but Berenice's tears were genuine as her husband was going off to
war. *aventum* in the conjecture of Munro for the MSS reading *parentum*, a reading
which has been defended on the grounds that the parents are happy at the wedding
of their daughter, but their joy (*gaudia*) is thwarted (*frustrantur*) by the tears of the
bride. The words *frustrantur ... gaudia* are, however, more appropriate to the
bridegroom than the parents; furthermore, these tears are shed *inside* the bedroom,
where parents would not be present to witness (an objection which Nisbet seeks to
counter by emending *intra* to *citra* (Nisbet (1995) 91). Clearly the ardent youths
have far more to be disappointed about if their brides cry; but the use of *aventes* to
mean *cupidi* is not paralleled and the emendation cannot be regarded as certain.
For the typical bride's tears cf. 61.81ff: for the reasons why they feel the need to

cry see 62.20-25. The marriage of Peleus and Thetis was not attended with tears _
though the Parcae sing a song which would make anyone cry – but the 'marriage'
of Ariadne and Theseus certainly was (e.g. 64. 71ff). The falseness of the bride's
tears is brought out by the pathetic diminutive *lacrimulis*: for the mocking use of
the diminutive cf. Lucretius 4.594, 4.1279 (*muliercula*): cf. also the pathetic use
of diminutives at Catullus 3.18, 17. 15, 65.6. The juxtaposition of joys next to
tears (*gaudia lacrimulis*) is pointed and effective. Venus is of course here
metonymic* for sex/marriage: she also has a function as a planet in the heavens,
as referred to at line 56.

17   **by the bucket:** adverbs ending -*im* are common in vulgar Latin and the effect
of *ubertim* is again comic and mocking: cf. Petronius 44.18 (*urceatim*). Here
there is a further rude edge to the word in the etymology from *uber* (the udder of a
cow).

18   **may the gods:** The word order is a fine example of hyperbaton* – contorted
and yet elegant. The sense of the line is easily disentangled but the initial reading
of the words would put *non ita me divi vera* together to suggest: '(other brides may
cry falsely but) not thus me gods true ... ' leading the reader to expect a
protestation of her own honesty, whereas in fact she is continuing her general
remarks about brides. Hyperbaton is quite common in Latin and Greek – even in
comedy – and the word order seems to have posed fewer problems for the hearer
than one might expect. *iuerint* is from *iuvo*, whose perfect tense is *iuui* and
perfect subjunctive is thus *iuuerim:* this shortens to *iuerim* to give the third
person plural form *iuerint*, as in Plautus (*adiuerit* in *Rudens* 305).

19   **me ... my:** Berenice is quite different from these other brides, as is well
brought out by the juxtaposition of *mea me*. Her queen wept, but the poet uses a
grander word (*querellis*) rather than the 'little tears' of other women (16).

20   **to see:** *inviso* is perhaps an unusual word here: it means 'go to see' rather than
'go to fight': cf. 31.4, 64.384. In this context it is euphemistic and perhaps
represents the sort of word a husband departing to battle might use to his anxious
wife. The fact that they have only just been married is again pointed out in *novo*.

21-2   **Did you:** the lock addresses Berenice directly in an abrupt apostrophe* straight
after referring to her in the third person. The lock teases Berenice gently about
why she was so upset to lose her husband: were her feelings those of a woman
robbed of her marriage bed, or those of a sister bereft of her brother? Ptolemy and
Berenice were in fact cousins, but are often referred to as brother and sister in
inscriptions. The lock is quite sure that it was not mere family feeling that wanted
Ptolemy back home, as she makes clear in the reference to marriage-bed (*cubile*)
and loneliness (*deserta*). The poetic amplitude of *fratris cari flebile discidium*
sounds like a mockery of formal mourning, as at Lucretius 3. 906-8.

23   **eat ... marrow:** For passion eating cut the marrow of the bones cf. 35.15 and
also Vergil's Dido (*Aen.* 4. 66). For high emotion running through the bones: cf.
e.g. *Aen* 2.120 (fear), Plautus *Most.* 243 (love). Here the line is extremely
emotional, with the spatial sense of 'deep down', the physical metaphor* of
'eating away', the marrow being pathetically 'sad' and the lugubrious assonance*
of *cura medullas*. For *cura* as referring to grief cf. 65.1: here it carries its other
common sense of the effects of love as in 64.62, Lucretius 4.1067.

24 The alliteration in this line of the letter 't' is striking, as is the enjambement*
    into line 25 and the next couplet. For the thought of *toto pectore* cf. 64. 69-70,
    of *sensibus ereptis* cf. the sensory deprivation of the speaker in poem 51.
26 **brave-hearted:**   The lock has been attached to Berenice and so is qualified to
    make this remark.   *magnanimam* is perfect for the context, suggesting both
    'brave' (i.e. able to stand suffering such as this) and also ' noble' (OLD s.v. 1)
27 **the brave deed:**   this was Berenice's part in murdering her first husband
    Demetrius, to whom she was married against her will by her mother and who
    transferred his affections from her to her mother. It was only by killing Demetrius
    that she was able to marry Ptolemy Euergetes and thus obtain the kingdom. We do
    not possess the requisite lines of the Greek original: Catullus presumably calls
    the deed *bonum* because Demetrius had been her mother's lover: the reference calls
    up other instances of abnormal sexual relations between the generations, as in
    poem 64. 403, 67.29-30.
28 **no braver deed:** The MSS reading *quod non fortior aut sit* is clearly wrong:
    reading *ausit* for *aut sit* is easy enough. This then leaves the sense of *fortior* as
    concessive ('even though he is braver ... ') which is weak. Muretus' suggestion
    quo fortius is an admirable emendation and almost certainly correct, focussing as
    it does on the deed itself as second to none in bravery. *alis* is a contraction of
    alius.
30 **you wiped:**   *tristi* has overtones of *tristis* (sad) as well as its primary meaning
    of 'you wiped' (being a contraction of *trivisti*). For the exclamation to Jupiter cf.
    48, 1.7.
31-2 **changed:**   Such sad behaviour is hard to square with the brave Berenice of old,
    and so the lock wonders which god transformed her – or is it simply love. The
    double possibilities produce a sort of bathos*, from the grandeur of *tantus deus* to
    the banal simplicity of lovers not wishing to be parted.
33/4 **sweet:** . the husband is called *dulci* just as the marks of their lovemaking were in
    line 13.
    bull's: The unusual adjective *taurinus* sounds arch – what the poet means of
    course is the sacrifice of bulls: the mention of blood is emphatic, as the bulls (not
    to mention the captive Asia) pay with their blood to keep his blood safe.
35 **return:**   the phrase *reditum tetulisset* is archaic and expresses the sense of a
    formal vow made in religious manner.
36 **captured Asia:** the purpose of Ptolemy's trip to Syria was to protect his sister
    (see note on line 12), but he continued his triumphant march across the Euphrates
    to the borders of India, thus adding territory to Egypt's kingdom. The litotes *haud
    in tempore longo* and the whole of line 36 sound very much like the language of
    encomiastic* inscriptions.
37 **For these deeds:** *quis* is a contracted form of *quibus*. The lock of hair has been
    duly given to the celestial gathering, both in the obvious sense of being
    sacrificed and also in the sense that she is now among the heavenly host of stars.
38 **old ... new:** *pristina ... novo* is a strong contrast. A *votum* was an offering of
    a gift, usually a promise that a specified gift would be made in the event of the
    prayer being answered; e.g. Horace *Odes* 1.5.14. Here the queen has promised the
    gift of the lock and so, on Ptolemy's return, must render the gift (hence *pristina*

vota): but the lock has been made into a constellation, which is both a new 'function' for a piece of hair (OLD s.v. 'munus' 1) and also a novel gift for the gods, as never before have *vota* been stars.

dissoluo is scanned as four syllables to give the necessary dactylic second half to the pentameter.

39-40 **O queen:** A couplet made famous by Vergil's imitation of it at *Aeneid* 6.458-60, where Aeneas seeks to apologise to Queen Dido whom he is about to abandon in Carthage in order to fulfil his mission. He pleads that he did not want to leave her and says:

> *per sidera iuro ...*
> *invitus, regina, tuo de litore cessi.*

('I swear by the stars ... I was reluctant to leave your shore, O queen').

The oath on the stars and then the direct quotation from a shorn lock now made into a star is striking, and scholars have been surprised that Vergil should use in a piece of high epic what Austin (ad loc.) calls here a 'piece of fun'. One possible explanation for that would be that both Catullus and Vergil are imitating a common but lost source which was high and serious: this allows Vergil to keep the seriousness while Catullus can quietly send it up. Alternatively, Vergil consciously used the Catullan/Callimachean original without any 'violation of literary taste' (Austin ad loc.), perhaps in ironic poignancy that a poem about a happy queen such as Berenice (who has only lost her lock of hair) can be quoted to so unhappy a queen who has lost everything. The emotion expressed here by the lock is of course parodistic: the dignified epanalepsis* of *invita ... invita* (no such repetition in the Greek original), the emotional apostrophe* *o regina*, and the misuse of the oath-formula of swearing by the head which is so absurdly appropriate for a lock of hair, are burlesque rather than high drama.

41 **Let anyone:** Such an oath is a serious matter, as is shown by the ritual curse on perjurers: again the style is reminiscent of laws.

42 **blade:** Catullus' heroic use of *ferro* meaning in the context simply 'steel' to cut hair but also suggesting 'sword' gives an epic bravado to the lines, to be continued in the rhetorical comparisons with Mount Athos to follow.

43-47 **even that mountain:** An example of the victory of steel over a mountain: if such a thing cannot withstand steel, then *a fortiori* neither can a flimsy lock of hair. In fact Mount Athos is not the largest mountain in Greece – the poet exaggerates for rhetorical effect.

43 **overturned:** *eversus mons* is expressively juxtaposed, the fantastic picture of a mountain being overturned. As befits a heroic effort on the greatest mountain on earth, the following line sees a heroic allusion to the 'offspring of Thia': that is, the sun god Helios, child of Thia and Hyperion. Thia was the wife of Hyperion and mother of the sun, the moon and the dawn as described by Hesiod (*Theogony* 371-4) and invoked by Pindar (*Isthmian* 5.1ff): she is the begetter of light in the universe, hence the juxtaposition of *Thiae clara*.

The incident described occured when the Persian king Xerxes in 483 BC dug through the isthmus behind Athos in order to avoid having to sail around the promontory which had seen the destruction (in a storm) of the Persian fleet in 492

B.C. (Herodotus 7. 22-24); not exactly turning the whole mountain upside down
...

45-6   **gave birth to:**   The fantastic nature of Xerxes' feat is brought out by the
striking metaphor* of giving birth to a new sea; followed by the image of the
youth of the Orient swimming through the middle of a mountain.

48   **Jupiter:**   For the exclamatory *Juppiter* cf. 30.
Chalybes were a tribe famed as the original metalworkers: they were supposed
to live on the shores of the Black Sea.

49-50   **who first:**   The ancients liked to identify the 'first discoverer' of each human
endeavour, if only (as here) to curse them when that endeavour goes wrong.
Catullus here gives a brief explanatory gloss of the work of the Chalybes (49-50);
it was an Alexandrian characteristic to be interested in the details of the lives of
working people (cf. Apollonius Rhodius 2. 374-6, 1001-7 on the Chalybes
themselves, and 3. 491-5, 4.1062-5 on the lives of working women). We find
similar interest in Homer *Iliad* 18. 369-477, Callimachus *Hymn* 3. 46-69 and
Vergil's description of the Cyclops at work in *Aen* 8. 416-53. The poet uses the
mots justes: *venas*, *stringere* (meaning to make the molten iron into 'pigs' or
stricturae). As often, poets in the tradition of Alexandrian literature strive to be
authorities on their subject-matter.

51   *abiunctae* is in the genitive case 'agreeing' with *mea* and thus meaning 'the
sisters of me who have been cut off': this is more likely than that it is nominative
agreeing with the sisters – Callimachus' original has *neotmeton* ('cut off')
agreeing with the lock as the object of the sisters' grief. (This is one of the
'ambiguities of expression' discussed in Levin (1959))

52-3   **the sibling of ... Memnon;**   Memnon's brother Zephyrus, the West Wind:
both of them children of the Dawn (Eos or Aurora), who is represented as a winged
horse. The rococo wit and allusions now multiply rapidly: Queen Arsinoe (wife of
the previous king Ptolemy II Philadelphus, sole ruler of Egypt from 282-246 BC)
was identified after her death with Aphrodite (Roman Venus) and had a temple at
Zephyrium, (a place near Alexandria founded by the Locrians, hence *Locridos* in
54), from where she derived the title of *Zephyritis* at line 57. It was to this temple
at Zephyrium that the lock was transferred from the Pantheon in Alexandria where
it was originally put.

56   **lap of Venus:**   i.e. in the temple of Aphrodite at Zephyrium: the suggestion is
that the Zephyr blew the lock mysteriously out of the Pantheon and into the
Zephyrium temple and onto the lap of the statue of the goddess.

57   **Zephyrium** has of course nothing to do with Zephyrus the West Wind, but both
Callimachus and Catullus use it as the vehicle for the pun whereby the mistress of
Zephyrium is also the mistress of Zephyrus.

58   **Canopus:**   Again, geographical allusion: Canopus was not far from Zephyrium
(local colour presumably clearer to Callimachus' Alexandrian readers than `o
Catullus' Roman audience): it was famous enough for the adjective to stand for
'Egyptian', and its people congratulated by Vergil *(Georgics* 4.287) for their good
fortune in having their fields irrigated by the Nile without their having to work, a
form of luxury enjoyed by gods and royalty and hence appropriate here of a deified
queen. Her Greek status derives from the Macedonian dynasty of the Ptolemies:

cf. again Vergil *Georgics* 4.287 where the town is called *Pellaei* after Pella the birthplace of Alexander the Great who conquered Egypt.

59-61   **crown:** The *corona Borealis* constellation is said to have been the crown given to Ariadne by Bacchus on their wedding and this is clearly what is referred to here. The first few words of the line are corrupt, however and require emendation. Postgate's *inde Venus* has been accepted by many with the awkward separation of *venus ... diva* an unfortunate hiccup. Friedrich's *hic liquidi* seems a better reading, as it would be unnecessary for the poet to name Venus but would be quite in keeping with his style to describe the heavenly destination, and the resulting line has a pleasing 'golden'* symmetry about it.

61-2   **I ... might shine:** the grandeur of the haughty lock elevated to the heavens is well brought out by the fifth foot spondee (*fulgeremus*) followed by the pompous self-description in four words arranged in chiastic sequence in the pentameter.

62   **blonde:**   Ariadne also had blonde hair (64.63); this may be a conscious comparison with the rival head, or (as Fordyce suggests ad loc.) an automatic attribution of blonde hair to heroes and heroines, or simply an appropriate colour for what is now a shining constellation – not even Conon would have spotted a brunette lock in the night sky.

63   **wet:** For the diminutive *uvidulam* cf. 15n. The lock is here complaining of the wetness she endured from the sea-spray in the seaside temple: a state of constant wetness throughout her time there, not a temporary wetness caused by the journey from Zephyrium to the heavens (presumably a vertical take-off involving no crossing of the sea). As well as the feeble complaining here of wetness note also the bumpy ride she gets to the heavens in the ending of the hexameter with a monosyllable, as well as focussing all the attention on little *me*. (cf. Lucretius 5.25 and see esp. Mynors on Vergil *Georgics* 3.255)

64   **put me:** The Narcissistic phrasing continues: note the collocation of *antiquis diva novum* with the contrast of old and new and the central divinity behind the promotion.

65   **Virgo ... Leo:** The constellation is in fact close to the constellations Leo (65), Virgo (65), Bootes (67), Corona Borealis (i.e. the crown of Ariadne, 60) and Ursa Major (66). The poet assumes knowledge of the constellations in the audience: astronomy was of course a popular subject in Alexandrian literature (cf. Aratus *Phaenomena*) and was equally popular in Latin didactic literature (Cicero translated Aratus: Manilius later composed his masterpiece *Astronomica* in five books).

The stars are not merely spots of light; any constellation called Leo must be savage, and the constellation Ursa Major (The Great Bear) is only mentioned allusively as Callisto daughter of the Arcadian king Lycaon (a companion of the virgin goddess Artemis who was turned into a bear by the angry Artemis when she found her with child by Zeus: she would have had her hunted down by the pack if Zeus had not placed her into the sky. (Graves *The Greek Myths* vol i. 22h: for a different version of the story see Ovid *Metamorphoses* 2.401-530))

67-8   **Bootes:** always referred to as slow, right from Homer *Odyssey* 5. 272; cf. also Aratus *Phaenomena* 581-5. Note the poetic intensification of *vix sero*.

69   **the footsteps of gods:** the gods live beyond the stars and are here visualised as walking on the 'floor of heaven' (cf. 7, Aratus *Phaenomena* 359, Manilius 1. 803), trampling on the lock. The lock is in the sky by night, but returns to the ocean as the constellation wheels round at dawn.

70   **Tethys** was the wife of Oceanus: see 64.29-30 and nn. The poet names her here to vary the language, having just mentioned Oceanus by name in line 68.

71   **Rhamnusian maiden:** i.e. Nemesis, who had a famous temple at Rhamnus in Greece. Nemesis might be rendered 'righteous indignation' and appears as a deification in Hesiod *Theogony* 223. where she is described as child of Night and 'an affliction for mortal men'. It is the expression of that public outrage at arrogant presumption; often linked with shame as the two forces which inhibit misbehaviour, the one internal, the other external (see Aristotle, *Nicomachean Ethics* 1108a32ff): here, as often, the force of divine displeasure at human pride and ingratitude. The lock ought to be grateful for her translation to the heavens, but is about to wish herself back on her mistress' head, risking the censure of the other stars for doing so (73).

72   **truth:** the lock's motives are honesty: to keep silent out of fear would be dishonest.

73-4   **tear me apart:** *discerpent* is here metaphorical* ('tear to pieces' exactly as in English). Swearing by the stars of heaven is relatively common (Vergil *Aeneid* 4.519, 6.458, Statius *Thebaid* 10.360) as the stars see everything and so can affirm the truth of one's words – the irony here is that the stars may tear her apart if she tells ... the truth!

74   **unfolding:** the metaphors in this line are mixed: *condita* suggests 'buried deep down' and in need of excavation from the depths of the breast, while *evoluam* literally means 'roll out' and would be more appropriate of unrolling a scroll (OLD s.v. 6). The use of *veri* with *pectoris* is a case of hypallage*, as it is the tale which is true, not the breast which contains it – but this way the lock manages to suggest that 'her heart is true' as well. The breast was seen as the centre of intellect as well as feelings by many ancient people: see Homer *Iliad* 2.142, 4.309, Plato *Phaedrus* 236c, Lucretius 3. 140.

75-6   **to be away:** expressive epanalepsis* of *afore ... afore*, here used for rhetorical wistful effect as also frequently in 64 (26-7, 61-2, 132-3, 259-60, 285-6, 321-2, 403-4). It was a particularly Hellenistic device: (cf. Callimachus *Hymn* 4.118-9, 5.40-41, Theocritus *Idylls* 9.1-2, 18.50-1) and used by other Roman poets also (e.g. Lucretius 5. 950-1, Vergil *Aeneid* 1. 108-9). The torment of the lock is expressed by the emphatic *discrucior,* similar to the *excrucior* used by the poet of his own feelings at 85.2. Note here how the poet translates the bare 'her's' in the Greek original into *dominae* in Latin (Zwierlein (1987)).

77-8   **cheap scent:** The lock explains her pain in bathetic* terms: it is the lavish scent which she misses more than anything, having had merely girlish scent until Berenice got married and then being cut off before she could enjoy the expensive perfumes for which Berenice was famous (Athenaeus xv. 689a). Just as she complained about being wet with sea spray at 63, so here she complains of the 'cheap scents' she had to endure, satirising herself and giving good grounds for her plea for libations.

Lobel's correction *vilia* for the MSS *milia* is made virtually certain by the Greek original *lita* ('cheap things').

79-86   The lock appeals for libations from the good but not from the wicked. As in 64, the poem ends with a 'moral' twist which brings the remote past and distant constellation into the everyday behaviour of the reader, a form of closure of which Catullus was clearly fond.

80   **affectionate:**   *unanimis* cf. 9.4, 30.1, Vergil *Aeneid* 4.8, Plautus *Stich.* 731.

81   **casting ... :**   the phrase is not necessary, as the meaning is quite clear from the previous line: but the sense is clearly that the brides should not indulge their sensory pleasures without giving the lock her sensory pleasure (hence *iucunda*). For the erotic thought cf. 64.65, Propertius 2.15.5.

82   **onyx** is here a perfume-jar. For the Greek and Roman taste in perfumes see Griffin (1985) 10-11. For the epanalepsis* see 75-6n.

83-4   **chaste:**   The contrast is drawn between the 'good' married people and the bad ones; *casto* here hardly means 'celibate' (as often, e.g. Lucretius 1. 98: see OLD s.v. 5) but simply 'faithful' as opposed to the *impuro* or adulterous.

85   **dust** is proverbially insignificant, (*levis*; cf. 61.199) but even dust will ruin the offerings of the impure. *irrita* is the perfect word to express the futility and waste of the perfume: cf. Vergil *Aeneid* 9.313. The high emotion of the line is brought out by the exclamation *a!*

87-8   **may harmony:**   Sounds like a pious prayer for domestic happiness and wifely good behaviour – or is it selfish longing to have offerings, seeing that the lock will only accept them from good people? The lock intensifies her prayer with the repetition of *semper* and the emphatic framing of line 88 *semper ... assiduus.*

89-92 Apostrophe to Berenice herself: the lock wistfully asks her former owner to remember her in her offerings.

90   **days:**   *luminibus* means simply 'days' but also has the sense of lights appropriate to stars in the sky.

91   **allow:**   *siris* is an archaic optative form from *sino,* contracted from *siveris* like *iuerint* at line 18. The ending of the line is metrically irregular and concentrates attention on the conjunction of *tuam me* (the lock is still Berenice's). For the effect cf. 63n.

93-4   **perish:**   A problematic text. The MSS read *sidera cur iterent utinam ...* which has been taken to mean: '(Give lots of gifts) to give the stars a reason for repeating "let me become a royal lock ... " '. i.e. make the other stars jealous of my good fortune. This reading leaves the last line to mean 'even if that makes Aquarius shine next to Orion' – i.e. even if we fall out of the sky and cause stars which are distant (Orion and Aquarius are in fact 100 degrees apart) to bunch up together. Quinn's reading of the last phrase as 'I don't care how bright Orion is ... ' relegates the phrase *proximus Hydrochoi* to being no more than a filler/piece of inessential information, and is for that reason unlikely to be correct. Lachmann's *corruerint* amounts to a defiant curse by the lock: 'let the stars go hang, I want to be a lock again, and I don't care if Orion shines next to Aquarius!' – that is, I do not care if my absence causes chaos in the heavens (although the stars managed quite nicely without the Lock until 247 B.C.: the lock's self-importance is ironically stated). The (fragmentary) Greek original certainly mentioned both Orion and Hydrochoos, exactly as in Catullus, but certainty about the precise point being made is likely to remain elusive.

6 7

After the lament of a lock in poem 66, a dialogue with a door: comic and salacious in
character, topical and local after the exotic Hellenistic flavour of poems 63-6. The form
of the poem is that of a rhetorical *diffamatio* ('lampoon' Copley (1949) 245) and, for all
its spicy colloquialisms, it follows closely many of the patterns of rhetorical theory and
practice (see Macleod (1983) for details). The question of the identity of the people
referred to remains a mystery: are the father and son mentioned in lines 1-6 the same as
the incestuous and impotent (respectively) pair in lines 23ff – as argued by Copley
(1949), Quinn and Goold (1983)? Why does the door mention Caecilius? Is he the son of
Balbus in line 23, as argued by Giangrande (1970), or the man with red eyebrows of line
46, as suggested by Macleod? To all these questions we can only propose tentative
answers, which might be summarised thus: Caecilius is the present owner of the house
and the door, but is neither the father nor the son being lampooned, while the wicked lady
in question must have committed her adulteries in Brixia (why else would Brixia know of
the tale?) and then come to Verona (where the door is (34)) to marry the younger Balbus.
She need not have been married in Brixia to commit adultery – Postumius and Cornelius
might have been married men – and this removes the need to postulate Goold's theory of
an earlier but unconsummated marriage in Brixia (somewhat unlikely in view both of the
woman's taste in lovers and of the parallel with 66.84 where *adulterio* also refers to
unmarried women misbehaving). The 'red-haired man' at the end of the poem might be
Caecilius – it would be a nice touch of ring-composition and would explain the otherwise
unexplained naming of Caecilius at the beginning of the poem.

The narrative outlined above can be inferred from the text, although its details are still
a matter of argument. It is perhaps more important to appreciate the literary and stylistic
qualities of the poem than to identify precisely whose dirty linen is being displayed, as
the poet was surely writing for a wider audience and also hoped that his work *plus uno
maneat perenne saeclo* (1.10) and so the topical references cannot be the sole or even the
main point of interest in the text. At least in discussing the style we are on firmer
ground.

The structure of the poem is as follows:
1-8   address to the door
9-14   door protests innocence
15-19   need for proof discussed
20-28   the wife was deflowered by her father
29-30   sarcastic response
31-48   the lady's other misdemeanours

We see at once that the sarcastic response at 29-30 neatly marks the end of one tale and
the beginning of the next, and that the questioning of the door's knowledge at the end
(37-41) mirrors the questioning of its probity at the beginning. The registers of
language used range widely: the crude (30), the direct and simple (36), the lewd comic
description (21-2), the heavy sarcasm (29-30), the playful use of unnecessary

description (32-4), rhetorical question-and-answer both 'real' (15-18) and anticipated (37), didactic manner (19-20), the topically allusive (45-48) and the morally outraged (24-5). As with the previous poem, we are in little danger of taking this poem too seriously: not only the scabrous contents but also the absurd setting and speaker make the text comic rather than serious, witty more than it is shocking. As with poems 64 and 66, the text ends with a topical closure which (again) distances the reader from the arch poetry which has preceded it, the final image in the mind of the reader being one of caricature and satire of a recognised individual.

The literary convention of having an inanimate object deliver an address is familiar enough from tombstones and was much used in Hellenistic epigrams (e.g. *Anth. Pal.* 7.64, 524) and continues the sequence begun in poem 64 with the dumb tapestry on the bed of Peleus and Thetis producing the tale of Ariadne (complete with speeches), through the speech of the forlorn lock of Berenice in poem 66. This poem is an interesting variation on the 'serenade' (*paraklausithyron*) where the lover, shut out from his beloved's house, speaks to the hard door begging admission, even smearing the step with perfume (Lucretius 4. 1177-9: for examples of the genre, see Asclepiades 5.167.1-2, 189.1-2, Propertius 1.16, Horace *Odes* 3.10, Copley (1956)). The poem opens with the language of the serenade, but it soon (5) becomes clear that the speaker has no wish to secure admission but only information (*dic ... quare* 7). The door – unlike the dumb and hard doors addressed in the typical serenade – goes on freely to give the information sought and more besides: it is worth pointing out however that the speaker both solicits the tale with a moral accusation (5-8) and is himself an agent of gossip (*dicunt* 3). If the door seems to tell the salacious details with a certain amount of relish, this is to be seen in the tradition of garrulous slaves gossiping in Roman comedy – the door is even described as a slave (5).

It is difficult not to see this poem as placed for deliberate effect between poems 66 and 68. Looking back to 66, the door is, like Berenice's lock, an inanimate object bound to an owner who knows and reveals personal details about them: the idyllic marriage of Berenice to her heroic husband is in stark contrast to the nameless adulteress in 67 whose nominal husband is ridiculously impotent and whose past is anything but fragrant. The lock is a sure sign of the reunion of the married couple, while the door ought to be – but has not been – the safeguard of marital fidelity. The lock was a helpless female in the hands of the brute sword (66.42-50), while Balbus' wife faced no danger at all from her husband's limp *sicula* (21); the lock refuses offerings from those women who commit adultery (66.84-6), while the door criticises Balbus' wife for similarly committing *malum ... adulterium* (67.36). The lock heard the sad words spoken by Berenice to her husband departing for the wars (66. 29), while the door heard the wicked wife boasting of her exploits in whispers to her slaves. The mock-heroics of 66 here become a savage burlesque of perverted comedy and parodied rhetoric (as analysed by Macleod (1983)). When we look at 68, however, the situation is reversed again: Laudamia is the type of the faithful wife, like Berenice but unlike Balbus' wife in 67 or Lesbia in 68. The 'moral' approval of fidelity assumed in the scathing scandal in 67 is given a more personal and more delicate handling in 68, where the heat of passion (73: cf. 67.25) is balanced against the grief of loss (both of his brother and of the fidelity of his lover) with the passion and the grief counterposed in the separation and the subsequent reunion of Laudamia and Protesilaus, mirroring the similar separation and reunion of Berenice and

Ptolemy: the fake pregnancy, which is a final caricature of farcical proportions in 67, becomes a late, unexpected and totally welcome childbirth in 68 (119-24) – a symbol both of the joy of Laudamia's union and of the peace of family life, in stark contrast to the joyless lust and the sordid scandals of poem 67. The closure* of all three poems is similar: the remote worlds of myth, of gossip and innuendo, of heroic legend are all in their different ways distanced and refracted into the stuff of poetry; and all three are brought into the lives of the reader and the world of the present at the end of the poems, as the lock utters stern advice to newly weds, as the door neatly shatters its own self-defence of loyalty by open criticism of its new master, and as the poet who has traversed the wide world of time and space ends his elegy with moving mention of his mistress.

1-3 The formal opening only names its addressee in line 3, to make the reader imagine that it is a woman who is being addressed. The irony then is: 1) that the real addressee will tell of a woman who is anything but pleasing to a beloved husband and parent and 2) that even this 'good' door has been unable to prevent the incest and adultery which went on behind it.

1　　　**Pleasing ... pleasing:**　For the repetition of *iucunda* cf. the hymenaeal repetitions in 62. 21-2, 28, esp. 42, 44.

2　　　**enrich:** *aucto* means 'to cause to grow' and would not appear to have a great deal of point when addressed to a door. It sounds like a conventional greeting: but perhaps there is a pun on the name Ops (mother of Jupiter).

3　　　**O door:**　Doors are expected to keep the household safe from adulterers and intruders and thus to preserve the honour and property of the family; the damage to the honour of this particular house (24) was committed behind the door and thus cannot be blamed upon the door. Balbus kept his door shut for both reasons, and managed to avoid being cuckolded himself: his probity does not exclude the possibility that he was the father who seduced his daughter-in-law, as suggested by Kroll and disputed eloquently by Giangrande (1970) 99-100. *ipse* has the sense of 'the master' as often (OLD s.v. 12), in contrast to the new young master who is anything but master of his house or his wife.

5-6　　**on the other hand:** *rursus* derives from *reversus*. The door's behaviour was perhaps mean towards the new master in being excessively indulgent towards his wife. *nato* is Froehlich's conjecture for the MSS *voto:* the mss reading can be defended as meaning 'marriage-vow' and hence 'marriage' (so Giangrande (1970) 86-7 and tentatively Macleod (1983) 187 n.4): this demands a metaphorical expression 'to be a slave to a marriage-vow' which is perhaps unlikely in the case of a door: to be the cheating slave of a 'son' is far more natural language, commanding 'the immediate comprehension which is indispensable in a *diffamatio*' (Copley (1949) 248).

6　　　**a bridal door:** An odd expression. The situation is clear enough – the old man dies and his son brings a wife to the house, thus giving the door the chance to be a 'bridal door' and have a bride carried over its threshold, if the wedding was subsequent to the father's death – for this applied sense of *maritus* cf. Ovid *Heroides* 2.41 ('Juno, who presides over the bridal bed (*toris maritis*)'). The phrasing here does suggest that the old man was a widower. The connection between the funeral and the wedding is well brought out by the sandwiching of *porrecto facta marita sene.*

7   **Come now ...** :   *dic agedum* is peremptory and colloquial. *feraris* (meaning 'you are talked about') links up with *ferunt* (5), *dicitur* (10), *fertur* (19), *dicitur* (24) *dicit* (31), *narrat* (35), *dixerit* (37), etc. The poem is a sustained piece of reported discourse, orchestrated gossip, as well as masquerading 'as a historical investigation' (Macleod (1983) 191) in the manner of Alexandrian poetry such as Callimachus' *Aetia.*

8   **long-standing:**   *veterem* could go with either *dominum* or *fidem* and is to be taken with both.

9-14 The door of course is not responsible for what its owners get up to, and here pleads its innocence. The saga of the woman's immorality will become ever more damning as the poem proceeds, so that 'no door, however well intentioned, could have protected her virtue, since she had none' (Copley (1949) 249).

9-10 **May it please ... :** This supposedly dumb piece of woodwork now begins to speak with simple eloquence and elegance. Notice the formal oath asserting innocence (Macleod ((1983) 188) compares Propertius 4.7.51-3, 11.37-42), the extreme separation of *non ... culpa* by the stylised parenthesis, and the elegant placing of the name Caecilius which allows the poet to give information subtly. For *ita* used thus cf. 61.189-90, 66.18, 97.1. The literal meaning is thus: ' it is not my fault – and may my disclaimer keep me in my new master's favour'. The surface meaning of an unpunctuated text is different and suggests: 'not in this way would I please my new owner' i.e. I have not changed to suit him but against my will. It is only when the reader reaches line 10 that he realises the real meaning of line 9; remember that ancient texts did not contain punctuation and parenthetical marks.

11   **wrong done by me:**   Doors cannot move of their own free will, let alone commit crimes: this is all part of the fabulistic technique of the poem. *potis/pote* alone means 'able', *possum* being a contraction of *potis sum* just as *nolo* = *non volo.*

12   **popular ... silence:**   a famous crux. The MSS reading *verum istius populi ianua qui te facit* is clearly corrupt: we need the line to supply an antecedent for *qui* in 13, and *populi* can do so (the people singular becoming people plural is no real obstacle to that). The point apparently being made is that the door's *good* behaviour is not mentioned in public, but it is blamed for anything *bad*: the suggested emendation of Munro *verum est ius populi: ianua quicque facit* ('but that's the justice of the people: the door does everything') is an improvement on Doering's *verum isti populo ianua quidque facit* ('but to that people the door does everything') and is possibly correct. Most plausible of all – and printed in this text – is Palmer's *verum istuc* (Heyse's correction of *istius) populi lingua quiete tegit*; this keeps the people as antecedent of *qui* and has the outraged note of perverse conspiracy whereby the people are deliberately covering up the door's innocence with incriminating silence. We then also have a pleasing sequence of *quiete ... qui qua ... -quid.*

13   **not right:** For *non bene factum* cf. 76.7-8. The style in these lines is of
studied simplicity, suggestive of the ingenuous naiveté of the door.

15-6 **It will not do ... :** a request for more information about the *non bene facta*
alluded to in 13: the poet wishes not only to hear a simple denial (*uno verbo*) but
to have an account which will make everybody 'feel and see' the events: a request
therefore for what ancient critics termed *enargeia* or 'clarity', 'realism'.

17   **Nobody asks:** The implication is that the door can only tell those who want to
know and so ask it questions, rather like the language of tombstones which will
only be read by the interested passer-by.

19   **In the first place:** The door begins its narrative proper in appropriate
didactic mode: *primum igitur*, even though there is no later/second story to come,
is one such feature, as is the summary of the syllabus preceding the main verb as at
(e.g.) Vergil *Georgics* 1.1-5, Lucretius 2.62-66, Ovid *Ars Amatoria* 1.35. The
subject of *falsum est* is the whole *quod* clause of the previous line: the whole
sentence is nicely pompous for the moralising door, disclaiming all
responsibility for the events it describes and transferring the blame onto others
(the rhetorical device known as *translatio criminis*, as Macleod observes ((1983)
189).

20   **husband ... first:** *vir prior* must mean her present and not any previous
husband (*pace* Kroll who wishes to make the tale more complicated than it already
is); if she had been married before, then her lack of virginity at marriage to Balbus
would hardly arouse scandal, as Macleod points out (Macleod (1983) 188). The
point here is that on her wedding she should have been a virgin; if not, then at
least it should have been her new husband who had deflowered her, but in fact of
the two men in her life (at the time) her husband was not the first to make love to
her, owing to his sexual inadequacy, and his place was taken by his own father.
Sex with a father-in-law was technically incest, and marriage between them would
have been forbidden by law (Treggiari (1991) 38). The illegality of the act does
not, of course, make the door's tale less plausible: Roman comedy contains
several examples of such lascivious old men (e.g. Cleostrata's husband in Plautus
Casina and other examples cited by Giangrande (1970) 100), including fathers
being rivals for their sons' girlfriends (as in Plautus *Asinaria*).

The MSS read *attigerit*, accepted by some as a generic observation – 'he will not
have touched her since (we all know) he is impotent' (see Giangrande (1970) 95
n.35 for discussion). The simple emendation to *attigerat* still has a concessive
force ('her husband had not (it is true) touched her, but ... ') and makes for better
narrative style.

21-2 **his sword ... :** A lively depiction of the man's impotence. The line puts the
two adjectives together at the beginning and the two nouns together at the end:
sicula ('a small dagger') appears only here as a metaphor for 'penis' (but cf.
commoner metaphors* such as *gladius, telum, arma* (discussed in Adams (1982)
19-22)) and is humorous in juxtaposition to *beta* complete with its description as
tenera. Adams (*op. cit.* 26) remarks that: 'Augustus' coinage *betizo = langueo*
(Suetonius *Augustus* 87.2) suggests that the plant *beta* was felt to resemble a
mentula languida ... but there is no evidence that *beta* was ever in use in an
anatomical sense.' The use of vegetable imagery for the penis is common: cf. the

Greek use of mushrooms (Archilochus 252 West), chick-peas (Aristophanes *Acharnians* 801, *Frogs* 545) and barley-corn (Aristophanes *Peace* 965). Such vegetable imagery is more appropriate than aggressive weapon-imagery for the limp lifeless penis: and *tener* is the perfect word for the context, suggesting as it does: 'delicate, soft, frail' (OLD s.v. 4) and also 'immature' (OLD s.v. 2): this latter sense is of course the link between the two objects, as there is no reason (except perhaps size, which is not at issue here) why a mature beet should have any more penile power than an unripe one, and so the addition of *tenera* can only be to increase the mockery of the penis: *tener* asserts that the man's penis is as that of a child (cf. Lucretius 3.447, Ovid *Fasti* 4. 512) and reduces him to the status of eunuch. His erection never even gets to the halfway mark on his tunic. Giangrande suggests less plausibly that the son is not impotent *tout court* but simply unequal to the task of deflowering a virgin: he would enjoy her 'once the road had been opened' (Giangrande (1970) 101) by his more virile father.

23-8 After the crudity of 21-2, the door now raises the tone to a more decorous moralising: *violasse cubile* is neatly conjoined with *conscelerasse domum* to denote the elements of impiety and adultery in the former and those of crime and domestic subversion in the latter, while the pair of alternative explanations (*sive ... seu ...*) are well in the rhetorical tradition (cf. e.g. a very similar passage in Gorgias *Encomium of Helen* 6: 'either it was ... chance and the ... gods and ... Necessity ... or because [Helen] was seized by force ... '). *miseram* often denotes the lovesick (especially in Lucretius, e.g. 4.1076, 1179) and here perhaps adds more than a simple comment on the 'wretched' state of affairs by implying that it is love which has sickened the household. *illusi* is an inspired emendation of Baehrens for the lacklustre *illius* of the mss. The word perfectly denotes the son who has been made a fool of, especially who has been thus cuckolded – and cf. the sexual senses of *ludere* at e.g. 17.17.

25 **ablaze with blind lust:** The imagery is violent: the mind is ablaze with the fire of unseen/blind passion. Love is *caecus* in both the active and the passive sense: not only do lovers not see clearly the defects of their beloved (as ridiculed by Lucretius at 4.1151-70) and so are 'blind', but they also bear their misfortune without any visible scars on the surface, and hence suffer from an 'unseen' passion. For the conventional image of the fire of love cf. (e.g.) Lucretius 1. 473-7, Vergil *Aeneid* 4.1-2. It is unclear here whether the father is motivated by simple physical lust for his daughter-in-law or whether he nurses an emotional infatuation with her; the general trend of the poem would suggest the former, as it seems to have been a matter of the availability of the woman and the incapacity of the husband rather than any finer feelings on anyone's part. *Amor* can mean simply 'sexual passion' (OLD s.v. 1) as well as 'love'.

26 **impotent:** The inertia and immobility of the son is well evoked in the cluster of consonants at -*rs st*-. The line as it stands might be taken to mean not that the son was impotent but rather that he was sterile, but then the ancients do not distinguish these two disorders as closely as we do: cf. Aegeus in Euripides *Medea* and also Phoenix in Homer *Iliad* ix 453-7 as well as the hapless would-be parents of Lucretius 4. 1233-8. One passage in Lucretius (4.1038) suggests that in fact it is the seed which causes the erection (*tument loca semine*) which would imply that

sterility will cause impotence. Infertility was a serious business, as childless men were under a disability in inheritance: hence the need to find an heir from somewhere, as beautifully depicted in 68.119-24. For this use of *iners* to mean 'impotent' cf. Horace *Epode* 12.17, Ovid *Remedia Amoris* 780.

27   **look ... to find:** The mss reading *quaerendus unde* would require a lengthening of the final *-us* and is rightly emended by Statius to *quaerendum unde unde* – the second *unde* having presumably dropped out of the ms by haplography, at which point a later scribe 'corrected' the text by removing the elision of *-um*. The repeated *unde unde* suggests the desperate search for virility anywhere. The sense of *nervosius* clearly plays on the sexual meanings of *nervus* as 'penis' as at e.g. Horace *Epodes* 12.19 and as 'sexual powers' at Ovid *Amores* 3.7.35. *illud* is looking forward to *quod* in the next line.

28   **untie ... belt:** For the 'undoing of the virginal belt' as a euphemism for deflowering, cf. 61.52-3, 2b.13.

29-30 **outstanding example:** There is sharp sarcasm in *pietate*. *pietas* is fidelity and commitment to the family, the gods and the state, the very quality which the old man lacks. *egregium ... mira* is less surprising ('outstanding ... amazing') until we find out the nouns to which they refer, both nouns left (as often in Catullus) until the end of the line.

30   **pissed:** the vulgar word *minxerit* comes as a bathetic* surprise after the sarcastic encomium* of line 30 (for this effect of high-flown language brought down to earth with a crudity cf. Aristophanes *Lysistrata* 706-715). The use of *minxerit* is interesting in that it appears to confuse urination with ejaculation: cf. Horace *Satires* 1.2.44, and note how similarly Lucretius moves straight from bedwetting to wet dreams at 4.1226-36. Adams (1982) 142 asserts that the use of urinary words in sexual contexts 'appear to have been applied particularly to squalid or humiliating sexual acts' – such as this cuckolding of an impotent man by his own father.

31-6 The door now introduces Brixia, the previous home of the lady in question. The door's language is a comic parody of the sort of gossip which it retails: the town claims that it 'knows for a fact' (*se cognitum habere*) not only the disgraceful story of the father and son, but also it can 'tell the tale' (*narrat*) ...

32   **Brixia** is the modern Brescia, in Catullus' time a town in Cisalpine Gaul. Cycnus was the name of the mountain overlooking Brixia, and was called after the Ligurian king and local celebrity Cycnus, son of Sthenelus, who was turned into a swan while mourning his friend Phaethon (Ovid *Metamorphoses* 2. 367-80, Hyginus *Fabulae* 154.5), Liguria being a large region of Italy north of Etruria and south-west of Brixia. Catullus adduces the geographical detail not only to send up gently the historical pretensions of the native Brixians (as Goold suggests) but also to add an appropriate irony here; the town itself (which knows all the gossip) has its own 'look-out post' (*specula*) named after a man who famously pined away with love, and so is ideally placed to spy out and judge the sexual peccadillos of its townsfolk.

32   **seated below ... :** carries on the description of the town in appropriate language. On the surface this couplet is a travelogue advertisement for the town,

and yet as such it surely has little point in the mouth of the Veronese door. The words chosen are all suggestive and carry on the sexual innuendo of the door's narrative even when (as here) it is not actually narrating at the moment. *flavus* is the colour of the beautiful heroine's hair (see 66.62n), *mollis* means 'effeminate' or even 'sexy' (cf. *OLD* s.v. 13, 15, 16) and the town is referred to as 'beloved mother' – although there is no evidence that Brixia in fact was the mother-city of Verona (for the maternal and erotic designation of the city, cf. Pericles words on Athens at Thucydides 2. 43.1, mocked at Aristophanes *Knights* 1340-4). The prurient door cannot even mention a town without unnecessary words of sexual comment, however inappropriate and (here) comic.

35 **Postumius and ... Cornelius:** Quinn suggests that Cornelius might be the Cornelius of poem 102; they were perhaps known to Catullus' contemporaries but are unfamiliar to us. It is sometimes assumed that they were Brixian as was the adulterous woman in question, but this then requires us to postulate that they carried on their affair with her in Verona and then 'told of their adventures when they returned home (i.e. to Brixia)' (Copley (1949) 252). *amore* here means 'love-affair'.

36 **shameful:** the door's feelings on the matter are conveyed in the unnecessary word *malum* – a rejection of adultery shared by the (equally inanimate) lock of hair in 66.84-5.

37 **someone might say:** The door here anticipates a challenge to its story – a common rhetorical device (*anteoccupatio*) to which Kroll compares Cicero *in Pisonem* 68.

38-9 **never ... away:** The force of the challenge is that such gossip as the lady's adultery with these men might be talked about in the town (*populum*) but that such talk would hardly reach the stay-at-home door; to which he replies that she talks to her maids about her good times in Brixia (42).

41/2 **secretive:** *furtiva* well conveys the guilty tones of a voice narrating improper love-affairs – cf. 7.8, 68.136. If adultery is the 'stealing' of another's partner, then such affairs are bound to be *furtivus* (*fur* = 'thief') as is the voice which gloats over them.

42 **misdeeds:** *flagitia* is the door's description of her doings, not the woman's, being a highly moralistic term of outrage (see OLD s.v. 3,4).

43 **naming ... spoken:** Note here the repetition *dicentem ... diximus*, the arch periphrasis avoiding any mention of the names of the men concerned. *utpote quae* + subjunctive is a causal relative clause ('she did this because she expected ... ') strengthened by initial *utpote* (similar in meaning to *quippe*: see Kennedy § 454).

44 **no tongue ... no little ear:** The door is not deaf and dumb as the woman supposed. For the diminutive *auriculam* cf. Lucretius 4. 594: the effect here is comic.

45-8 **red eyebrows:** The identity of the 'man with red hair' remains a puzzle. The door 'refuses to name him' but describes him both by his appearance and his notorious courtcase in such a way as to make his identity (presumably) obvious to the poet's contemporaries. Macleod's suggestion (Macleod (1983) 191) that it refers to Caecilius – thus rounding off the poem with a 'sting-in-the-tail' reference back to the door's present owner (otherwise unmentioned in the poem, *pace* those

202   CATULLUS

commentators who believe that Caecilius is the impotent youth) is the best
answer to the puzzle so far adduced. The courtcase presumably concerned either 1)
a fraudulent claim of his that his wife had produced a child in order to inherit his
father-in-law's estate (a situation remarkably similar to that of the dying old man
in 68. 119-24 whose new baby grandson is to inherit his property: see nn ad loc),
or 2) a fraudulent claim on a woman's part that this red-haired man had made her
pregnant.

47   **tall:** The size of the man is neatly proportional to the size of the lawsuit.
48   **fake ... belly:**   The final line is excellent: four words, concentrating the
        dishonesty in the first half with the juxtaposition of *falsum mendaci* and then
        putting the two 'childbirth' words together in a cartoon-like figure of the woman's
        womb 'telling lies' and landing the man in court.

6 8

This poem is 'probably the most extraordinary poem in Latin' (Lyne (1980) 52) and has aroused a good deal of controversy about its unity or lack of it. The apparent discrepancy between the two addressees (lines 11 and 30 on the one hand and 41 on the other) has led many editors to regard the text as a mistaken amalgamation of two – or even three – quite separate poems into one. There is nothing absurd about this possibility: the last sixteen poems in the collection (101-116) were all put together in the archetype (Wiseman (1974) 89), as were 56-58b, 69-71, 72-6. The question is partly textual (see 11n below) and partly one of literary taste – can either of the two sections stand alone as a poem in itself, or are there compelling reasons to regard the text as a single coherent creation? The classic case for the unity of the poem is still that of Williams (1968) 229-30, who demonstrates *inter alia* that 149-50 is complementary to the apologia of 31-2. Furthermore, cryptic remarks in the poem are explained elsewhere in it, such as *hospitis* (12) explained at 67ff where the poet narrates exactly what sort of a 'guest' he was in Allius' house, and the philosophical attitude of the poet towards his lover's infidelities (131-42) is ideally addressed to the man whose own love-life was clearly in turmoil (3ff).

The discrepancy over the names is still a major problem, however: the name in line 50 must begin with a vowel for the line to scan, and so attention has been given to the name addressed in the first section. Attempts have been made to emend the mss reading *mali* in line 11 to *mi Alli* to make the referent the same – a reading accepted in this text but involving an unusual elision in the sixth foot which is not paralleled elsewhere. Other scholars have seen the two names as both belonging to the same man, whose full name was Manius Allius – however the use of the *praenomen* alone here would be the only such use in the whole of Catullus' poetry and would set up a tone of 'solemnity amounting to sarcasm' (Tuplin (1981) 114 n. 4 quoting Macleod (1974) 82 n.3). The alternative is to see Manius or Manlius of line 11 as a different man from Allius in line 41, and print the text as separate poems. Many scholars print the text as 68a and 68b, or even 68a, 68b and 68c (Goold).

One possible way out of the dilemma which has perhaps not been suffiently considered is as follows: the first section is an apology and an introduction, explaining the poet's difficulty in writing verse in his state of fraternal grief. Lines 41-148 are an extended love elegy recounting the poet's love and his debt of gratitude to the friend whose house received him and his mistress. There is no *a priori* reason why the poem written *about* Allius should not have been sent *to* somebody else – after all, the first section addresses its recipient in the second person singular, while the second section describes events in the third person, slipping into the second person address again at the end. It is clear that the person addressed in line 150 is the same as the person who lent Catullus the house, but not that this is the same as the addressee of lines 1-40. The unity of the poem is thematic and artistic rather than narrative, making the 'gift' of lines 41-160 appropriate for the friend addressed in 1-40. In particular, the combination of grief and joy in 41-160 is tailored for the friend who needs raising from his own grief to a happier state. I have printed the 'consistent' text – but the poem may still be a unified creation even if the names do not both belong to the same man. Other posssible explanations are easy to find: Allius may be a light pseudonym for the man whose generosity would not find universal approval – or indeed the whole scenario of lover and Allius' house may be a complete fiction designed to please the grief-stricken addressee.

If the unity is accepted, we are then left with a poem within a poem such as we also find in 64, or at least with a short epistolary poem 'covering' a succeeding poem as in 65-66; in 68 the letter frames the poem to the Muses, and the poet mixes the topical and the universal, the contemporary and the mythical, love and grief, in a seamless synthesis. The theme of love (for his mistress, for his brother, of Laudamia for Protesilaus) mingles with that of grief (for the same people) tied by common elements such as Troy (where Protesilaus and the brother died) and the shared abode (the mistress like Laudamia entering the home of the lover). There are also ironic contrasts between these elements which force the interpretation of the poem away from any simple 'moral' standpoint: his mistress, for instance, is married, like Laudamia, but not to her lover: and the adultery of another married woman (Helen) caused the Trojan War and the death of Protesilaus (the moralising language of 103-4 is incongruous in the mouth of the poet whose own lover was also a *moecha*). Adultery is painful for the betrayed – even for the 'greatest of the heaven-dwellers' Juno (138) – but it can produce heroes such as Hercules whose own exploits are of great benefit to mankind (111-116). The death of loved ones is also painful (and Catullus is inconsolable about his own grief (19-24, 91-100)) but other people's grief is more readily explicable as frustrated passion (80-84). The gender-correspondences of the *exempla* are teasingly inconsistent also: Catullus is a man in love with a woman, but he is time and again compared to the female in the role-models adopted – he is Laudamia to her Protesilaus, Laudamia to his brother's Protesilaus, Juno to his lover's Jupiter.

There are then other themes at work. The theme of the house (*domus*), for instance, neatly ties the different 'poems' together, as the poet's reference to his home in line 34-5 leads on to the lending of a surrogate 'home' for a pretend marriage in lines 68 – the *domum* to which Laudamia is going is a real home, while his lover's destination is only a borrowed house; but then, the home which Laudamia was going to was 'begun in vain' (75), while the house of the poet's lovemaking is a *domum* with a *dominam*. Furthermore, the death of the poet's brother has murdered his home (22-3, 94-5). This theme focalises the image of marriage – real but unfulfilled (Laudamia and Protesilaus) or unreal but fulfilled (Catullus and his mistress), real and fulfilled (the happy childbirth in 119-124), unreal and unfulfilled (the celibate life of 28-9). This in turn reflects the ironic contrasts of promiscuity: the poet's admission of his own past in 15-18 looks forward to his description of his lover's similar behaviour in 135-6, just as the adjoining similes of lines 119-128 contrast faithful family life and the promiscuous affections of the dove.

Over against all this sexual theme is the theme of death, which also overarches the entire poem. The poet is asked to raise his addressee from the doorway of death (4) but cannot do so as he is himself drowning in grief (13). The poet can rescue the name of Allius from the decay and death of oblivion (45-50; cf. 151-2) but is still inconsolable at the death of his brother (91-6). The love of Laudamia and Protesilaus was doomed in the Trojan War which made Troy the 'shared tomb' of Asia and Europe – a war caused by the love of Helen and Paris. The linking of love and death in love poetry is of course not new in this poem (cf. poem 5), and these coherences and ironies are obvious: the reader is led along a series of interconnected images and ideas without any single theme or 'moral', the simple message of gratitude towards Allius being both qualified and embodied in the poetic variation to which the poet subjects it. More subtle still, however, is the poet's use of similes* in the poem. Ever since Homer, poets had been composing similes in their narratives, for the effects of variation, of decoration, of analogy, even of proof (as in Lucretius). Singular experience – of death in battle, for instance – is compared to universal experience, often of the natural world of flowers, animals and the weather. Lucretius uses the simile to allow the reader to visualise the invisible world of atoms in the visible world (of sheep on a hillside, for instance, at 2.317-322), or to demonstrate a scientific proposition (the optical illusions at 4.324-468 prove that the senses are nonetheless reliable) or combine science with a emotional edge (the pathetic image of the calf slaughtered in 2.350-366). Later Love Elegists often compare themselves and their beloved to figures from heroic legend: Propertius for instance sees himself as Milanion to Cynthia's Atalanta in his first poem. It is not enough for the poet to be himself; the love-poet uses the wider literary tradition to create elegy out of love. These comparisons elevate the ordinary world of the lover and his girlfriend into the extraordinary stuff of heroes, and sometimes also set up ironic contrasts – such as in Propertius 1.3. where the sleeping Cynthia is 'idealised' until she wakes and is terrifyingly 'real'. Catullus in this poem sets up similes which do more than simply decorate a story with fairy-tales. In a very real sense, the similes are what the poem is all *about*. (In what follows I am indebted to Feeney (1992)).

For the choice of similes is bizarre: the poet selects his subjects with the obvious intention of surprising the reader, just as the labyrinthine thread of poem 64 startles the reader at every turn. Comparing the depth of Laudamia's love to a deep pit dug by Hercules or the glee of a grandfather is unusual and forces the reader to re-assess at every turn the exact relationship between the 'tenor' (i.e. the thing compared – e.g. Laudamia's love) and the 'vehicle' (the thing to which it is being compared, e.g. the pit). All ancient poets are sensitive to the possibilities of subtle manipulation of the reader by the delicate slippage between coherence and contrast, between reinforcement of image and ironic questioning of it. This becomes more urgent in this poem if only because of the quantity of simile involved: in lines 41-160, 45 lines are 'straight' simile. The simile comparing the poet's beloved with Laudamia encloses its own similes to illuminate Laudamia's love, the simile within the simile mirroring the poem within the poem. If we remove the similes, there is precious little left here: Allius lent me a house for love-making and my brother has died. Hardly enough to qualify as 'gifts of the Muses and of Venus'.

The similes shift focus constantly. The poet early on (53) describes himself as blazing with passion like Mount Aetna or the hot springs of Thermopylae – the fire of Aetna countered with the water of the spring, but with a common element in both being hot: this heat is then compared to that of a hot dry summer which a spring relieves with its cool irrigation from the top of a mountain (like Aetna?). So the figure of the heat becomes a figure of its cure, the same elements (mountains and springs) being used to express both heat and coolness. Add to this the reference to the poet's tears and the simile takes on a further dimension of tears pouring down his face (55-6) falling like a stream down a mountain. What was first the hot water of passion or the volcanic mountain of fire becomes the hot tears of a poet and then the cool mountain spring refreshing the weary wayfarer. The wayfarer then gets more water than he wants as he becomes a sailor out at sea desperate for the storm wind to become a gentle breeze, the aid of the gods invoked to deliver salvation, the similes brought to rest in the metaphor of line 67 w..ere Allius is said to have 'opened up a closed path' thus concluding the wayfarer theme. This series of similes is especially surprising if one recalls the tenor behind them: the poet's burning passion for his beloved, relieved by the loan of a house. The house is thus the cool stream to his Thermopylae of passion, the breeze to his storm, the gods invoked delivering his *candida diva* (70). The sequence is elegant and seamless, but the extravagant vehicles are disproportionate to the tenor: whatever is going on here, the poet is not simply seeking to move the reader's sympathy for his plight.

The beloved arrives, and her foot is planted on the threshold. The poet then leaves her mid-step for sixty lines while he travels in time and space to Troy. The simile of Laudamia has obvious points of contact with the poet – love and the loss of a beloved at Troy – but many ironic elements. Laudamia is married to her lover, unlike the poet's lover, who is unfaithful, while Laudamia is not: Laudamia's lost beloved is her husband, while Catullus' grief is for his brother: Laudamia's love was stolen from her as a result of Paris stealing the love of the adulterous Helen, which makes Catullus and his mistress closer to Paris and Helen than to Laudamia and Protesilaus. Within this lengthy simile are embedded other sub-similes such as that comparing the depth of Laudamia's love to the depth of the pit dug by Hercules – again, a simile rich in associative power when we recall that Hercules carried out the labour in order to win an immortal bride (just as Catullus had his *diva* (70)), and again a simile of ambiguous intent in that the imagery of the *barathrum* more commonly denotes dismal death than joy, is more often a symbol of destruction rather than simply 'depth of feeling': the word is used frequently of 'the underworld' (as in Plautus *Rudens* 570, Lucretius 3.966, OLD s.v. 2). In using a 'death' word to describe 'love' Catullus manages to unite the two themes of the central part of the poem – his love for Lesbia and his grief for his brother – and then caps it by denying that the simile is adequate to describe the love anyway (117). The poet then adds two more similes – the late-born grandson and the wanton dove – neither of which is ideal vehicle but both of which add a great deal to the texture of the poem. The late-born grandson presents an idyllic picture of family life which succeeds in foiling the villainous *captator* and maintains the family inheritance with unbroken fidelity: this hardly has any direct bearing either on Laudamia (who has no children) or on the poet's lover (who is contaminating her family inheritance by her affair with the poet). Again, the point of comparison – the joy and delight – is almost swallowed in the mass of extraneous and oblique detail. The dove is even more oblique – her promiscuity recalling that of Catullus' youth (17) and also of his lover (135-6), her ambiguity shown in the clash between her love for her mate and her wanton reputation. To make the irony even more acute, the dove is called *compar* – meaning both 'mate' and also 'similar' – the poet thus referring to the process of comparison in the middle of his simile, a gesture of self-conscious allusion (Feeney 41-2). Once again, the poet ends by rejecting the simile as a suitable description of Laudamia – 'you outdid the great passions of all these ... ' (129) just as he has done over the pit (117) and just as he will do in referring his mistress to Laudamia (131). The poet constantly shifts the focus of our vision and constantly draws our attention both to the process itself and to its inadequacy.

Nor, finally, is this merely arch pretentiousness. The figure of the poet's lover is seen from different oblique perspectives in a manner which lies at the heart of what the poem is trying to do. When she first appears she is not human at all – she is his *candida diva* (70) as she sets her foot on the threshold. 'It is indeed a climactic moment, and it is pivotal. It is the high point of romance; but in seconds Lesbia will enter the house and then she will *change*. She must change. She will be a creature of flesh.' (Lyne (1980) 55). When she does cross the threshold sixty lines later she is still mythicised with Cupid flitting about her (133-4), but the romance is at once dashed by the poet's honesty about her lack of fidelity – she is not even faithful in her adultery, let alone her marriage. Her former status of 'goddess' is revised in the light of this and she becomes Jupiter to his Juno – appallingly promiscuous and a source of anger to her beloved – rather than Hebe to his Hercules. The simile of Laudamia which appeared to be showing the idyll of the poet's love in fact showed the opposite. The only things which he had in common with Laudamia were his grief – grief born of love, and all the more painful for that – and his sexual desire. The legend of love and heroism in the similes is shattered in the grim realisation of the truth: his 'wife' is somebody else's wife, his *domus* is somebody else's house, his actual home is one of loneliness, grief and frustration (27-35).

And yet the poem does not end on a note of disillusion. Far from it: she is his 'light' who makes his life worth living. For all her manifest faults she is as flesh and blood preferable to the tissue of plaster heroines and nature-similes with which he has been comparing her throughout the poem. The closure of the poem – as so often in this collection – brings us back to the real world, just as do the codas of poems 63, 64 and 66. The end-result is a delicious irony whereby the reader – having been entertained and moved by a sequence of dazzling poetic inspirations – is finally convinced that the slippage in this poem is not simply between the tenor and the vehicle of the many similes but goes deeper than that: it is between the language of poetry and the language of truth, between the image of the beloved held in anticipation of her visit and the reality of the love-making itself – an act which Catullus (himself no prude) did not describe – between the world of fantasy and the world of myth. The poet's grief for his brother is of course part of the 'real world' – and is not subjected to the sort of comparisons which the poet's lover receives – and acts as a counterweight to the legend of heroic death in Troy with the brute truth about real death in Troy. This is not a didactic 'message' against poetry – that would be absurd. What the poet leaves us with, as at the end of 64, is the sense that poetry has the power to transform the everyday and the banal into the purest fantasy; and that the value of the poetry lies not in its fidelity to historical truth but rather in its own hermetic world of language and of sensitivity. At the end of this poem we are left with a poet having it both ways: to close a gloriously successful piece of poetic imagination he leaves us with a self-deprecating glimpse of the reality which transcends the poem which has embodied it.

The structure of the poem is symmetrical in the extreme: the following is a slightly simplified version of the analysis in Bright (1976), showing the mathematical symmetry of the line numbers and also the thematic ring composition:

		Number of lines
A (1-40)		
a	1-10 Allius' request for consolation	10
b	11-14 Transition to C's plight	4
c	15-26 C's plight	12
b	27-30 transition back to Allius	4

1   **The fact that:** For the *quod* clause outlining the topic to be defined as *gratum*
        in line 9, cf. 67.19-20. *acerbo* is to be taken with both *fortuna* and *casu*.

2   **written in tears:**. the pathos of *conscriptum lacrimis* is continued in the
        diminutive *epistolium*.

3   **shipwrecked:** the metaphor* here (as at 13) may also contain the 'implicit
        myth'* of Odysseus rescued from the waves, later imitated by Horace in *Odes* 1.5.

4   **threshold of death:**   cf. 76.18 for the notion of love-sickness being death's
        door.

5   **holy ... soft:**   Venus is surrounded by two adjectives appropriate to her:
        sancta ('holy') and also *molli* ('effeminate', 'sexy'). Catullus presumably implies
        that the would-be lover's non-existent sex life leaves him insomniac with
        frustration rather than asleep in exhausted bliss. For the idea that the loneliest
        time for the lover is the night cf. Propertius 3. 15.2; here the suggestion is that
        the lover is unable to sleep due to his unhappiness and frustration.

6   **bachelor:**   A *caelebs* is a single person, who may be either a bachelor, a
        widower or divorced. The word is here applied to the bed itself: as often in Latin
        love poetry, the bed is thought to share the status and the feelings of its occupant,
        as in Propertius 2.15.2: in 67.6 the door is addressed as having 'got married' when
        Balbus the younger brought home a wife. The combination of *desertum ... caelibe*
        reinforces the point.

7   **nor do the Muses ... :**   Notice how the line begins with the two adjectives
        and then adds the two nouns before finishing with the proper noun *Musae*. The
        addressee is lying awake bereft of his lover and is too distraught even to find
        solace in the reading of old (i.e. presumably Greek) poets. Fordyce tartly

observes that *veterum* must mean 'Greek' because 'neither Catullus nor anyone who shared his tastes would have used *dulcis* of the older school of Latin poetry'.

8   **troubled:** For *anxius* used of the dissatisfied lover, cf. Lucretius 3.993.

9   **me ... you ... me:** Notice the deliberate concentration of personal pronouns *mihi me ... tibi*, and also the linking of *tibi dicis amicum*: this sets up a nice pattern of dative – accusative; dative-accusative. The repetition of a word in a different case (polyptoton*) is used sparingly by Catullus.

10 **gifts:** The addressee has complained of lacking both Venus and the Muses: Catullus neatly picks up both points here in reverse order. Catullus could normally supply both the poetry and the love (i.e. love-poetry): commentators remark that it was a familiar feature of early Greek poetry to speak of the 'gifts of the Muses' and the 'gifts of Aphrodite' (most obviously combined by Anacreon Fragment 96 D). It is also worth remarking that Venus is linked with *venustas* as a term of approbation for elegant poetry in 35.17 or charm in general (as at 86.3), and that Lucretius asks Venus to be his 'ally' in composing verses (1. 24): Lucretius also claims the patronage of the Muse Calliope (6.92-5) but describes her in a manner clearly echoing his description of Venus in book 1 (*requies hominum divumque voluptas* 6.94: *hominum divumque voluptas* 1.1), suggesting that the links between the Muses and Venus are strong.

11 **In case ... not known:** The litotes* *ne sint ... ignota* meaning simply 'to see that you know of ... ' is elegant and understated: notice also the close position of *tibi ... mea*, making a neat five-word pattern up to the caesura (*sed tibi ne mea sint*), followed by an expressively assonant *ignota incommoda. incommoda* looks forward to *commoda* in line 21.

The mss read *mali*, which has been taken to conceal the name of the addressee and which has major implications for the unity of the poem. The possibilities are:-

a) Manlius (i.e. Manlius Torquatus, the addressee of poem 61). The name Allius is virtually certain at line 50, so this would force us to treat 1-39 as addressed to a different addressee than the man referred to in 40-160.

b) Manius as the *praenomen* of Manius Allius: this satisfied Lachmann and Williams ((1968) 230 n.2) but has been strongly doubted by recent editors (e.g. Macleod 1974) 82 n.3, Bright (1976) 89)

c) emend to Schöll's *mi Alli*: this at least allows us to maintain the unity of the poem, a unity supported by internal literary coherence of theme and mood, but requiring us to elide at a place where Catullus does not elsewhere elide (Hutchinson (1988) 314 n.75)

12 **friend:** *hospes* is a difficult word to translate, meaning as it does both 'host' and also 'guest' and referring to the reciprocal relationship whereby the stranger in a country is to be looked after generously in the assurance that the host himself will be generously treated if he goes to his guest's country (Greek *xenia*). Commentators here remark that the addressee must have looked after Catullus when he came to Rome from Verona. A major part of the host's duty was to provide 'guest-gifts' of hospitality (such as are demanded of Polyphemus by Odysseus in Homer *Odyssey* 9. 267-8) and the poet/host here apologises for not providing the *munera* demanded: there is an echo of the implicit myth* of

Odysseus again (cf. 3n, 64.62, 64.97, 65.4) in his elaborate self-description as being *merser fortunae fluctibus* (13). The poet pictures himself as Odysseus washed up on the shores of Phaeacia and being in need himself of *hospitis officium*: all the more reason, then, why he cannot provide guest-gifts for his addressee, let alone rich ones (14).

14   **good fortune ... pitiful:** *miser* and *beatus* are clearly oxymoronic* here: *miser* often denotes the lovesick (cf. 67.24n), while *beatus* often suggests the rich (either in money (as at 10.17) or simply in the good things of life (e.g. 9.10)).

15-20 Catullus contrasts his carefree youth which has now ended at the death of his brother.

15   **white garment:** Boys wore a distinctive *toga praetexta*, a toga with a purple border: at the age of about 15 they assumed the plain *toga virilis*.

16   **flowery ... spring:** The metaphor* here of youth as the flowery spring of the year of life is an obvious one to use (cf. Ovid *Met.* 10. 85: it is the first of the list of metaphors by analogy in Aristotle *Rhetoric* 1411a3, where he quotes Pericles' famous remark that the youth killed in the war were gone from the city as if someone had taken the spring from the year, a remark used also by Herodotus (7.162)), but has added point here in the contrast between the whiteness of the toga and the flowery season of the year.

17-18 **sported:** *ludo* often denotes sexual affairs (Cicero *Pro Caelio* 42), as well as playful poetic exercises at 50.2; Catullus, it is implied, used to 'play' in both senses and now is incapable of playing in either. The goddess, however, 'who mixes sweet bitterness with passions' is certainly Venus: note the litotes* of *non ... nescia* (cf. 11n), the oxymoron* of *dulcem ... amaritiem* (deriving from Sappho 47 L-P *glykypikron*) and the *figura etymologica** in *amaritiem* (reminding the reader of *amare*, to love). For *cura* used of passionate love cf. 66.23n. The poet is here self-deprecating: he has had many – well, enough – affairs, and the goddess is not ignorant of his existence – though he is hardly top of her list of great lovers – and the love has not been totally happy and successful either.

19   **But the death ... :** The smooth elegant and playful life of love and poetry, so elegantly portrayed in lines 15-18, is now rudely broken in the jarring rhythm of this line, where the final monosyllable refuses the customary coincidence of ictus and accent at the ending of the hexameter: Catullus can find no 'resolution' of his artistic and emotional turmoil: the sentence runs on (enjambement*) into the next line and leaves the final word (*abstulit*) in as emphatic a position as possible, being at the end of a sentence and the beginning of a line. The pause after this strong verb (with its expressive cluster of consonants -*bst*-) is followed by the open vocalic sound *o*, expressive of deep emotion and assonant* with the final syllable of *misero*, just as the vowels of the following two words are assonant, although the quantities vary: *frater adempte*. The word *studium* refers more easily to the poetry than to love: cf. Vergil's famous self-description as *studiis florentem ignobilis oti* (*Georgics* 4.564) ('flourishing in the pursuits of unpretentious peace').

20-26   A passage which finds echoes in more than one place in Catullus' work: in this poem lines 92-6 are a close repetition of 20-24: and poem 101 picks up the theme of his brother's death once again. Notice here the ease with which Catullus slips into addressing his dead brother directly (apostrophe*), with the strong emphasis on the second-person pronoun (*tu ... tu ... tecum ... tecum ... tuus* 21-24) and on the word *frater* (*fraterna ... frater ... frater*).

21   **shattered my pleasures:**   *fregisti commoda* is a striking phrase. The sense of the verb (of shipwreck (cf. OLD s.v. 1c)) picks up the imagery of 3 and 13 – and note also the emphatic alliteration* with *frater*, just as *tota* gives a similar alliteration with *tecum* in 22. *commoda*, as in Lucr 3.2 (*commoda vitae*), may have been a common rhetorical word, if Arrius is anything to go by (poem 84). There is also the paradox of a man being able to break things in the act of dying.

22-3   **our ... you:**   Notice the incantatory repetition of *tecum una tota ... omnia tecum una* and the assertion that just as the brother is buried, so also the whole household is buried (in grief) along with him, and just as the brother has died, so also have all the joys of life died along with him.

25-6   **At his decease:**   picks up 19-20. *deliciae* is a difficult word to render in English: it often refers to the conscious seeking of pleasure as an end in itself, but it is also used by Catullus to mean the thing which provides the pleasure (e.g. Lesbia's pet in 2: cf. Trimalchio's catamite described as his *delicias* (Petronius *Satyricon* 64.5)). Fordyce's note on 50.3 renders it as 'naughtiness' and sees it as part of the hedonistic anti-moralistic stance taken by the New Poets in contrast to the censorious disapproval of such frivolity thundered by men of *gravitas* such as Cicero and Cato. The word here is delimited by *animi* to show that it refers only to mental pleasures (i.e. poetry) and not physical love-making: grief has clearly depressed the pleasure-centres of the mind and taken the enjoyment out of Catullus' former enthusiasms.

27-30   Roman texts had no punctuation, let alone indications of a change of speaker. The MSS reading *Catulle* here would indicate that the poet is quoting the exact words of his friend back at him and require speech marks to begin after *scribis*. The principal difficulties in these lines are as follows:

1) Fordyce comments that the verbatim quotation is unparalleled and improbable, and that the *quod* clause is therefore referring to the words rather than quoting them.

2) If Catullus is quoting words *verbatim*, then *hic* in line 28 must mean Rome, where the addressee is, whereas if the words are indirectly reported, the word will mean Verona. In what sense, then, is it shameful for the best people in Verona to warm their cold limbs in a deserted bed?

3) If it refers to Rome, as Quinn suggests, then there is perhaps a reference here to his lover's selective seduction of 'anybody of the right class' – a state of affairs which is decidedly shameful for her lover; and one, furthermore, which he could well describe as *miserum* (lovesick, used precisely in this sense of the romantic lover besotted with a woman who does not deserve such devotion in Lucretius 4. 1173-5). Many editors take lines 28-9 to be a warning to Catullus that while he is in Verona his lover is warming the limbs of upper-class Romans in her 'deserted' bed (referring simply to the absence of Catullus). One wonders at this point just how blunt and rude Catullus' friend could be

about the behaviour of Catullus' beloved and still expect to stay his friend and receive
poems to order. The phrase would have more jocular and friendly force if it referred to
Verona and simply means that the young aristocrat in Verona 'could not engage in
amorous pursuits with the same freedom as in the capital' (Goold (1983) 257).

4) The MSS reading *tepefacit* is obviously wrong as it is unmetrical. If the whole
sentence is in *oratio obliqua* then we need a subjunctive such as Bergk's *tepefactet*: if the
phrase is direct quotation, then *tepefactat* is to be read – as the corrector of the MS R
suggested.

5) Is it likely that Allius' letter was composed in verse? If not, then Catullus is not
here quoting the text *verbatim* but rendering it into verses.

These are formidable problems. A possible solution which has not been suffiently
considered is that the 'quotation' consists only of *Veronae turpe Catulle esse*
(understanding *est*), and that the following phrase is an explanatory gloss added by the
poet. This allows the MSS reading *Catulle* to be kept without the difficulties of reading
hic as 'at Rome'. The reference *hic* is then a gentle jibe at the expense of the sexual desert
which is Verona rather than a direct stab at Catullus' beloved, of whose behaviour he
would not wish to be reminded.

28   **of higher quality:**   *nota* is a metaphor from the wine-cellar (Fordyce):   the
         effect of the whole phrase is parodistic deflation of the sort of pretentious
         snobbery which cannot however procure sexual excitement.

29   A 'golden line'*:   cf. 64.125, 64. 314, 66.1, 67.21 etc.

30   **more ... pitiful:**   *magis* here is colloquial: cf. 73.4.   *miserum* is often used of
         sexual misery: particularly the frustration produced by not having a sexual outlet,
         whether because the lover refuses anybody except the one beloved (as in Lucretius
         4. 1066-7) or because there are simply no partners available.

31-2   **you ... me:** Notice the parallelism of *mihi ... tibi* to explain that the grief of
         the one causes the lack of gifts to the other. *munera* picks up the same word in
         line 10.

33   **writings:** *scriptorum* could be the genitive plural of either *scriptores* ('writers')
         or *scripta* ('texts'):   the poet explains his inability to furnish a poem by saying
         either that he has not got his own (new) writings with him or that he needs to
         consult a larger library to be able to compose 'learned' verses modelled on
         Alexandrian Greek poetry. The *quod* clause is picked up clearly by the *hoc* of line
         34, suggesting perhaps that the remark about Catullus not having a plethora of
         texts with him was also part of the original letter; 'as for your comment about my
         not having ... well that's because ... '; alternatively, it means 'the fact is, I haven't
         ... because ... '.

34-5   **I live in Rome:**   Catullus' family home was presumably in Verona, but he
         spent his time in Rome. Notice here the way the verb *vivimus* comes after the
         caesura in the pentameter, putting the word strongly with *illa domus*. Note also
         the tricolon crescendo* in *illa ... illa ... illic*. For the meaning of *carpitur* cf.
         Austin on Vergil *Aeneid* 4.2: '[*carpere*] implies the action of taking a part from a
         whole, and so the completion of something by successive stages, as in *carpere
         viam, opus*'. There is also perhaps a sense of the Fates plucking away at the thread
         of his life as at 64.310.

36   **book-boxes:**   a *capsula* was a cylindrical box in which scrolls (*volumina*) would be carried. *sequitur* suggests that the box travelled in the manner of a servant, travelling with but 'behind' the passenger himself (OLD s.v. *sequor* 11a).

37-8   **spite:**   *mente maligna* and *animo non satis ingenuo* are not exactly parallel phrases: the first indicates deliberate malice, the second, while conceding that the poet does not act out of malice, argues an inability to do otherwise owing to the poet's lack of good breeding.   For the 'indirect wish' subjunctive *statuas* following straight on from *nolim* cf. Kennedy 419a + n. 1.

40   **unasked:**   *ultro* is in deliberate contrast to *petenti*: if I had a large store of poems you would not need to ask for them.

41   **Allius:**   the name is probably correct here. Quinn points out that the name, whatever it is, must have begun with a vowel in line 50 to scan.   For the problems of the identity of the named addressees, see introduction to this poem.
       goddesses: the Muses, who are invoked both to give immortal fame to Allius' good deeds (43-4) and also to pass the word on to many other people (45-6)

43   **time ... night:**   a most striking phrase: the time flies past in generations which forget the deeds contained in former ages: this is well developed in the image of night being 'blind' in line 44.

45   **you ... you:**   for the polyptoton* of *vobis vos* cf. 9n. The repetition is especially strong here because of the repetition also of *dicam ... dicite*.

46   **old page:**   *anus* is a neat surprise: the book is to continue speaking even when it is ancient.   The joke here of course is the caricature of the book as a garrulous old woman (cf. 78.10 *fama loquetur anus*), a tradition in ancient literature going back to (e.g.) the Nurse in Aeschylus' *Choephoroi*. The grammatical gender of *carta* assists in the description.

47   **so that ... death:**   At least one line has here dropped out of the archetype: Baehrens suggested the following text to fill the gap:
       versibus ut nostris etiam post funera vivat
       ('so that in my verses he may live even after death').

48   **dead ... grow ... famous:**   there is a paradox here: *mortuus* is concessive ('although he is dead'), and yet the name is to grow more and more famous owing to the spreading further and further of his fame through the agency of the Muses.

49-50 **spider:**   The image is one of a spider weaving a web over the deserted monument bearing the name of Allius: this is not so much a literary commonplace, as Quinn suggests, comparing Homer *Odyssey* 16.34, where Telemachus is expressing satisfaction that the bed of his father Odysseus has been saved from oblivion by the arrival of the hero back to Ithaca: he had feared that his mother would marry somebody else and so render the bed 'lacking in bedding and having shameful spiders' webs on it'.   Catullus alludes to the happy reunion of Odysseus and Penelope in comparison, perhaps, to the later union of Catullus and his beloved. Notice here the added detail of the adjectives: *tenuem ... sublimis ... deserto*: the spider is high up (on a monument?), the name is abandoned and alone, the spider's web is only thin and slight (and so easy to remove, but nobody would take the trouble).   There is also a faint hint that Catullus himself is doing what the spider will not do: he is creating a work (*opus*) out of the (otherwise deserted) name of Allius, a work which is elegant and slight *(tenuem)* and which the poet weaves like a spider.

51-66 An excessively stylised and verbose hymn of thanks to Allius for his help in Catullus' love-life.

51   **Amathusia** is the goddess Venus, so called after her cult-centre Amathus in Cyprus. She is *duplex* in that she gives out both good and bad fortune to people (cf. 18), and she sets people on fire with scorching passion.

52   **way in which** seems otiose as Venus only operates in one sphere.

53-4   **Trinacrian ... Malian:**   Catullus compares the heat of his passion to two famous hot phenomena in the ancient world: *Trinacria rupes* is Mount Aetna in Sicily, and the 'Malian water' refers to the hot springs in Malis which gave Thermopylae its name. In both of them Catullus is comparing small with great in a mannered and highly elegant allusive style: not only the allusive nomenclature of 'Trinacrian rock' and the concentration of geographical names in *Oetaeis Malia Thermopylis* but also the paradoxical equation of the fire of Etna with the waters of Thermopylae, the two terms set next to each other over lines 53-4.

55   **eyes ... weeping:** Mention of the hot springs of Thermopylae brings to mind the hot springs of the poet's tears. Notice again the golden* symmetry of the line (adjectives, verb, nouns) and the choice of *tabescere* connoting both 'wasting away' in a general sense and also 'melting away' (OLD s.v. 2a) highly appropriate to eyes awash with tears. The eyes do not cease to weep, and the sentence fittingly runs over into the next line, which itself has elision where the caesura should be.

56   **shower of sadness:** The shower of tears is 'sad' by hypallage*.

57-65   **stream ... breeze:**   Some editors argue that the first simile looks forward to 66ff, the stream bearing welcome relief just as *(tale* 66) Allius did to the poet: others see it as referring back to the suffering of the poet whose tears well over his cheeks like the mountain stream. Catullus will surely have known the Homeric passage where: 'Agamemnon stood up pouring tears like a black-watered spring which pours its murky liquid down the sheer rock-face' (*Iliad* 9.13-15). What the poet has done is to begin with a backward-looking image of suffering and then to transform it – as Allius transformed the suffering itself – into a benevolent image. The spring of tears becomes an oasis of sweet water for the thirsty: having then changed the mood of the passage from pain to pleasure, he continues in the same vein with the next simile comparing Allius with a welcome wind to sailors on the sea.

57   **just as ... :** The style is highly visual and dramatic: the mountain is 'airy', the stream gleams on the top of the mountain, the stream falls over the end of the hexameter in appropriate enjambement* and leaps forward over a mossy stone. Such details are in a sense unnecessary but add greatly to the poetic colour and form the *munera Musarum* which it is the poem's purpose to provide (10).

59   The alliteration* is striking: *prona praeceps ... valle volutus*. The image of the water tumbling reminds us of the girl's apple falling out of her lap in 65.23. There is a nice sequence of movement here as the water begins at the top *(vertice)*

and then rolls down the slope (*prona*), going through the middle (*per medium*) before reaching the ground where the heavy heat is opening up the earth (62) .

60   **road thronged:** Fordyce well points out that the busy highway is contrasted with the lonely heights. There is also a jingle of *transit iter* (cf. 3.11).

61   **tired:** *lasso* could of course be taken with either *viatori* or with *sudore* (by hypallage*). Baehrens' suggestion *salso* would clear up the confusion and paint a neat picture of the salt sweat of the travellers being relieved by the fresh water of the spring. Catullus here has it both ways: the grammatical sense forces *lasso* to go with *viatori*, but the placing of the caesura after *viatori* naturally leads us to treat *lasso in sudore* as a single phrase, the sweat being 'tired' because it is produced by a tired traveller. *levamen* is also something of a surprise – water is heavy to carry and so only metaphorically* could it be said to 'lighten' the weary traveller: this is made more paradoxical in the description of the heat in 62 as *gravis*: in fact of course heat rises while water falls (as the simile has shown so beautifully). The image of the 'traveller' gains extra point when we learn that Allius' big favour to Catullus was to provide him with a *pied-à-terre* to conduct his affair in – giving the poet and lover somewhere to rest.

62   The sound of the line contains a number of expressive *u* and *st* sounds: *exustos aestus hiulcat*. The water is welcome to the traveller: it would also be welcome to the land, but the land is not drinking it, and the burning thirst of the land is expressive both of the heat of the season and the thirst of the traveller.

63/4   **favourable breeze ... sailors:** the sailors are at sea and there is already a wind blowing but it is a storm wind (*turbine*) and to their relief a second/favourable breeze (*aura*) – barely a wind at all – breathes (*aspirans*) – rather than blows – more gently (*lenius*). The storm is 'black' (OLD s.v. 'niger' 4a) as at Horace *Odes* 1.5.7 (where see Nisbet-Hubbard *ad loc*).

65   **prayers:** A neatly phrased line: *iam ... iam* dividing it into two halves, but with the names of the two gods side-by-side in chiasmus*; and rounded off with the neoteric fifth-foot spondee (on which see Introduction # 'Metres'). Castor and Pollux were the Sons of Zeus, twins traditionally prayed to for rescue on the sea: (see Fordyce on 4.27) they were a constellation providing help to mariners.

66   **that was ... to me:** This line comes as something of a bathetic* letdown after the high epic style of the preceding passage.

67-72 Allius' help is at last described in detail. The language is almost hymn-like in its praise – note the repeated *is* and the quasi-miraculous feats performed.

67   **opened up a closed field with a broad path:** an enigmatic phrase to be explained in the lines which follow. The line is almost golden* in its adjectives-verb-nouns symmetry and is deliberately mysterious to build up the sense of heroic/divine exploits, only to bring matters down to the mundane in the following line.

68   **mistress:** *dominam* is difficult: Allius provided the house for the lovemaking – he did not also supply the girl, it is argued. Fordyce attempts to justify *dominam* as a 'chatelaine' or compliant housekeeper to admit the lovers; that leaves the subject of *exerceremus* unspecified until the *candida diva* appears in 70, but that is not an insuperable problem; more serious is the later passage where the *domina* is

mentioned as joining in the fun and games at 156, which rather suggests that the word cannot mean a 'housekeeper', however compliant. The word *domina* later came to bear the meaning of 'beloved, mistress', but there is no clear proof that it had this meaning yet (for all the similarity of Catullus' use of *era* in 136): the poet does goes on to describe the girl in the next line as a 'white goddess', however, which makes 'mistress' a less extravagant term of adoration by comparison, and the notion of Allius providing the house and (by providing the facility, also providing) the mistress is a neat ellipsis fully in the manner of Catullus. Worth noting is also Macleod's suggestion that the mistress in question is the goddess Venus herself. (Macleod (1974) 86 n.8).

69   **mutual:** The love was not – or not entirely – one-sided.

70   **gleaming:**   *candida* means primarily 'white' and then comes also to signify 'beautiful' in a society where only the rich could keep out of the sun enough to render their complexion pale. The poet builds up the praise of the girl with the juxtaposition of *molli candida* (ideal both to touch and to see) before calling her simply *diva*. The idealised portrayal of the girl is to be qualified later with his more realistic assessment of her character (135-48); for a satirical treatment of precisely this sort of idealising romantic love of a 'divine girl' see Lucretius 4.1149-91.

71-2   The associations are diverse here:

a) marriage-ceremonies (crossing the threshold)

b) divine apparitions – the emphasis on her foot (*fulgentem plantam ... arguta ... solea*) is redolent of (e.g.) the divine footwear of Athene when she appears to Telemachus in Homer *Odyssey* 1. 96-8, or of Hermes in *Iliad* 24.340.

c) a very specific sound, as Lesbia taps (*arguta*) on the threshold with her sandal.

Above all, the poet leaves the foot poised on the doorstep for 60 lines, before resuming the account of their encounter at line 132.

73-86 Protesilaus and Laudamia (I). According to Homer (*Iliad* 2.698-702) Protesilaus was the first to disembark from a Greek ship at Troy and was the first to die there: he died leaving a weeping wife Laudamia and a house only half-built. Catullus focusses on the frustration of Laudamia and the anger of the gods, neither theme pronounced in Homer: the identity of the *hostia* (76) and the connection with lines 70-72 are still open to conjecture (see 75n.).

73   **blazing with love:** Catullus compares the ardour of his lover visiting Allius' house with the ardour of Laudamia coming to the house of her new husband Protesilaus: the link is therefore carnal desire – but the poet also later finds a further link in the grief which both he suffers for his brother and Laudamia for her husband.

74   A rare 3-word pentameter, *Protesilaeam* being the first half. The poet succeeds in naming the two lovers together, after a non-specific introductory line 73.

75   **a house** was only half built when Protesilaus went to Troy, a detail of the story which goes right back to Homer (*Iliad* 2. 701): here the treatment suggests that the marriage was conducted and the bride taken home before the house was fully built. The building of the house was also begun in inordinate haste before the requisite sacrifices had been made. Quinn prefers to take it that 'Laudamia did not

wait for the ceremony seeking divine approval of her union with Protesilaus', but the explanatory *cum* clause comes straight after *inceptam frustra* and would seem to be a gloss upon it. The 'moral' of the tale seems so far to be a counsel against haste.

The identity of the *hostia* is not specified: the most obvious candidate would be Iphigeneia, the daughter of Agamemnon sacrificed to make the wind blow and release the fleet stuck at Aulis (cf. Lucretius 1.84-101). This however assumes that Protesilaus stayed in Greece and began his house between the fleet setting out from Greece and the sacrifice of Iphigeneia, when all the ancient accounts quite reasonably assume that he went with the fleet as soon as they set sail. Furthermore, the only sense in which Iphigeneia's blood could be described as *sacro* is that it was 'dedicated to a goddess'.

76   **appeased:** *pacificasset* is taken as a reference to the *pax deorum*, the bribing of the gods with sacrifices to prevent them obstructing a human course of action (cf. Ogilvie (1969) 23), the implication being that the gods will subvert human ambitions unless paid off (cf. Herodotus 1.32, 'gods are envious of human prosperity and like to trouble us'). The reference here might simply be the inference that if Protesilaus' house was built in vain (and it was as he was doomed to die in Troy) and his marriage to Laudamia was cut off too soon, then they must have neglected to appease the gods with the right sacrifices.

77   **May nothing ... :**The poet applies the 'moral' (of the need to observe patience and humility before the gods) to his own life; cf. the closure at the end of poems 63 and 64 with their autobiographical 'god-fearing' epilogues. The Rhamnusian maiden is the goddess Nemesis, who had a famous temple at Rhamnus in Attica; see on 66.71.

78   **rashly:**   *temere* picks up *frustra* at 75, just as *eris* picks up *eros* in 76 and *suscipiatur* picks up *inceptam* in 75.

79-80   **How much ... :** The indirect question comes first, as often: cf. 67.19-20. The blood is *pius* by hypallage*, as e.g. at 61 above, and also Horace *Odes* 3.23.20. *ieiuna* is literally 'famished' and is here applied to the altar itself as being 'starved of blood', as if the altar itself were addicted to the sacrificial offerings it receives, a sort of pathetic fallacy* like to the door being 'married' in 67.6. It may also suggest the notion that the gods actually need our sacrifices or else they go hungry – a comic idea found in e.g. Aristophanes *Birds*, explained seriously by Ogilvie (1969) 42. The word is appropriate here of course because the gods are as greedy for sacrifice as the lovers are for sex (cf. *avidum* 83), and the greed for sex will not be satisfied (83) unless the greed for sacrifice is sated first. The implication of line 80 is almost that the gods, deprived of their rightful blood-offerings, took the life of Protesilaus instead. The form of line 79 is again almost golden*, with its adjectives separated from their nouns by a central verb.

81   **forced ... :** The line is notable for its strong alliteration of <u>c</u>oniugis ... <u>c</u>oacta ... <u>c</u>ollum, the affection between them beautifully depicted in the thumbnail sketch of the wife forced to release her new husband's neck.

83-4   **could have satisfied   ... passion:**   A touch of realism, perhaps: if Laudamia had had a few more years with him, she would not have been so upset at his death. The poet specifies winters and then points to its 'long nights' which gave more time for sex. Line 82 once again has elision over the diairesis as the years melt into each other in the passage of time.

83   **passion:** Their *amor* was still *avidus* but could be satisfied in time: Lucretius well describes the madness of sexual desire but does not allow for the idea of such desire ever being satisfied permanently (4. 1086-1120). Catullus has the more cynical attitude that a good deal of the passion is generated by novelty (*novi* 81) which could not last more than a couple of years, and also that Laudamia's grief is at least partly sexual frustration which a longer marriage would have removed (84).

85   **the Fates:** For the *Parcae* see 64.303ff. The subject of *quod* is the rupture of the marriage.

86   **he went ...:** Protesilaus was fated to be the first to die at Troy if he was the first to disembark from the ships; Catullus simply reports his fate as being fixed if he went as a soldier to the walls of Troy: in fact the tale of Protesilaus has a nice symmetry in that he alone leapt down from the ships when all the others hesitated (Graves (1955) vol ii § 162b p. 295), just as here the failure to be patient and prudent caused the trouble (75-6).

87-90   **Troy:** A brief explanation of the Trojan War leading up to the poet's personal reasons for hating Troy in that it was the scene of his brother's death.

87   **stealing of Helen:** The leaders of the Greeks mobilised their forces to recover Helen, the errant wife of Menelaus king of Sparta: Helen had been seduced by Paris the Trojan prince and taken back with him to Troy, from where the Greeks sought to recover her. The language here is suitably epic: for the grandiose *primores Argivorum* cf. Lucretius' *ductores Danaum delecti, prima virorum* (1.86).

87-8   **Troy ... draw to itself:** The poet indulges in the conceit that Troy attracted men to itself for them to die there: there is also perhaps an implicit myth* that Troy is like the Sirens luring sailors over the sea to their doom (Homer *Odyssey* 12.39-54)

88-90   **Troy:** The name Troia repeated three times in plangent rhetorical tones: first of all the simple statement that Troy attracted men to itself, then that Troy was a common burial-ground for Asia and Europe, finally the most emotional statement that Troy is the 'bitter ashes of all men and all manly qualities.'

89   **(what wickedness!):** The parenthetic *nefas* is later imitated by Vergil (*Aeneid* 7.73, 8.688), a poet who uses exclamatory parenthesis a great deal: the first impression here, however, is that *nefas* is to be taken directly with *commune* ('a shared sin'). *Nefas* is the opposite of *fas* and denotes what is not pleasing to the gods; presumably the parenthesis is intended as a personal response by the poet rather than a theological point.

   shared grave: the rhetorical idea of 'a shared tomb' goes back perhaps to Pericles' Funeral Speech (Thucydides 2.43.3: 'the whole earth is the tomb of famous men') but here the rhetoric of a funeral speech (which often invokes phrases such as *virum et virtutum*) is inverted: the glory and the goodness of the dead men is nothing more than a total waste and a sin. The traditional consolation that the dead have their everlasting memorial (e.g. Simonides 5 Diehl) is here subverted into a bitter rejection of the decision to send them to their deaths in the

COMMENTARY: 68   219

first place. The bitterness of the outburst is mirrored in the ugliness of the metre
itself: the series of elisions *(sepulcrum Asiae Europaeque)* distorts the rhythm
completely.   .

90   **manly qualities:**   *virtus* is of course the quality which defines a *vir*, but the
       phrase is not tautologous. The rhetoric is hyperbolic* in that Troy for all its evil
       did not destroy *all* men. The reference to 'ashes' is appropriate both in the
       reference to cremation and in the sense of destruction and bitterness left behind:
       cf. e.g. 101.4, Callimachus' epigram in *Anth. Pal.* vii.80. 5.

91-100 Catullus laments the death of his brother: this is the personal reason for the
poet's hatred of Troy.

91   **which also:** The MSS reading is clearly corrupt, and Heinsius' emendation to
       quaene has found general approval, being a form of the relative: it has affirmative
       force (see OLD s.v. *'ne'* 7), and picks up *Troia* from the previous line, making the
       last decisive point about the place. *fratri* is deliberately placed at the end of the
       line for emphasis, as is the pause after *attulit* in 92, exactly as at 19-20.

91-3   Notice the repetitions of *miserabile fratri ... misero frater ... misero fratri* in the
       repetitious nature of lamentation. Both the brother and the poet are alike *miser* in
       the death, and the brother is *ademptus* from the poet just as the light has been
       ademptum from himself. This whole passage is echoed from lines 19-24 and again
       in poem 101: the repetition of 22-4 at 94-6 reminds the reader of the initial
       reluctance to compose the poem and the reasons behind it. It is however the only
       example of repetition of a sequence of lines in Catullus' extant work – usually
       repetition is confined to a single line (e.g. the first and last lines of poems 16,
       36, 52, 57 and the incantatory line 64.327 repeated eleven times). For repetition,
       cf. Lucretius 1. 146-8 (= 2. 59-61, 3. 91-3, 6. 39-41).

97-100 The fate of Catullus' brother, buried in a foreign land, is the fate of all those
Greeks who fell at Troy. The Romans saw the family as a continuum, whose permanence
was especially shown in funerals where the masks of ancestors were paraded before the
dead person, followed by the living relatives. Family tombs sometimes maintained the
coherence of the fam'ly unit even in death (on which see Hopkins (1983) 205-6): the
poet here compares th₃ happier fate of those whose ashes rest among the remains of their
relatives – a romantic notion that the philosophers would have had no time for (cf. e.g.
Lucretius 3. 870-93).

98   **laid to rest:** *compono* is the *mot juste* for 'laying to rest' (see OLD s.v. 4c) and
       also makes for a neat alliteration of *cognatos compositum cineres.*

99   **held:** Troy which had a name for luring men to their death in 88 is now keeping
       the brother locked up *(detinet)* in the furthest place on earth *(extremo* cf. 11.2) and
       is a land which is foreign.
       Troy: Emphatic repetition of the accursed *Troia* again (as at 88-90). *obscena*
       was originally a term of augury and connoted 'ill-omen' (Mynors on Vergil
       Georgics 1.470) which is appropriate here in the context of the doom of both
       Protesilaus and Catullus' brother. *infelice* is ablative going with *Troia.*

101-4 Troy : A quick resumé of the Trojan War, picking up the theme from 90. The themes are still constant: the youth of Greece 'hastened' (Protesilaus' besetting fault) and left their household gods (just as Catullus' brother is buried in a foreign land) in case Paris might enjoy the pleasure of his mistress (as Catullus enjoyed his married mistress in Allius' house).

101/2 is said: *fertur* is a neat combination of 'travelled' (OLD s.v. 4) and 'is said to have' (OLD s.v. 33).

102   homes and hearths: *penetralis* reminds us of the *di penetrales*, the tutelary gods of the Roman household: *focos* refers to the hearth as the centre of the worship of the tutelary god the *Lar familiaris*. There is something disturbingly appropriate about death coming to those who have 'deserted their household gods' – in the light of the poet's strictures about divine displeasure at human neglect in lines 75-8.

103-4 getting away ... : The lines are teasingly fitting for Catullus, the poet of the life of love, whose whole ethic is one of love and *otium*. *libera* has the sense 'get away with ... '. *moecha* is a Greek word and always has the sense of 'forbidden lover' (as in Horace *Satires* 1.4.113), usually because the woman is married to somebody else – as of course was Lesbia whose 'divine' love the poet celebrated so rapturously in lines 70-72. The combination of *gavisus libera ... otia pacato* is extremely appealing: *pacato* may have been chosen to remind the reader of *pacificasset* in line 76 – this bedroom did have the blessings of the gods, and unlike Laudamia they had 'time in plenty, without interference' (Quinn).

105-118 Laudamia (II)

105   o most ... : The poet easily slips into apostrophe* of Laudamia. What is a deliberate attempt by the Greeks to restore Helen is to her simply a misfortune (*casu*).

106-7 marriage: The lines run on by enjambement*, ending with a strongly emphasised *coniugium*: cf. how Catullus i..plies that her loss was primarily sexual (see 83n above). Her marriage was dearer to her than her life and her soul, a hendiadys in that the *anima* was the 'spirit' which distinguished a living body from a corpse (Lucretius 3.128-9): for the phrasing cf. 64.215.

107-8 tide ... whirlpool: The power of Laudamia's love is compared to a swelling tide. *vertice* here means a swirling whirlpool, *aestus* a swelling tide; the two words sandwich *amoris* which can be taken with either or both. *aestus* also connotes 'heat' (OLD s.v. 5a) and is thus peculiarly fitting for the passion of love here. How flattering is this comparison, however? Laudamia is told that her love has dragged her down into a pit like the underground excavations at Phemius.

108   pit: *barathrum* is a Greek word transliterated: it is usually used in a highly pejorative sense of the pit of Tartarus – and would not be a place where anybody would like to end up.

109   just like the one ... :   refers to the subterranean channels at Pheneus in Arcadia, which drained the floods from the river Olbius from the plains below Mount Cyllene and were said to have been excavated by Hercules. Note here the concentration of proper names, the attribution of the tale to the Greeks and the fifth-foot spondee. The passage 'smells of the lamp' according to Quinn: but the connection of thought is well-executed and shows a highly sophisticated poetic and scholarly temperament – what one would expect of a *doctus poeta*.

110 The alliteration* of *s* and *p* is notable here, as is the juxtaposition of *siccare emulsa* – the drying is the result of the draining away, and the result is a plain which is rich (*pingue* cf. OLD s.v. 3b) because well-irrigated.

112 **heart of the mountain:** The mountain is credited (by the pathetic fallacy) with quasi-animal bones (*medulla* properly means the marrow of the bones, and then by extension the vitals or the heart) for Hercules to excise – exactly the sort of labour he would attempt.

112 *audit* is a direct translation of the Greek idiom using *akouein* ('to hear' to mean 'to have it said of one that ... '). Amphitryon was married to Hercules' mother but she was actually impregnated by Jupiter – hence the epithet *falsiparens* here – and the tale became the source of both comedy (Plautus and later Molière) and serious drama (Kleist). This line is 'Alexandrian' in every sense – the Greek usage, the compound adjective, the elaborate allusive patronymic, the metrical ingenuity which can produce a perfect pentameter with three words, the second half of the line consisting of a single word.

113 **Stymphalian:** Hercules' fifth labour was to kill the man-eating birds of Stymphalus on the other side of Mount Cyllene from Phenius. The bow which he wielded was 'unerring' in that it never missed its target – a bow which Hercules bequeathed to Philoctetes on his deathbed and which kept the hapless Philoctetes alive on Lemnos when he was stranded there by his perfidious companions during the Trojan War after a snake-bite gave him an incurably malodorous foot. This same Philoctetes was nephew of Protesilaus. For a sceptical view of Hercules' skill at killing *monstra* cf. Lucretius 5.22-42. The Stymphalian birds are the first of three 'bird' images, the others being the vulture (124) and then the dove (125-8), all three being in one sense or another appetitive.

114 **master inferior:** *deterioris eri* echoes Heracles' own words at Homer *Odyssey* 11. 621 where he describes Eurystheus as an 'inferior man'.

115 **so that the doorway ... Hebe ... virginity:** The reason for the phrasing is firstly to remind the reader of *trito ... in limine* (71) where a *candida diva* crossed the poet's threshold, secondly to remind the reader of the marriage theme – just as Laudamia and Protesilaus do, just as the poet and his mistress do, so also Hercules and Hebe consummate their sexual love, all of them enjoying long amours except Laudamia and Protesilaus. The reference to the Stymphalian birds is 'justified' by the need to explain what Hercules was doing in that part of the world when he excavated Pheneus, but this couplet has no other purpose than to link the passage with the network of imagery and ideas which unite the poem.

117 **love ... deeper:** returns the reader to the *barathrum* metaphor (107-8) for Laudamia's love which set the poet on to the Hercules story in the first place. Notice the rhetorical repetition of *altus ... altior*.

118 **broken in ... yoke:** The sequence of thought appears to be: Laudamia was not 'broken in' as a wife, but nonetheless her desire taught her to 'bear the yoke'. The unflattering metaphor for wifely sex (parallel passages in Adams (1982) 207-8) does not contribute to our picture of her as *pulcherrima* (105).

119-28 A further series of similes* expressive of Laudamia's love for Protesilaus. The first is the fondness of an old man for his new grandson who will thwart the legacy-hunters, the second is that of loving doves.

119-24 The figure of the *captator* or legacy-hunter is a common satirical target in Roman literature: see especially Martial 1.10, 2.26, Juvenal 12. 93-130, Hopkins (1983) 238-247. The image successfully 'isolate(s) affection from sexual attraction, as in 72.3-4' (Quinn). Fordyce remarks that under the *Lex Voconia* of 169 BC a single heir to a large fortune had to be male – even an only daughter could not receive more than half and so the elderly father of an only daughter would find his more distant relatives raising their hopes; but the situation was rather more complex than this – see Treggiari (1991) 365-6 + nn, where she shows that the old man here was engineering one of the standard ways to bypass the law by leaving the money to the child of a daughter, knowing that the money would be *de facto*, if not *de iure*, in her hands thus. There is also here an echo of Homer *Iliad* 9. 481-2, where Phoinix reports how Peleus received him 'and loved me as a father loves his one dear son who is heir to great possessions', but it is noteworthy how the poet has made the setting unmistakably Roman with the terminology of inheritance.

The poet extracts as much pathos as possible out of the situation: the child is a *carum caput* born of his one and only daughter (*una nata*) as a late birth (*seri*) just in time (*vix tandem*) when he is racked with old age (*confecto aetate*): the picture is also focussed on the mother breastfeeding her infant (*caput ... alit*).

122   **name ... will:**   seems rather prosaic but is after all the key incident in the passage as it is this legal step which thwarts the legacy-hunter. The *tabulae* were of course the old man's will (OLD s.v. *tabula* 8b) which could now bear the child's name if it were inscribed in the presence of witnesses (*testatas*).

123   **wicked:**   *impia* as being equivalent to wishing the old man dead. There is a moral touch of *Schadenfreude* to the juxtaposition *impia derisi:* his impious joys deserved to be made a fool of, and the removal of his joy is a source of joy to the old man. The word *gentilis* is specific: if no immediate heir were forthcoming, the estate had to stay inside the *gens* by being passed to the nearest male relative within it. The disappointed man's only claim to the fortune was to have been a member of the *gens*.

124   **the vulture** is of course a metaphor* for the legacy-hunter: it also ties in neatly with the Stymphalian birds (similar to the vulture in every way) and leads us nicely to the loving doves (birds still, but *loving* birds). *capiti* reminds us of *caput* in 120 – the baby's *caput* protects the old man's *caput*. *suscitare* is a good word to evoke the act of shooing the bird away, *cano* evokes the pathos of the old man's plight.

125-8 The faithful love of the dove, renowned for quiet fidelity rather than sexual passion (Pliny *Natural History* 10.104) and yet doves are here seen as 'wanton' in a surprising manner.

125   **dove:** the female dove is singled out, her lover being snowy white as Catullus' love is *candida* (70).

126   **shameless:**   *improbius* is a strong word to use of the dove: it connotes behaviour which relentlessly seeks its own way without regard for others (see

Austin's note on Vergil *Aeneid* 4. 386) and is more often applied to eagles and wolves than to doves. The traditional picture is of the dove billing and cooing with its mate: here the poet sees the love as more greedy than the most promiscuous of women.

127/8 **nibbling:** For the affectionate pecking cf. poem 2.3-4. There is a paradoxical clash between soft *oscula* and hard *mordenti* which reminds one of poem 8.18 and Lucretius 4. 1080-1 (*[lovers] smash their teeth on little lips and inflict kisses …*).

promiscuous: The compound *multivola* is found only here but is similar to compounds such as *omnivoli* (140) and *vulgivaga Venere* (Lucretius 4. 1071). The poet suggests that the dove shows more affection for her one mate than the most promiscuous woman shows for all her many lovers – and the picture is bound to remind the reader of the poet's laments over Lesbia's 'three-hundred' lovers in poem 11.18.

129-30 brings the reader back to Laudamia.

129 **passions:** *furor* is often used of the 'madness' of romantic love (cf. 64.54; other exx at OLD s.v. 3a). It might possibly be used of the dove but hardly of the old man's love for his grandson, and so *horum* must refer to the dove and her mate (although the male's reactions to the female's affection is not recorded by the poet). The force of *sola* is that Laudamia had more love in her than all these others put together, and when put with *vicisti* a metaphor of combat is introduced whereby she took on all comers in an affection competition – and won.

130 **fair-haired:** *flavo* is the colour of many epic heroes and heroines: see 64.63.

131-48 The poet returns to his mistress, whose foot is still poised on the doorstep.

131-2 **brought herself:** *se … contulit* reminds us of *se … intulit* at 70-71. *lux mea* – as Cicero calls his wife at *ad Fam* 14.2.2. The poet's lover, for all her beauty and affection, has to be placed second to Laudamia.

133 **Cupid** is the child of Venus, a personified force of sexual desire often seen in works of art and usually depicted naked bearing his famous bow with which he fires arrows into the hearts of those he wishes to infatuate: for a famous parallel example cf. Vergil *Aeneid* 1. 657-94. Cupid here is clothed in a saffron gown, attending the lovers as in poem 45. Winged Cupid flitting here and there of course reminds us of the doves whose love we have just witnessed, just as it is fitting that a 'divine girl' should have a divine attendant.

134 **brilliantly … saffron:** Note the colour contrast of *crocina candidus*. Catullus' beloved was described as a *candida diva* who ought to have a divine *candidus* attendant.

135-40 The poet becomes more realistic after the fanciful picture of Cupid. His mistress may be divine at least in the manner of promiscuous gods – she is certainly as promiscuous as any of the Olympians. This wry twist is fully in the manner of Catullus.

135 **Catullus:** The poet names himself as at 27.

136 **infrequent … modest:** *rara verecundae* is deliberate juxtaposition to weaken the accusation of promiscuity – her deceptions are few and she is discreet about

them.   This   attitude   is   somewhere   between   the   idealism   of   109   and   the
recriminations of poems 11 and 58. *furta* are literally 'thefts' and denote the
'stealing' of another's spouse for adultery: Catullus' own affair is itself a *furtum* –
later on the elegists proclaim that the nominal husband has no real claim on the
beloved and that their love is higher and more deserving than his legal claim (cf.
e.g. Ovid *Amores* 1.4). The beloved here is called the *era* – as the gods were earlier
called in line 76: for the elegiac conception of the poet's beloved as his 'mistress'
or *domina* and his *servitium amoris* see Lyne (1979).

137   **nuisance ... stupid:** recalls the rueful attitude of the poet in poem 8: it is the
mark of the stupid man to complain about his mistress' infidelity when she will
make no effort to curb it: he only makes a fool and a nuisance (*molestus* cf.
10.33) of himself.

138-40   **even Juno:**   The poet compares himself to Juno – if the greatest of the
goddesses (*maxima caelicolum*) could not curb her partner's amours, then *a fortiori*
this wretched poet cannot.   The argument justifying human adultery from the
model of divine adultery goes back to Aristophanes *Clouds* 1076-82 but was not
used seriously: besides which, even a cursory acquaintance with Greek mythology
will show that Juno did not simply swallow her anger but rather took systematic
revenge on the females on whom Zeus' fancy fell (e.g. Io, Semele, Alcmene) or
who simply assisted him (Echo) – unless events secured their punishment through
other agencies.

139   **misbehaviour:** For *culpa* meaning 'sinful love-affair' cf. Vergil *Aeneid* 4. 19,
172.   The MSS read *cotidiana* which is clearly corrupt: Lachmann suggested
concoquit iram ('she swallowed her anger') which has found favour with many
editors – while Hertzberg's suggestion *contudit iram* also recommends itself,
denoting the stamping out of the flames (*flagrantem*) of her wrath, a better
metaphor to use with this participle.

140   **all-desiring:**   *omnivoli* is a compound adjective formed like *multivola* (128):
Zeus' indiscriminate promiscuity was legendary in the ancient world – indeed part
of his divine power was that he could indulge his sexual desires wherever and
whenever he chose. It is assumed in the tale of Gyges and his magic ring in Plato
Republic book 2, 360-1 that anybody who could get away with murder and
seduction would do so, as the gods do. *furta* picks up 136.

141   **And yet ... :**   This line undercuts the whole basis of the preceding three:
Jupiter and Juno are a) divine and b) married, while his human mistress is only
married to somebody else (143-6). Most editors assume a lacuna after 141, and
Goold's filler is worth quoting *exempli gratia*.:

>   *nec mala, quot Juno, quantave nos patimur*
>   *tolle igitur questus et forti mente, Catulle,*

('and I do not undergo as many sufferings as Juno did.   Cease your
complaining, therefore and with sturdy mind, Catulle, ... ').

142   **pick up:** *tolle onus* would naturally mean 'lift up the burden' and makes the
reader think of (e.g.) Aeneas lifting the aged Anchises onto his shoulders. How
this links with the context is baffling, and so editors take the line as meaning
rather 'stop being a thankless burden like a doddering parent': *tolle* meaning
'remove' as at Vergil *Aeneid* 10.451, *onus* being an active sense of 'burdening'.

The line ends up teasing the reader, whereby its apparent meaning (do your duty) is exactly the opposite of its real meaning (stop being a killjoy). Marcilius suggested that perhaps more than a single couplet has fallen out of the MS at this point. It is at any rate clear that the mention of *parentis* in 142 leads happily on to *paterna* in 143.

143-6 The poet's mistress is not married to him: he dwells on the details of the wedding ceremony (the *deductio*, the father, the perfumes) only to dwell even more on the secret love affair which they enjoyed. The father did not take part in the *deductio* to the bride's new home, in fact: but the point here is that his lover's father did not hand over his daughter to Catullus – the passage implies the reverse, that her father would be horrified at the adulterous liaison they enjoyed (cf. the *rumores senum severiorum* in poem 5).

144 **Assyrian:**   in fact Roman perfumes were produced in Arabia rather than in Assyria or Syria (the two being often confused) For more details see Pliny *Natural History* 13.4-8. The new bridal home has been sprinkled with perfume.

145-6 **stolen:**   Adultery is 'stolen' (cf. *furta* 136) from under the husband's nose, mocking the poor cuckold as at 17.12-22 with the repeated *ipsius ... ipso* dwelling on the danger and the risk of the undertaking. The phrase also recalls line 132: she came to my *gremium* with gifts stolen from his *gremium*. Her gifts are small (*munuscula*). *mira* (mss reading 'wondrous') is defended stoutly by Quinn but rejected by most editors in favour of Heyse's *muta*.

147-8 I am content if she gives me her best days, even if she shares other days with other lovers, i.e. if I am her favourite. The image of marking with a whiter stone comes from the tradition of the Cretans dropping a white stone into their quiver to mark a happy day, a black stone to mark an unhappy day (Porphyrio on Horace *Odes* 1.36, quoted by Quinn).

149-60 Epilogue to Allius.
149   **gift:** The poem was the gift described in line 10.
150   **in return for many kindnesses:**   including the provision of a house for Catullus' love-making, as described in line 67-72.
151/2   **foul rust:** a striking image of neglect: cf. 64.42, Vergil *Georgics* 1.495.
        another ... another ... :   The repetitive sequence of similar words well evokes the endless sequence of days, as in the repetition of numbers in 5.7-10. The poet can confer immortality through his verse, a common topos* of ancient poetry and one of its principal functions. See e.g. Horace *Odes* 3.30, Homer *Iliad* 6.357-8.
153   **Themis** is the personified spirit of Justice and the poet indulges in a nostalgic wish for the gifts of Justice as in the good old days to be conferred on Allius – exactly as missed and lamented at 64. 397-408 (Fordyce compares also Aratus *Phaenomena* 112.) *antiquis ... piis* encloses the line: and the poet wishes for divine gifts in the context of a poem which is a gift requested by one to whom he owes a gift.
155   **May you ... :**   A wish for marital/amorous happiness. as at 66.87-8. *tua vita* sounds like Allius' beloved – for the phrase cf. 45.13, 104.1, 109.1.

156 **mistress:** If *domina* is correct and is the subject of *lusimus*, then the word must surely refer to the poet's beloved mistress, not Fordyce's compliant chatelaine (68n) – unless we punctuate to put *in qua lusimus* into parenthesis, as Goold does. This is possible but faces the objection of all interpretations based on editorial punctuation of being entirely a modern importation into an ancient unpunctuated text. For *lusimus* cf. 17n.

157 A corrupt line and a *locus conclamatus*. The mss reading *terram dedit aufert* is meaningless and must be emended. Behind *aufert* may lurk a name or a reference to a name, behind *terram* it is plausible to see *te: te tradidit* is Scaliger's brilliant emendation for *terram dedit* and is almost certainly correct. Who, then, was the person who gave the mistress to Catullus? Goold argues that Caelius Rufus (former lover of Clodia, defended by Cicero in the *pro Caelio* and formerly on the staff of the provincial governor in Africa) could recognisably be referred to as *Afer* (first suggested by Munro) – recognisable, that is, to contemporaries but not to medieval scribes who 'corrected' this to the gibberish we have in the mss. Other suggestions include *auspex* (Lipsius, referring to the augur who was present at the wedding ceremony, OLD s.v. 2), *Anser* (Heyse, perhaps referring to the erotic poet of that name mentioned in Ovid *Tristia* 2.435). Certainty is beyond reach: but the reading printed is at least sense.

158 The hiatus over the central caesura is unusual, but cf. Quinn on 10.27. Haupt first proposed adding *mi* to remove the difficulty.

159 **me ... I:** *mihi ... me* for emphasis.

160 **my light:** *lux mea* recalls 132, *qua viva* implies that even the death of the brother (who is himself described as *iucundum lumen* in 93) is not an insuperable obstacle to happiness as long as Lesbia lives. Note the stress in juxtaposing *viva vivere*, and the sense that life and love are for the poet almost synonymous, as at 5.1.

Appendix

Callimachus fragment 110 (Pfeiffer)

This is the extant remains of the poem of which Catullus 66 is a translation.
A literal translation follows the Greek.

Πάντα τὸν ἐν γραμμαῖσιν ἰδὼν ὅρον ἦ τε φέρονται   1

†η με Κόνων ἔβλεψεν ἐν ἠέρι τὸν Βερενίκης   7
βόστρυχον ὃν κείνη πᾶσιν ἔθηκε θεοῖς

[σύμβολον ἐννυχίης ... ἀεθλοσύνης?]   13/14

[μεγάθυμον?]   26

σήν τε κάρην ὤμοσα σόν τε βίον   40

].[43
ἀμνά]μω[ν Θείης ἀργὸς ὑ]περφέ[ρ]ε[ται,
βουπόρος Ἀρσινόη[ς μ]ητρὸς σέο, καὶ διὰ μέ[σσου   45
Μηδείων ὀλοαὶ νῆες ἔβησαν Ἄθω.
τί πλόκαμοι ῥέξωμεν, ὅτ᾽ οὔρεα τοῖα σιδή[ρῳ
εἴκουσιν; Χαλύβων ὡς ἀπόλοιτο γένος,
γειόθεν ἀντέλλοντα, κακὸν φυτόν, οἵ μιν ἔφ⸤ηναν
πρῶτοι καὶ τυπίδων ἔφρασαν ἐργασίην.   50
ἄρτι [ν]εότμητόν με κόμαι ποθέεσκον ἀδε[λφεαί,
καὶ πρόκατε γνωτὸς Μέμνονος Αἰθίοπος
ἵετο κυκλώσας βαλιὰ πτερὰ θῆλυς ἀήτης,
ἵππο[ς] ἰοζώνου Λοκρίδος Ἀρσινόης,
.[.]ασε δὲ πνοιῇ με, δι᾽ ἠέρα δ᾽ ὑγρὸν ἐνείκας   55
Κύπρ[ι]δος εἰς κόλπους   ἔθηκε   ·
αὐτή⸥ μιν Ζεφυρῖτις ἐπὶ χρέο[ς
.... Κ]ανωπίτου ναιέτις α[ἰ]γιαλοῦ.
ὄφρα δὲ] μὴ νύμφης Μινωίδος ο[
.....]ος ἀνθρώποις μοῦνον ἐπι.[,   60
φάεσ]ιν ἐν πολέεσσιν ἀρίθμιος ἀλ⸤λ⸥ὰ γένωμαι

καὶ Βερ]ενίκειος καλὸς ἐγὼ πλόκαμ[ος,
ὕδασι] λουόμενόν με παρ' ἀθα[νάτους ἀνιόντα
Κύπρι]ς ἐν ἀρχαίοις ἄστρον [ἔθηκε νέον.

                    ]   65

                ]

ͺπρόσθε μὲν ἐρχομεν.. μετοπωριγὸνͺ Ὠκ]εανόγδε
                 ].ο[
  ἀ]λλ' εἰ κα[ι   ].....ν
               ].. ιτη[70
μὴ   ]κοτέσῃ[ς, Ῥαμνουσιάς· οὔτ]ις ἐρύξει
βοῦς ἔποσͺ   ]η...[   ].[ ].βη
           ].[.]ελε.[   ].θράσος ἀ[στ]έρες ἄλλοι
         ]νδινειε.[   ]ο̣σο̣σο[.]τεκ.[.]ω·
οὐͺ τάδεͺ μοι τοσσήνδε φͺέͺρͺεͺι χάρͺιͺν ὅσ̣[σο]ν ἐκείνης   75
  ἀ]σχάλλω κορυφῆς οὐκέτͺι θιξόμεν[ος,
ἧς ἄπο, παρ[θ]ενίη μὲν ὅτ' ἦν ἔτι, πολλͺὰ πέͺπωκα
  λιͺτͺά, γυναικείων δ' οὐκ ἀπέλαυσα μύρων   78

. .   ·   ·   ·
ο.[89
    μͺε[·   ·   ·   ·
νͺυ[   ].[
  το.[   ]νθιͺ[
γεί[τονες   ]ωσ[
  α.[   ]. Ὑδροχ[όος] καὶ[Ὠαρίων.   94
χ[ ], φίλη τεκέεσσι.[94a
 .[   ]....[.].ν.[94b

Translation

1   Having seen the whole of the charted sky, and where move...

7   Conon saw me also in the air, the lock of Berenice, which she
dedicated to all the gods..

13/14   [token of the nightly struggle]

26	[great-hearted]
40	I swore by your head and by your life...
44	Thia's bright descendant travels...
45	the obelisk of your mother Arsinoe, and through the middle

of Athos the deadly ships of the Persians went.
What can we locks of hair do, when mountains like that give way
to iron? May the race of Chalibes perish
who first revealed it, an evil growth rising up from the earth,

50 and taught the work of the hammer.
My sister locks were missing me when I had just been newly
shorn:
at once the brother of Memnon the Ethiopian
whirring his swift wings round, the gentle breeze,
the horse of Locrian Arsinoe of the violet girdle,

55 seized me with his breath and bearing me through the moist air
...set me down in the bosom of Aphrodite.
Aphrodite of Zephyrion, who dwells on shore of Canopus,
<chose> him for that purpose.
And so that not only the <crown> of the Minoan bride

60 might <cast its light> on men
but that I also might be counted among the myriad lights
I the fair lock of Berenice
as I went up to the immortals, washed in the waves
Aphrodite set me up, a new star among the old.

65	. . . . . .
67	..first going in autumn towards the ocean...
75	These events bring me not so much pleasure as misery

that I shall touch that head no more
from which, when Berenice was still a girl, I drank many

78	cheap scents, but did not enjoy the married woman's perfumes...
93	neighbours...
94	Hydrochoos and Oarion
94a	dear one, to..children...

Glossary of Literary Terms

Aetiological: a form of narrative which explains the origin of a custom or event.

Alliteration: the repetition of a consonant sound, often at the beginning of successive words: e.g. 64.92–3.

Anaphora: the repetition of a word, often at the beginning of successive phrases, e.g. 64.28-29, 64.132–4 *(sicine ... sicine ...)* 64.215–6.

Apostrophe: the poet addresses a character in the tale directly, e.g. the address to Peleus in 64.26–30, or the address to the dead brother at 68.20-24 and to Laudamia at 68.105.

Assonance: the repetition of vowel sounds, e.g.: *anxia in assiduos absumens lumina fletus* (64.242).

Asyndeton: the omission of connective words in a series of nouns or verbs: e.g. the verbs at 63.85–6

ataraxia: the Greek word used by Epicurus to denote the 'unruffled' calm which is happiness, a state of serenity in which there is no pain and no pleasure but simply static contentment.

Bathos: a sudden drop in the register of language, from the sublime to the ridiculous or vulgar: e.g. *minxerit* at 67.30

Chiasmus: an arrangement of words or phrases in A-B-B-A form; e.g. 64.152–3 *dilaceranda (A) feris (B)..alitibusque (B) praeda (A)*

Closure: the degree to which the ending of a work is satisfyingly final, and the extent to which new perspectives and readings are available to it. See Fowler (1989).

ecphrasis: the digression from the narrative to describe a secondary narrative descriptive of a work of art or at least a visual landscape: e.g. the digression on the tapestry at 64.50-266.

Encomium: literary expression of extravagant praise.

Enjambement: the 'running-on' of the sentence over the end of one line and into the next, e.g. 64.32–3, 136–7, 68.57–8: the opposite of this is the 'end-stopped' line where sense comes to a complete halt (with punctuation) at the end (e.g. 64.34)

Epanalepsis: the repetition of a word after a few other words, often in consecutive lines as at 64.26–7, 66.39–40, 66.82. It was a particularly Hellenistic device: (cf Callimachus *Hymn* 4.118–9, 5.40–41, Theocritus *Idylls* 9.1-2, 18.50–1) and used by other Roman poets also (e.g. Lucretius 5.950–1, Vergil *Aeneid* 1.108–9).

Figura etymologica: a punning use of words which suggests their derivation: e.g. *amaritiem* at 68.18 to imply an origin in *amare* (to love), 64.204.

Golden Line: the poet puts the two adjectives first at the start of the line, followed by the verb and then the two nouns at the end. e.g. 64.172, 68.29

Hypallage: transferred epithet: a word which strictly should apply to one word is made to agree with a different word for effect: e.g. 64.57, 66.74 *condita ... veri pectoris* when the phrase 'means' *condita vera pectoris* (the tale is true, not the breast which contains it.), 68.56 (the 'sad' shower).

Hyperbaton: unusual word order, used for effect: e.g. 66.18

Hyperbole: exaggeration for emphasis: e.g. Ariadne conceiving love as a fire right down to the marrow of her bones at 64. 92–3.

iconic: having the sensory appearance of the thing represented -- such as a drawing of a dog. The word 'dog' does not look like a dog (and so is arbitrary and not iconic).

Implicit myth: the use of imagery which suggests a familiar tale from the world of mythology, e.g. 68.88

Litotes: understatement brought about by a double negative, such as 68.11 *ne sint* ... *ignota* ('so that they may *not* be *un*known' for 'so that they may be known'), 61. 191-2.

Metaphor: a figure of speech in which one thing is described in terms appropriate to another, such as marriage being described as the 'breaking in' an animal to 'bear the yoke' at 68.118

Metonymy: 'change of name'; commonly the use of the name of a patron god for the area of which (s)he is patron, such as Venus (for 'sex') at 66.15.

Mise-en-abyme: an enclosed narrative structure which has tales within tales, such as the tale of Ariadne being enclosed within the tale of the wedding of Peleus and Thetis in poem 64.

Onomatopeia: sound-effects, whereby the sound of the word imitates the sound being described; e.g. *euantis* at 64.391.

Oxymoron: the juxtaposition of words with opposite meaning, e.g. the 'sweet bitterness' of *dulcem ... amaritiem* in 68.18.

para prosdokian: Greek term denoting a paradoxical form of expression which appears untrue – such as the root of the vine touching its topmost tendril at 62.52.

Pathetic Fallacy: the poetic conceit where inanimate objects are credited with human feelings: e.g. 64.179, 68.79, 68.111.

Pleonasm: a word which is redundant, its meaning already being supplied by other words (cf. 64.22)

Polyptoton: the repetition of a word in a different case: e.g. 68.9 *mihi me.*

protreptic: a style of writing designed to educate or persuade the reader.

simile: a description of a thing or an event which compares it to another thing or event: e.g. the battle of Theseus with the Minotaur is compared to a tree being laid out by the wind (64.105-9) the 'tenor' being the thing compared and the 'vehicle' the thing with which it is then compared. See on this especially the Introduction to 68.

syllepsis: a figure of speech where a word brings together two constructions, as at 64.84.

synecdoche: a form of metonymy where a part of a thing is mentioned as standing for the whole thing: e.g. 64.6 'salt ways' (= seas), 'poop' (=ship).

tautology: repetition of ideas and words; saying the same thing twice over, such as *regia ... regali* at 64.44-6

toponymic: a name derived from the place of origin, e.g. 64.287.

topos: a stock literary theme or scene, e.g. 68. 151-2.

tricolon crescendo: a set of three phrases, usually beginning with the same (or a similar) initial word and growing in length; e.g. 68.34-5 *illa domus//illa mihi sedes// illic mea carpitur aetas.*

Bibliography

This is a list of the works I have found most useful in preparing this edition. Where abbreviations are used in the commentary, these are indicated after each listing below.

Works of Reference:
The Oxford Classical Dictionary (2nd edition, Oxford 1970) (OCD)
The Oxford Latin Dictionary (Oxford, 1982) (OLD)
Kennedy, B.H. The Revised Latin Primer (London, 1962)

Editions of Catullus:

Ellis, Robinson (Oxford, 1889)
Lenchantin de Gubernatis, M. (Turin, 1953)
Mynors, R.A.B. (Oxford Classical Text 1958) (OCT)
Fordyce, C.J. (Oxford, 1961)
Pighi G.B. (Verona, 1961)
Kroll, W. (Stuttgart, 5th edition 1968)
Bardon, H. (Brussels, 1970)
Quinn, K. (London, 1970)
Thomson, D.F.S. (Chapel Hill, 1978)
Garrison, D.H. (London, 1989)
Goold, G.P. (London, 2nd edition 1989)

Books and Articles
Adams, J.N.   The Latin Sexual Vocabulary (London, 1982)
Avallone, R.   'Il carme 66 di Catullo e la Chioma di Berenice di Callimaco' Euphrosyne 4 (1961) 23-48
Baker, R.J.   'Domina at Catullus 68.68: mistress or chatelaine?' Rheinisches Museum 118 (1975) 124-9
Barber, E.A.   'The Lock of Berenice: Callimachus and Catullus' in: Greek Poetry and Life: Essays presented to Gilbert Murray (Oxford 1936), 343-363
Bramble, J.C.   'Structure and Ambiguity in Catullus LXIV' Proceedings of the Cambridge Philological Society 1970 22-41
Bright, D.F.   'Confectum carmine munus: Catullus 68' Illinois Classical Studies 1 (1976) 86-112
Cairns, F.   'The Nereids of Catullus 64.12–23b' Erazer Beiträge 11 (1984) 95–101
Clausen, W.V.   'The Marriage of Peleus and Thetis' The Cambridge History of Classical Literature (Cambridge, 1982) 2.2 13-19
————————   'Catullus and Callimachus', Harvard Studies in Classical Philology 74 (1970) 85-94 (= Kallimachos, hrsgb. von A.D. Skiadas (Wege der Forschung 296, Darmstadt 1975), 395-400

Copley, F.O.   The "riddle" of Catullus 67' *Transactions of the American Philological Association* 80 (1949) 245-53

---------   Exclusus Amator: *A Study in Latin Love Poetry* (Baltimore, 1956)

Courtney, Edward 'Moral Judgements in Catullus 64' *Grazer Beiträge* 17 (1990) 113-122

Curran, Leo C. 'Catullus 64 and the Heroic Age' *Yale Classical Studies* 21 (1969) 171-92

Daniels, Marion L. 'Personal Revelation in Catullus 64' *Classical Journal* 62 (1966) 351-6

Dee, James H. 'Catullus 64 and the heroic age: a reply' *Illinois Classical Studies* vii.i (1982) 98-109

Duban, J. 'Verbal Links and Imagistic undercurrent in Catullus 64' *Latomus* 39 (1980)777-802

Edwards, M.J. 'Invitus regina' *L'Antiquité Classique* 60 (1991) 260-5

Elder, J.P. 'Catullus' Attis' *American Journal of Philology* 68 (1947) 394-403

Fedeli, P. *Catullus' Carmen 61* (Amsterdam, 1983)

Feeney, D.C. 'Shall I compare thee...?': Catullus 68a and the Limits of Analogy' in: Woodman and Powell, *Author and Audience in Latin Literature* (Cambridge 1992), 33-44.

Ferguson, J. *Catullus* (Greece and Rome New Surveys in the Classics) (Oxford, 1988)

Forsyth, P.Y. 'The marriage-theme in Catullus 63' *Classical Journal* 66 (1970) 68-9

Forsyth, P. 'Catullus 64: The Descent of Man' *Antichthon* 9 (1975) 41-51

Fowler, D.P. 'First Thoughts on Closure: Problems & Prospects' *Materiali e Discussioni* 22 (1989) 75–122

--------- 'Narrate or describe: the problem of *ecphrasis*' *Journal of Roman Studies* 81 (1991)25-35

--------- 'Postmodernism, Romantic Irony and Classical Closure' in: De Jong I.J.F. and Sullivan J.P. *Modern Critical Theory and Classical Literature* (*Mnemosyne* supplement, Leiden 1994)

Fraenkel, E. 'Vesper adest' *Journal of Roman Studies* 45 (1955) 1-8

Giangrande, G. 'Das Epyllion Catulls im lichte der Hellenistischen Epik' *L'Antiquite Classique* 41 (1972) 123-47

Godwin, J. (Ed) Lucretius, *de rerum natura 4* (Warminster, 1986)

Graves, R. *The Greek Myths* (Harmondsworth, 1960)

Griffin, J. *Latin Poets and Roman Life* (London, 1985)

Guillemin, A. 'Le poeme 63 de Catulle' *Revue des Études Latines* 27 (1949) 149-57

Harmon, D.P. 'Nostalgia for the Age of Heroes in Catullus 64' *Latomus* 32 (1973) 311-31

Herrmann, L. ' Le poeme LXIV de Catulle et l'actualite' *Latomus* 26 (1967) 27-34

Hopkins, K. *Death and Renewal* (Cambridge 1983)

Horvath I.K. 'La technique de traduction de Catulle à la lumière du Papyrus de Callimaque retrouvé à Tebtynis', *Acta Antiqua* 10 (1962) 347-56

Hunter, R. 'Breast is best: Catullus 64.18' *Classical Quarterly* 51 (1991) 254-5

Hutchinson, G. *Hellenistic Poetry* (Oxford, 1988)

Jenkyns, R. *Three Classical Poets* (London, 1982)

Kenney, E.J. 'Doctus Lucretius', *Mnemosyne* 23 (1970) 366-92

--------- (Ed): Lucretius *de rerum natura 3* (Cambridge, 1971)

Kidd, D. ' Some Problems in Catullus LXVI' *Antichthon* 4 (1970)

234   BIBLIOGRAPHY

Kinsey, T.E.   'Irony and Structure in Catullus 64' *Latomus* 24 (1965) 911-931
Klingner, F.   'Catulls Peleus-Epos' *Studien zur griechischen und römischen Literatur*
                 (1956) 156-224
Knopp, Sherron   'Catullus 64 and the conflict between Amores and Virtutes' *Classical
                 Philology* 71 (1976) 207-213
Konstan, David *Catullus' Indictment of Rome: the meaning of Catullus 64*, (Amsterdam,
                 1977)
Laird, A.   'Sounding out ecphrasis: Art and text in Catullus 64' *Journal of Roman
                 Studies* 83 (1993)18-30
Levin, D.N.   'Ambiguities of expression in Catullus 66 and 67' *Classical Philology* 54
                 (1959) 109-11
Lyne, R.O.A.M., 'Servitium Amoris' *Classical Quarterly* NS 29 (1979) 117-130
----------   *The Latin Love Poets* (Oxford, 1980)
McKie, D.S.   *The Manuscripts of Catullus: Recension in a Closed Tradition* (diss.
                 Cambridge University, 1977)
Macleod, C.W.   'A use of myth in ancient poetry', *Classical Quarterly* 24 (1974) 82-93 (=
                 Collected Essays (Oxford, 1983) 159-70)
----------   Homer, *Iliad Book 24* (Cambridge 1982)
----------   'The Artistry of Catullus 67' in *Collected Essays* (Oxford 1983) 187-95
Martin, C.   *Catullus* (Yale, 1992)
Martindale, C.   *Redeeming the Text: Latin Poetry and the Hermeneutics of Reception*
                 (Cambridge, 1993)
Mossman, Judith: *Wild Justice: a Study of Euripides'* Hecuba (Oxford, 1995)
Most, Glenn: 'On the arrangement of Catullus' *Carmina maiora*' *Philologus* 125 (1981)
                 109-25
----------   'Neues zur Geschichte des Terminus 'Epyllion'' *Philologus* 126 (1982)
                 153-6
Mynors, R.   (Ed.) Virgil: *Georgics* (Oxford, 1990)
Newman, J.K.   *Roman Catullus and the Modification of the Alexandrian Sensibility*
                 (Hildesheim, 1990)
Nisbet, R.G.M.   *Collected Papers on Latin Literature* (Oxford 1995)
Ogilvie, R.M.   *The Romans and their Gods* (London, 1969)
Perrotta, G.   'L'elegia di Catullo ad Allio' in *Scritti Minori I* (Rome 1972) 189-212
----------   'Il carme dell' *ianua*: Catullo 67' in *Scritti Minori* i (Rome 1972) 157-88
Putnam, M.C.J.   'Catullus 66. 75-88' *Classical Philology* 55 (1960) 223-8
----------   'The Art of Catullus 64' *Harvard Studies in Classical Philology* 65 (1961)
                 165-205
Quinn, K.   *The Catullan Revolution* (London, 1969)
----------   *Catullus: An Interpretation* (London, 1972)
Ross, David O. Jr., *Style and Tradition in Catullus* (Harvard, 1969)
Rudd, N.   (Ed) Horace *Epistles* Book II and *Epistle to the Pisones* (Cambridge,
                 1989)
Russell, D.A.   *Criticism in Antiquity* (London, 1981)
Sandy, G.N.   'The Imagery of Catullus 63' *Transactions of the American Philological
                 Association* 99 (1968) 389-99

BIBLIOGRAPHY 235

---------- 'Catullus 63 and the Theme of Marriage' *American Journal of Philology* 92 (1971) 185-95

Sarkissian, J.   'Catullus 68: an Interpretation' *Mnemosyne* supplement 76 (1983)

Schafer, E.   *Das Verhältnis von Erlebnis und Kunstgestalt bei Catull.* (Wiesbaden 1966)

Schmid, W.   *Catullus: Ansichten und Durchblicke* (Göppingen 1974)

Shipton, E.M.W.   'The Attis of Catullus' *Classical Quarterly* 37 (1987) 444-449

Syndikus, H.P.   *Catull: eine Interpretation (zweiter Teil: die großen Gedichte 61-68)* (Darmstadt 1990)

Tatham, G.   'Ariadne's Mitra: a note on Catullus 64.61-4' *Classical Quarterly* 40 (1990) 560-1

Thomas, R.   'Catullus and the polemics of poetic reference' *American Journal of Philology* 103 (1982) 144-64

Thomas, R.F.   (Ed) Vergil *Georgics* (Cambridge, 1988), 2 vols.

Townend, G.B.   'The Unstated climax of Catullus 64' *Greece and Rome* 30 (1983) 21-30

Treggiari, S.   *Roman Marriage* (Oxford, 1991)

Tuplin, C.J.   'Catullus 68' *Classical Quarterly* 31 (1981) 113-139

Webster, T.B.L.   'The myth of Ariadne from Homer to Catullus' *Greece and Rome* 13 (1966) 21-31

Whatmough, J.   'Pudicus Poeta: Words and Things' in *Poetic, Scientific and other Forms of Discourse* (California 1956) 29-55

Wilamowitz, U.v. *Reden und Vorträge* (Berlin, 1913)

----------   *Hellenistische Dichtung in der Zeit des Kallimachos* (Berlin, 1924)

Williams, G.   *Tradition and Originality in Roman Poetry* (Oxford 1968)

----------   *Figures of Thought in Roman Poetry* (Yale, 1980)

Wiseman, T.P.   *Catullan Questions* (Leicester, 1970)

----------   *Catullus and his World: a Reappraisal* (Cambridge, 1985)

Wormell, D.E.W.   'Catullus as Translator' in *The Classical Tradition* (ed. L Wallach) (Cornell, 1966), 194-201

Zetzel, J.E.G.   'Catullus, Ennius and the Poetics of Allusion' *Illinois Classical Studies* viii.2 (1983) 251-266

Zwierlein, O.   'Weihe und Entruckung der Locke der Berenice' *Rheinisches Museum* 130 (1987) 174-90

Aris & Phillips Classical Texts – Published Books

AESCHYLUS: THE EUMENIDES; THE PERSIANS
APPIAN: THE WARS OF THE ROMANS IN IBERIA
ARISTOPHANES: ACHARNIANS; BIRDS; CLOUDS; ECCLESIAZUSAE, FROGS; KNIGHTS; LYSISTRATA; PEACE; WASPS; WEALTH; THESMOPHORIAZUSAE
ARISTOTLE: ON THE HEAVENS; ON SLEEP AND DREAMS
AUGUSTINE: SOLILOQUIES *and* IMMORTALITY OF THE SOUL
CAESAR: CIVIL WAR I & II; III
CASSIUS DIO: ROMAN HISTORY 53.1-55.9
CATULLUS: THE LONGER POEMS; THE SHORTER POEMS
CICERO: TUSCULAN DISPUTATIONS I; II & V; ON FATE with **BOETHIUS**, CONSOLATION V; PHILIPPICS II; VERRINES II,1; ON STOIC GOOD AND EVIL; LAELIUS ON FRIENDSHIP and THE DREAM OF SCIPIO; LETTERS OF JAN.–APR. 43
EURIPIDES: ALCESTIS; ANDROMACHE; BACCHAE; CHILDREN OF HERACLES; ELECTRA; HECUBA; HERACLES; HIPPOLYTUS; ION; IPHIGENIA IN TAURIS; ORESTES; PHOENICIAN WOMEN; SELECTED FRAGMENTARY PLAYS I; TROJAN WOMEN
GREEK ORATORS: I ANTIPHON, LYSIAS; II DINARCHUS 1 & HYPERIDES 5–6; III ISOCRATES Panegyricus and To Nicocles, IV ANDOCIDES; V DEMOSTHENES On the Crown; VI APOLLODORUS against Nearia
HELLENICA OXYRHYNCHIA
HOMER: ODYSSEY I & II; ILIAD VIII & IX
HORACE: SATIRES I; SATIRES II
JOSEPH OF EXETER: THE TROJAN WAR I-III
LIVY: XXXVI; XXXVII; XXXVIII; XXXIX; XL
LUCAN: CIVIL WAR VIII
LUCIAN: A SELECTION
LUCRETIUS: DE RERUM NATURA, III; IV; VI
MARTIAL: THE EPIGRAMS
MENANDER: SAMIA; THE BAD TEMPERED MAN
OVID: AMORES II; METAMORPHOSES I-IV; V-VIII; IX-XII, XIII-XV
PERSIUS: THE SATIRES
PINDAR: SELECTED ODES
PLATO: APOLOGY; MENO; PHAEDRUS; REPUBLIC V; X; STATESMAN; SYMPOSIUM
PLAUTUS: BACCHIDES
PLINY: CORRESPONDENCE WITH TRAJAN FROM BITHYNIA
PLUTARCH: LIVES OF ARISTEIDES & CATO; CICERO; MALICE OF HERODOTUS; LIFE OF THEMISTOCLES
PROPERTIUS I
THE RUODLIEB
SENECA: LETTERS (a selection); FOUR DIALOGUES; MEDEA
SOPHOCLES: AJAX; ANTIGONE; ELECTRA; PHILOCTETES
SUETONIUS: LIVES OF GALBA, OTHO AND VITELLIUS
TACITUS: ANNALS IV; V & VI; GERMANY
TERENCE: THE BROTHERS; THE SELF-TORMENTOR; THE MOTHER-IN-LAW; THE EUNUCH
THUCYDIDES: HISTORY II; III; IV-V.24; PYLOS 425 BC, IV, 2-41
WILLIAM OF NEWBURGH THE HISTORY OF ENGLISH AFFAIRS I
XENOPHON: HELLENIKA I-II.3.10; II.3.11-IV.2.8; SYMPOSIUM; WITH **ARRIAN** ON HUNTING

Printed and bound by CPI Group (UK) Ltd, Croydon, CR0 4YY

09/06/2025

14685953-0002